AMERICA'S SUBURBAN CENTERS

TITLES OF RELATED INTEREST

Accommodating inequality
S. Watson

The carrier wave
P. Hall & P. Preston

Cities and telecommunications
M. Moss

Cities and society
R. J. Johnson

Computer applications in geography and planning
R. Barr & D. C. Bannister

Cost-benefit analysis in urban and regional planning
J. A. Schofield

Development and the landowner
R. J. C. Munton & R. Goodchild

Distribution-free tests
H. R. Neave & P. L. Worthington

Gentrification of the city
N. Smith & P. Williams (eds)

High tech America
A. Markusen *et al.*

Housing and urban renewal
A. D. Thomas

Intelligent planning
R. Wyatt

International capitalism and industrial restructuring
R. Peet (ed.)

Localities: a comparative analysis of urban change
P. Cooke (ed.)

Location and stigma
C. J. Smith & J. Giggs (eds)

London 2001
P. Hall

London's Green Belt
R. J. C. Munton

Optimal control of spatial systems
R. J. Bennett & K. C. Tan

The politics of the urban crisis
A. Sills *et al.*

Property before people
A. Power

Regional development and settlement policy
R. Dewar *et al.*

Regional dynamics
G. Clark *et al.*

Regional economic development
B. Higgins & D. Savoie (eds)

Remaking planning
T. Brindley *et al.*

Silicon landscapes
P. Hall & A. Markusen (eds)

Technological change, industrial restructuring and regional development
A. Amin & J. Goddard (eds)

Town and country planning in Britain
J. B. Cullingworth

Urban and regional planning
P. Hall

Urban hospital location
L. Mayhew

Urban problems in Western Europe
P. Cheshire & D. Hay

Western sunrise
P. Hall *et al.*

AMERICA'S SUBURBAN CENTERS

The land use–transportation link

ROBERT CERVERO

University of California, Berkeley

Boston
UNWIN HYMAN
London   Sydney   Wellington

Unwin Hyman, Inc.
8 Winchester Place, Winchester, Mass. 01890, USA

Published by the Academic Division of

Unwin Hyman Ltd
15/17 Broadwick Street, London W1V 1FP, UK

Allen & Unwin (Australia) Ltd,
8 Napier Street, North Sydney, NSW 2060, Australia

Allen & Unwin (New Zealand) Ltd in association with the
Port Nicholson Press Ltd,
Compusales Building, 75 Ghuznee Street,
Wellington 1, New Zealand

First published in 1989

Library of Congress Cataloging-in-Publication Data

Cervero, Robert.
America's suburban centers.

Bibliography: p.
Includes index.
1. Commuting—United States. 2. Choice of transportation.
3. Suburbs—United States. 4. Business parks—United States.
5. Traffic congestion—United States. 6. Land use—United States.
I. Title.
HD5717.5.U6C47 1989   388.4'13143'0973   88–37836
ISBN 0–04–445333–7 (alk. paper)

British Library Cataloguing in Publication Data

Cervero, Robert
America's suburban centers : the land use – transportation link.
1. United States. Transportation. Policies
I. Title
380.5'068

ISBN 0–04–445333–7

Typeset in 10/11 point Times
Printed in Great Britain by
Cambridge University Press

Preface

After completing a book several years ago, entitled *Suburban gridlock*, I became convinced that marked changes in how suburban workplaces are designed and built are absolutely essential if regional mobility is to be safeguarded in both the US and abroad in coming years. This initial research into suburban transportation issues suggested that the low-density, single-use character of many suburban work centers was a root cause of the congestion problems being faced in suburbia. While vehicles tend to circulate almost effortlessly once inside most suburban office parks and developments, roadways leading to them are all too often jammed because of the preponderance of automobiles with a single occupant. Thus, what we have witnessed during the 1980s is the construction of spacious, nicely landscaped suburban work settings that have had the unfortunate consequence of compelling most workers to commute alone, clogging up regional thoroughfares in the process.

To explore the extent to which this is true, I sought to carry out an empirically based study of the relationship between the physical design characteristics of suburban workplaces and the commuting choices of their workforces. This work represents the results of that effort. The research would not have been possible without the generous contributions of a number of organizations and individuals. Foremost, my thanks goes to the Office of Budget and Policy of the Urban Mass Transportation Administration, US Department of Transportation for their financial backing of this study. I am particularly indebted to Kenneth Bolton and Rob Martin for their inputs in both conceptualizing this project and revising earlier drafts. I also owe a debt of gratitude to the Rice Center for Urban Mobility Research both for administering the grant for this research and furnishing me with volumes of background material that went into the analysis. Gary Brosch, Jon Martz, David Hitchcock, and Philip Loukisas of the Rice Center all provided valuable assistance during various phases of the research. I also thank Bob Dunphy of the Urban Institute for making numerous reports and data sources available to me at the outset of the study. Finally, numerous individuals associated with the case sites used in this study, including developers, business association staff, local planners, and private employers, provided data, reports, and other support materials which allowed this research to be conducted. All were generous with their time and shared their many insights on a host of suburban mobility and growth issues. Without their assistance and interest in the topic, this work could never have been completed.

Robert Cervero
April 1988

Acknowledgments

Financial support for this study was provided by the Urban Mass Transportation Adminstration, US Department of Transportation. I thank the Administration, along with the many agency staff and private developers, too many to list here, for their kind assistance and applaud them for having the foresight to support basic research on land use and transportation relationships in America's suburbs. I also thank Andy Oppenheimer and Roger Jones of Unwin Hyman, London, for their assistance in seeing this work to production. I alone, however, am responsible for any errors or omissions that might remain.

Contents

Preface   *page* vii

Acknowledgments   ix

List of tables   xv

List of figures   xvii

1 Introduction: suburban office growth and congestion   1

   1.1 The suburban mobility crisis   1
   1.2 Study purpose   2
   1.3 Hypotheses   3
   1.4 Suburban growth and congestion   4
   1.5 International context   10
   1.6 Study outline   12
       Notes   14

2 Probing the suburban land use–transportation link:
   definitions and research methodology   15

   2.1 Defining terms   15
   2.2 Methodology   18
       Notes   28

3 Land use, employment, and transportation
   characteristics of America's SECs   29

   3.1 Characterizing SECs in the United States   29
   3.2 Scale, locational, and employment characteristics of SECs   30
   3.3 Density, site design, and property ownership characteristics 33
   3.4 Land uses and mixed-use activities   40
   3.5 Jobs–housing balancing and on-site housing provisions   46
   3.6 Transportation facilities and services in SECs   54
   3.7 SEC commuting and traffic conditions   61
   3.8 Summary   68
       Notes   69

4 Classifying suburban employment centers   72

   4.1 Forms of suburban growth   72
   4.2 Factors for classifying SECs   74
   4.3 Classification of case sites into SEC groups   78

4.4 Brief case summaries of SEC groups   86
4.5 Summary   101
    Notes   102

5   Comparison of land use and transportation
    characteristics among SEC groups   104

    5.1 Introduction   104
    5.2 Differences in size, location, and employment among
        SEC groups   105
    5.3 Comparisons of densities, lotting, and ownership
        patterns among SEC groups   108
    5.4 Comparison of land use compositions among SEC groups   113
    5.5 Transportation facilities and services   120
    5.6 Comparison of commuting choices and local traffic
        conditions among SEC groups   124
    5.7 Summary: policy inferences   131
        Notes   132

6   Land use and work site factors influencing
    commuting choices in SECs   134

    6.1 Introduction   134
    6.2 Factors influencing mode choices in SECs   135
    6.3 Factors influencing traffic conditions around SECs   142
    6.4 Factors related to parking standards at SECs   147
    6.5 Factors related to jobs–housing levels around SECs   151
    6.6 Factors related to property ownership patterns in SECs   153
    6.7 Case summary of work site factors influencing
        commuter choices in Pleasanton, California   154
    6.8 Summary of hypothesis tests   164
        Notes   167

7   Case studies of land-use transportation issues in
    SECs in greater Seattle, Chicago, and Houston   168

    7.1 Introduction   168
    7.2 Seattle area case study   169
    7.3 Chicago area case study   176
    7.4 Houston area case study   184
    7.5 Summary   193
        Note   194

8   Linking land use and transportation in SECs   195

    8.1 Overview of research findings   195
    8.2 Institutional responses   196
    8.3 Legislative and regulatory responses   198
    8.4 Density initiatives   201

8.5 Site design initiatives 202
8.6 Parking considerations 205
8.7 Mixed-use and jobs–housing initiatives 206
8.8 Closing remarks 209

Appendix 1 National survey on land use and travel
characteristics of major suburban employment centers 211

Appendix 2 Cluster analysis summary 217

Bibliography 219

Index 226

List of tables

1.1   Ranking of the 20 US metropolises with the most
      traffic congestion in 1984.   *page*   9
2.1   Listing of case sites by state, metropolitan
      area, and jurisdiction.   22–3
3.1   Size, locational, and workforce characteristics of 57
      large SECs in the US (1987).   31
3.2   Density, lotting, and land ownership characteristics of SECs.   34
3.3   Land use and mixed-use characteristics of SECs.   45
3.4   Housing provisions within and near SECs.   52
3.5   Transportation facilities and services.   55
3.6   Travel characteristics of workforce and areawide
      traffic conditions.   62
4.1   Factor loading and summary statistics for SECs.   76
4.2   Listing of cases within the six SEC groups.   80
4.3   Low-to-high thresholds for six SEC groups.   81
5.1   Comparison of size, location, and employment
      among SEC groups.   106
5.2   Comparison of density, lotting and ownership patterns
      among SEC groups.   108
5.3   Comparison of land use compositions and housing
      provisions among SEC groups.   115
5.4   Comparison of transportation facilities and services
      among SEC groups.   121
5.5   Comparison of workforce travel characteristics and
      areawide traffic volumes among SEC groups.   126
6.1   Stepwise regression results on factors influencing
      percentage of work trips (drive-alone mode).   136
6.2   Stepwise regression results on factors influencing SEC
      drive-alone commuting relative to regional averages.   137
6.3   Stepwise regression results on factors influencing
      percentage of work trips, by rideshare modes.   139
6.4   Stepwise regression results on factors influencing
      percentage of work trips, by walking and cycling modes (I).   140
6.5   Stepwise regression results on factors influencing
      percentage of work trips, by walking and cycling modes (2).   141
6.6   Stepwise regression results of factors influencing average
      commuting speeds.   143

6.7   Stepwise regression results of factors related to average
       journey-to-work travel time.   144
6.8   Stepwise regression results on factors related to level of
       service on main freeways serving SECs.   145
6.9   Stepwise regression results on factors related to level of
       service on main surface arterials serving SECs.   146
6.10 Stepwise regression results of factors related to parking
       per employee standards.   148
6.11 Stepwise regression results of factors related to parking
       per square footage standards.   149
6.12 Stepwise regression results of factors related to on-site
       jobs–housing ratios in SECs.   151
6.13 Stepwise regression results of factors related to ration of
       jobs to nearby housing units.   152
6.14 Stepwise regression results on factors related to property
       ownership patterns.   153
6.15 Stepwise regression results on factors related to developer
       land ownership shares.   154
6.16 Binomial logit results on likelihood of selecting share-ride
       modes.   159
6.17 Binomial logit results on whether employee commutes
       outside of both peak hours.   162
A.2   Dendogram of cluster analysis of 57 SECs.   218

List of figures

1.1 Comparison of office growth in Boston area
     suburbs and central city, 1979–86   *page* 6
2.1 Location of 57 case sites in the United States.   24
2.2 Los Angeles–Orange County cases.   24
2.3 San Francisco–San Jose cases.   24
2.4 Denver cases.   24
2.5 New York–New Jersey–Connecticut cases.   24
2.6 Miami–Ft. Lauderdale–Palm Beach cases.   25
2.7 Atlanta cases.   25
2.8 Chicago cases.   25
2.9 Baltimore cases.   25
2.10 Washington, DC cases.   25
2.11 Boston cases.   25
2.12 Detroit cases.   26
2.13 Minneapolis–St. Paul cases.   26
2.14 Philadelphia cases.   26
2.15 Cleveland cases.   26
2.16 Dallas cases.   26
2.17 Houston cases.   26
2.18 Seattle cases.   27
3.1 Distribution of job classifications in SECs.   32
3.2 Alternative configurations of a 500-acre parcel.   38
3.3 Percentage of SECs in three growth categories,
     exclusive of corridors.   40
3.4 Percentage of floorspace in land use categories.   44
3.5 Percentage of work trips to SECs, by mode.   63
3.6 Percentage breakdown of average level of service
     on main roadways serving SECs.   67
4.1 New England Executive Park site plan.   89
4.2 The sub-city of Tysons Corner.   98
5.1 Share of workforce in professional job
     categories, by SEC type.   107
5.2 Plot of FAR versus employment size, by three
     SEC groups.   109
5.3 Average stories of lowest and highest buildings,
     by SEC groups.   110
5.4 Average building square footage per employee
     in five SEC groups.   111
5.5 Average setbacks for front and sides of
     buildings, by SEC groups.   111

5.6   Percentage of floorspace in retail and office
      uses, by SEC groups.   113
5.7   Percentage of floorspace in retail versus
      office use, by three SEC groups.   114
5.8   Comparison of land use entropy index among
      five SEC groups.   116
5.9   Average number of retail centers with floorspace
      over 50,117 square feet.   117
5.10 Plot of number of retail centers versus FAR,
      by three SEC groups.   117
5.11 Average jobs–housing ratios for five SEC groups.   119
5.12 Plot of dwelling units versus employment,
      by three SEC groups.   119
5.13 Average number of companies sponsoring vanpools
      and vans operating in SECs.   123
5.14 Average per cent of SECs with rideshare
      coordinators and offices.   124
5.15 Average per cent of work trips made to SECs,
      by drive alone versus ridesharing.   127
5.16 Average traffic volumes as per cent of
      capacity on main roadways serving SECs.   130
6.1   Plot of parking supply versus FAR, by three
      SEC groups.   149
6.2   Plot of percentage of floorspace in retail
      use versus supply, by SEC groups.   150
6.3   Location of Pleasanton in the San Francisco
      Bay Area.   157
6.4   Probability of shared-ride commute, by one-way
      trip length for employees of Pleasanton, California.   160
6.5   Probability of shared-ride commute, by number
      of employees at work sites in Pleasanton, California.   161
6.6   Probability of travel outside of a.m. and p.m. peak
      hours, by number of employees at work sites in
      Pleasanton, California.   163
7.1   Location of Bellevue CBD.   170
7.2   Residential locations of Oak Brook, Illinois
      employees.   182
7.3   Residential locations of Schaumberg, Illinois
      employees.   183
7.4   Major activity centers in Houston.   185
7.5   West Houston Energy Corridor.   189
8.1   Alternative road layouts within an office
      development.   203
8.2   Separate pedestrian and cyclist path system.   204

1

Introduction: suburban office growth and congestion

═══════════

1.1   The suburban mobility crisis

Suburban America today finds itself in the throes of a mobility crisis. In greater Atlanta, Boston, Los Angeles, and at least a dozen other metropolitan areas around the country, bumper-to-bumper conditions are as common on cross town routes and outlying beltloops as on major downtown connectors. Along the Katy Freeway in suburban Houston, on Route 101 south of San Francisco, and along sections of Interstate 25 southeast of Denver, traffic crawls at under 12 m.p.h. during much of the morning and evening commute hours. Getting stuck in traffic jams, once a dubious distinction of downtown commuters, today affects nearly all Americans.

By and large, the suburbanization of congestion in America has paralleled the suburbanization of jobs throughout the 1980s. Surges in suburban office employment over the past ten years have fundamentally altered commuting patterns, giving rise to far more cross-town, reverse-direction, and lateral movements than in years past. The dispersal of both jobs and commuting has been a mixed blessing. While on the one hand it has relieved some downtowns of additional traffic and brought jobs closer to some suburbanites, on the other hand it has flooded many outlying thoroughfares with unprecedented volumes of traffic which they are incapable of handling and seriously threatened the very quality of living that lured millions of Americans to the suburbs in the first place.

The way suburban workplaces are being designed no doubt bears some of the blame for worsening congestion. Many suburban offices have been built at densities far below those of their downtown counter-parts, rendering mass transit an impractical travel option. The scaling of offices on a lateral rather than a vertical plane has spread out most buildings, creating a form of horizontal skyscraper, and made walking, cycling, and most forms of group travel far less convenient than (and less competitive with) the private automobile. Many suburban job centers, moreover, have a single dominant use, usually as offices; traditional downtown centers, by contrast, tend to have a rich variety of offices, shops, restaurants, banks, theaters, and other activities which intermingle. While downtown workers can easily walk to a restaurant or a merchandise store during lunch, those who work in many campus style office parks are virtually stranded in the midday if they do not drive their own car to work. If these kinds of built environments continue to evolve, the suburban workplace of tomorrow will become one which is hostile to commuting and circulating by almost any means other than the private automobile. This is the crux, it is believed, of the mobility crisis which is fast enveloping America's suburbs. The intent of the study which follows is to explore whether indeed this is the case and, if so, what can be done about it.

1.2   Study purpose

Suburbia's traffic problems have received considerable attention during the 1980s. A flurry of articles, research reports, and media accounts has identified suburban congestion as one of the most pressing problems in the transportation field today and, most probably, one that will hold center stage in the transportation policy arena for years to come (Cervero 1984, 1986b, Dunphy 1985, Leinberger & Lockwood 1986, Orski 1986a, 1987). To date, most research on the topic has focused on the economic and demographic forces that have given rise to suburban congestion as well as the most promising approaches to managing travel demand and financing infrastructure improvements.

The one area where there has been far less research and where a considerable knowledge gap remains is the relationship between suburban development patterns and mobility. More specifically, how the size, density, and land use make-up of suburban office and commercial centers affect the travel choices of their tenants' employees as well as areawide traffic conditions remains unclear and, at best, is treated in the literature mainly through anecdotes. Since transportation is a derived demand, i.e., people travel in order to access activities occurring in different places, transportation scholars have long argued that coordinated land use planning offers the most effective and enduring basis for improving mobility over the long run. And since congestion is largely a problem associated with the peak period, commute trip, the spatial proximity of residences and workplaces can have a particularly strong bearing on suburban travel patterns and traffic conditions. Accordingly, this study probes the relationship between the development characteristics of suburban job centers and worker travel choices as well as local traffic conditions and, based on its findings, recommends land use practices and policy initiatives that are most consonant with high levels of regional mobility.

Since suburban congestion has been most acute around large employment centers, this book concentrates mainly on the linkage between mobility and commercial–office development. This linkage is examined for major suburban office centers and corridors in America's largest metropolitan areas, with primary attention given to how the travel choices of workers and local traffic conditions are influenced by the following site characteristics: (a) employment densities; (b) site designs; (c) land use composition, particularly the level of mixed use activities; (d) suburban levels of jobs housing balance; (e) land lotting and ownership patterns; and (f) parking provisions. Only through a better understanding of how these factors, both singly and collectively, shape the travel choices of suburban workers can meaningful land use measures be introduced to safeguard mobility and head off what some forewarn is an impending suburban mobility crisis.

1.3 Hypotheses

The central proposition of this study is that congestion problems and declining mobility are inescapably linked to the emerging land use environment of suburban employment areas. The land use and physical design characteristics of most suburban workplaces are believed to have contributed directly to the decline in suburban mobility by inducing most employees to drive alone to work. Specifically, this study hypothesizes that the *low density*, *single use*, and *non-integrated* character of many suburban office–commercial centers and corridors has compelled many workers to become dependent on their automobiles for accessing work and circulating within projects. These factors, combined with the abundance of free employee parking, inadequate road facilities, and meager levels of suburban transit services, it is argued, have contributed to unprecedented levels of congestion. Many suburban work settings are designed principally for private automobile access and circulation and, consequently, are insensitive to the needs of pedestrians, cyclists, buses, and other commute options – what some critics have called "transit hostile" environments. Severe jobs–housing imbalances in many outlying growth areas, moreover, are thought to be a root cause of growing auto dependency and, as a result, worsening congestion. The emergence of suburban workplaces with densities equivalent to those of small downtowns, rich mixtures of land uses, and nearby affordable housing, it is felt, could do at least as much to mitigate congestion over the long run as any mix of traffic management or roadway expansion programs, and perhaps far more. The analyses which follow attempt to test the soundness of these propositions, relying on a balance of statistical investigations and case analyses. As a prelude, the remainder of this introduction offers an overview on suburban growth and congestion issues in the US and abroad, and a chapter by chapter outline of the rest of the book.

1.4   Suburban growth and congestion

The office boom

The migration of traffic jams to the suburbs has followed in the wake of what some have called America's "third wave" of suburbanization. The first wave involved the mass movement of middle class and upper income residents to the outskirts of cities throughout the 1900s in search of spacious living conditions and detached, single family homes. The construction of inter urban streetcar lines and modern motorways literally paved the way for this exodus (Warner 1962, Adams 1970). The second wave of decentralization, which occurred primarily during the three decades following World War II and continues today, witnessed the migration of commercial and industrial activities to the outskirts, attracted to the vast reservoir of potential consumers and workers living in the suburbs. The opening of massive indoor shopping malls and the emergence of commercial strips and industrial parks along axial motorways perhaps best characterized this transformation of America's suburbs from predominantly bedroom communities to more urban-like places.[1]

The third wave of suburban expansion – the arrival of workers, particularly those in the office and high-technology sectors – has brought many American suburbs full circle. With the addition of a day-time workforce population, many suburbs have become virtually indistinquishable from traditional urban centers, featuring a mosaic of places, from office towers and executive parks to fern bars and performing arts centers. No longer do Americans vacate suburbs each morning; today's suburbs have become primary destinations themselves. Unfortunately, suburbs have also suffered many of the ills that accompany maturation, most notably traffic congestion.

The pace of suburban employment growth has been nothing short of phenomenal. In 1980, 57 per cent of all office space in the US was located in urban centers and 43 per cent in the suburbs; by 1986, the situation was reversed – 60 per cent was in the suburbs, compared to 40 per cent in cities (Pisarski 1987, Office Network 1987). Attracted by cheaper land, closer proximity to regional airports, smart buildings laced with fiber optic cables and advanced telecommunications equipment, and country-like amenities, the overwhelming majority of the nation's high-technology firms today have chosen a suburban address (Urban Land Institute 1986, 1987). Many firms in the financial/insurance/ real estate (FIRE) sectors, one of the nation's fastest growing, have likewise opted for the suburbs, moving their back office and clerical workers to branch facilities that are hooked up to the main offices *via* telephone lines and communication satellites. Low land prices and the availability of pools of (primarily female) second wage-earners have been the primary lures attracting FIRE firms to the urban fringes (Dowall 1987, Kroll 1986, Urban Land Institute 1986).

While the suburban office boom has been most pronounced along the America's sunbelt crescent (Cervero 1986b), the trend has been truly nationwide in scope, occurring even in older industrial areas. In greater Philadelphia and St. Louis, for instance, suburban employment grew by 8 and 17 per cent respectively between 1982 and 1986, contrasted with a loss in central city jobs over the same period (Orski 1986a, Urban Land Institute 1987). Office decentralization has also been swift in New England, the region of the country enjoying the healthiest economic growth over much of the 1980s. As shown in Figure 1.1, the suburbs' share of the total office market in the greater Boston area rocketed from 20 per cent in 1979 to 60 per cent in 1986, an average annual gain of over 5 percentage points. Many expect the decentralization trend, if anything, to accelerate in coming years as America's economy continues to shift from a "smokestack," manufacturing base to a service and information-processing emphasis, enabling more and more firms to relocate to the lower cost suburbs.

The physical appearances and make-up of suburban employment areas are as diverse as the types of businesses and activities that are locating in them. Some of the larger, nodal developments have been varyingly referred to as *suburban downtowns*, *urban villages*, and *megacomplexes* – clusters of office and commercial development that resemble the downtowns of many medium-sized cities in both scale and density (Leinberger & Lockwood 1986, Orski 1986a, 1987). The archetypal suburban downtown is City Post Oak, eight miles west of downtown Houston, where 30 million square feet of office, retail, and hotel floorspace (including a 65-story skyscraper) has been added within the past two decades. Other notable examples are Tysons Corner in northern Virginia, Las Colinas west of Dallas, and South Coast Metro in Orange County, California. The speed at which these

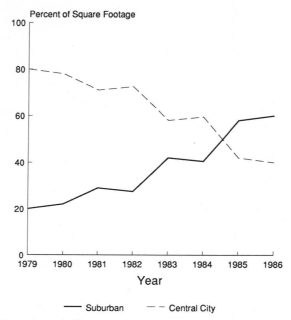

Figure 1.1   Comparison of office growth in Boston area suburbs and central city, 1979–86.

new outlying downtowns have been built has been dizzying. While traditional downtowns have evolved gradually, allowing a buildup of road improvements over time, suburban downtowns with over 10 million square feet of commercial floorspace have sprouted in as few as five years, overloading the local infrastructure in the process. Quite often, these "instant downtowns" have produced "instant congestion."

At the other end of the workplace spectrum have been *master-planned office parks*, ranging from small business compounds to massive expanses of low-lying office buildings spread over 500 acres or more, such as Bishop Ranch east of San Francisco and Technology Park northeast of Atlanta. Many business parks resemble modern college campuses, designed to provide a premium, rural-like work environment for highly skilled, professional workers. Most are characterized by nicely groomed landscapes, glass-textured buildings with impressive atrium entrances, plentiful parking, and employment densities that are a fraction of those found downtown. All support one primary activity – office functions, which normally account for over 95 per cent of total floorspace. For all intents and purposes, office parks are designed at the outset almost exclusively for automobile circulation. While traffic often flows freely once inside these spaciously designed premises, in many instances the convergence of thousands of motorists driving to and from these parks has jammed connecting arterials and freeways.

Suburban job growth has also been less nodal and focused, situated instead along suburban corridors – generally loosely organized strips of freestanding office buildings and retail complexes, typically aligned along axial freeways and arterials. Most of the better known corridors are host to some of the nation's most prestigious high-technology firms. Notable among these "silicon strips" are the "Princeton Zip Strip" in central New Jersey (Route 1), the Sunset Corridor west of Portland, Route 128 encircling Boston, and the Silicon Valley north of San Jose (Route 101) (Fulton, W. 1986). While the traffic impact of individual projects along these corridors tend to be modest, the cumulative effects of numerous unrelated and speculative projects have frequently clogged up areawide thoroughfares.

Still another form of suburban development that has gained recognition is that of megacounties – massive, often amorphous, swaths of urban-like growth that have leaped over to once-tranquil counties ringing major urban centers, such as Gwinnett County northeast of Atlanta, Du Page County west of Chicago, and Oakland County north of Detroit. In the case of Oakland County, 40 per cent of all of Michigan's job growth between 1982 and 1986 occurred there, spread fairly evenly throughout the county (Church 1987). This countywide version of urbanization has often overwhelmed secondary roads that only five or ten years earlier functioned as leisurely farm-to-market roads.

The traffic boom

Job dispersal has had a profound affect on commuting patterns in America throughout the 1980s. No longer focused on a single downtown, America's metropolises have far more complex patterns of travel than ten or fifteen years ago. For most urbanized regions, a pathwork of criss cross and lateral movement streams has replaced radial commutes as the dominant pattern. National statistics underscore this. Between 1960 and 1980, the share of work trips which began and ended in the suburbs increased from 30 per cent to nearly 42 per cent within US metropolitan areas with a population larger than 250,000 (Fulton, P. 1986). During this period, moreover, intra-suburban commuting garnered around 83 per cent of the metropolitan growth in travel, a pattern that was uniform across the nation. In greater Boston, Detroit, St. Louis, and Pittsburgh, nearly two thirds of work trips today take place wholly within suburbs.[2]

There has also been a surge in commuting between metropolitan and non-metropolitan areas in the United States. Over ten per cent of the non-metropolitan counties in the US, for instance, have more than 15 per cent of their employed residents commuting to central counties in urbanized areas (Pisarski 1987). This growth in ex-urban flows, what geographers call "extended commuting," has virtually blurred the distinction between city and county in a number of regions across the country (Berry & Gillard 1977).

These trends do not square well with the nation's urban highway and transit networks, most of which are of a hub and spoke variety, designed to funnel commuters downtown. Those making lateral and cross-town journeys are all too often forced on to secondary arteries and ring roads that were never designed or oriented to serve large volumes of traffic. Circuitous trip making and clotted roadways have all too often resulted. The dispersal of travel bodes unfavorably for mass transit as well since buses and trains are poor substitutes for the automobile when trip origins and destinations are widely spread. Journey-to-work statistics confirm this: in 1980, only 1.6 per cent of all suburb-to-suburb work trips in the United States were made *via* public transit (Fulton, P. 1986).

Traffic is spreading out not only spatially, but temporally as well. Stop- and-go conditions can be found throughout the day in many areas. Dallas's North Central Expressway, Chicago's Dan Ryan Expressway, Los Angeles's Ventura Freeway, Washington's Beltway, and the Long Island Expressway are frequently as jammed during the noon hours as they are at 7.30 a.m. and 5.30 p.m. (Orski 1986a).

Within limits, one should be reminded, traffic congestion is desirable – a sign that a region is economically vibrant and has refrained from overinvesting in highways. And, of course, congestion is relative – residents of Manhattan, St. Louis, and Boise perceive congestion quite differently. Recent public outcries and the rash of initiatives to halt growth, however, suggest that congestion in America in the 1980s and 1990s has exceeded acceptable limits and may indeed be approaching the intolerable. From 1975 to 1985, the share of rush hour freeway traffic in urbanized areas that flowed under 35 m.p.h., what traffic engineers consider to be congested, increased from 41 per cent to 56 per cent (Lindley 1987, US Department of Transportation 1985). In over a dozen metropolitan areas across the country, public opinion polls indicate that traffic congestion is viewed as the number one urban problem. In the San Francisco Bay Area, residents have cited congestion as the worst public menace for six years straight, outdistancing its closest rival air pollution, by more than three-to-one. Such widespread dissatisfaction reflects the fact that congestion in the US now afflicts nearly all metropolitan commuters to some degree – whether they are headed downtown, reverse-commuting, or traveling on a secondary, county road. While only a decade ago congestion was the scourge of downtown, rush-hour commuters, today it is pandemic, pervading the freeway and arterial networks of most American metropolises at all hours of the day.

Table 1.1 shows which American cities suffer the severest congestion when expressed in delay per mile of travel. Many areas with the worst

Table 1.1   Ranking of the 20 US metropolises with the most traffic congestion in 1984.

Rank	Urban area	Congestion severity index[1]	Annual recurring vehicle-hours of delay (millions)[2]
1	Houston	11,112	39.5
2	New Orleans	10,576	7.7
3	New York	8,168	62.7
4	Detroit	7,757	16.2
5	San Franciso	7,634	72.9
6	Seattle	7,406	18.5
7	Los Angeles	6,376	78.3
8	Boston	5,538	10.0
9	Charlotte	5,263	1.3
10	Atlanta	5,034	15.8
11	Minneapolis	4,704	11.2
12	Dallas	4,630	16.3
13	Norfolk	4.505	5.0
14	Chicago	4,501	19.7
15	Denver	4,454	7.5
16	Washington, D.C.	4,188	16.3
17	Hartford	4,111	1.9
18	San Antonio	3,938	5.2
19	Pittsburgh	3,216	6.5
20	San Diego	2,823	8.6

[1] Congestion severity index = total hours of delay/million vehicle-miles of travel.
[2] Reflects roadway segments where there are recurring congested conditions.
Sources: Lindley (1987, Tables 2 and 3) and US Department of Transportation (1986).

congestion, like Houston, New Orleans, and Los Angeles, are fast growing sunbelt metropolises that have experienced meteoric increases in suburban employment during the 1970s and early 1980s. In Houston, for instance, the American city suffering the worst traffic jams, only 39 per cent of all office construction was outside of its downtown in 1970; by 1982, the share had catapulted to 87 per cent (Rice Center 1983). Even older, traditional manufacturing centers of the US with stifling levels of traffic congestion, such as the greater Detroit area, are experiencing a suburban office building boom. In Detroit, for instance, employment in the city proper grew only 2.1 per cent between 1982 and 1986, while during the same period jobs increased 14.1 per cent (Orski 1986a).

The mounting congestion crisis poses a grave threat to the high standard of mobility that Americans have long cherished and taken for granted, as well as a threat to continued economic growth in many regions of the country. Infuriated by traffic's ever-increasing presence, more and more suburbanites are insisting that future commercial and office growth be regulated, be it through downzoning, moratoria on the issuance of building permits, or height restrictions placed on new buildings. In California, 47 growth control initiatives were placed before voters in 1986 alone, of which nearly two-thirds were passed (Cervero 1988). Along Boston's Route 495, restrictive zoning by-laws in many towns have restrained housing construction and driven up prices. This new wave of initiatives, it might be noted, differs in kind from the celebrated growth controls of the 1970s in places like Petaluma (California), Ramapo (New York), and Boulder (Colorado); whereas these earlier initiatives sought to limit new housing construction and thus to ease the burden placed on local treasuries, today we are seeing steps aimed squarely at banning new commercial and office growth – that is, the number of shoppers, workers, and other "outsiders" driving their cars into established communities. Because such measures tend to push growth elsewhere in the region, quite often farther out along the urban periphery, and because increases in traffic headed to surrounding communities frequently clog these places regardless, some argue that efforts to control growth at a municipal level are doomed to failure (Work *et al.*, 1987, Cervero 1986b). High stakes are involved where rampant suburban office and commercial growth fuel fierce political controversy, and the rising ground swell of resentment to mounting traffic jams can only be expected to spawn even more confrontations among builders, residents, and city councils in coming years. The battle to halt suburban growth will no doubt intensify in the 1990s, with traffic being the dominant issue around which battle lines are drawn.

1.5   International context

The suburbanization of office growth and traffic jams has certainly not been restricted to the North American continent. On the peripheries of a number of British and Scandinavian conurbations, several self-contained satellite centers of commerce and industry have emerged during this century, notably Vallingby and Farsta outside of Stockholm, Albertslund west of Copenhagen, Tapiola near Helsinki, and Milton Keynes, Letchworth, and Stevenage north of London. As planned developments with large numbers of people living and working in the community, however, most of these satellite new towns have experienced little in the way of American-style traffic congestion. More recent concentrations of suburban office development in Europe have been the Courbevoie district of high-rise, first class office space west of Paris, the massive complex of multinational company headquarters north of Luxembourg City, and the assemblage of high technology firms and branch plants east of Reading, England, among others. In the cases of these more recent renditions of European suburban office growth, rush-hour traffic tie-ups are becoming far more commonplace on the fringes of metropolitan areas.

As in the United States, the decentralization of jobs as well as traffic flows in many European conurbations can be directly linked to the on-going modernization and reindustrialization of traditional manufacturing-based economies. Throughout Europe, employment in agriculture, mining, and manufacturing has steadily declined over the past decade while the workforces of service and information-related industries have expanded (Fothergill & Gudgin 1982, Greenwood 1982). In many instances, the decline in manufacturing jobs stems from the heavy dependence of larger, older cities on steel production, ship building, textiles, and other labor-intensive industries which have suffered employment and sales losses stemming from increased international competition, advances in manufacturing and assembly technologies (such as robotics), and the use of plastics and other weight-reducing synthetic substitutes in many consumer products. In Great Britain, service industry jobs increased 11 per cent from 1959 to 1975, whereas manufacturing employment fell over 2 per cent over the same period (Fothergill & Gudgin 1982). Similarly, pronounced economic shifts occurred in other industrialized nations of the world.

No longer tied to rail spurs and waterports, more and more firms during the post-industrial era have become "footloose" i.e., they are able to move freely to wherever they can maximize their net advantage, which generally means to places where input costs for land, labor, and capital are the lowest. One spatial repercussion of this footlooseness has been a widely publicized "sunbelt" pattern of movement to climatically milder settings. In Great Britain, companies have been steadily flocking from Liverpool, Manchester, Birmingham, the West Midlands, and other parts of the industrialized north to urban and semi-rural settings along England's southern coast since the early 1970s. A similar geography of job flows can be found in France where companies are migrating from the industrialized Rhone-Alps and Lorraine areas to the nation's four southernmost regions. Since 1975, high-technology employment has grown six times faster in France's southwestern provinces than in the nation's northwestern ones (Ayadalot 1984). And in West Germany, the greater Stuttgart and Munich areas in the southern Bavarian provinces have been the chief recipients of the nation's employment growth since 1980.

While the sunbelt shift has captured wide media attention, it has been the relocation of jobs to the outer spheres of established areas that is having the most profound influence on the geomorphology of European metropolises and levels of mobility within them. The suburbanization of jobs appears to be almost on a par with America's experiences in some regions. In Manchester, England, for example, total employment in the inner area declined 6.3 per cent between 1975 and 1980 whereas jobs increased 4.3 per cent in outer Manchester (Webster *et al.*, 1985). In West Germany, every major city, with the exceptions of Cologne and Hanover, lost population and manufacturing jobs between 1970 and 1984, while over the same period many suburban communities and small towns tripled both their population and employment bases (Kasarda & Friedrichs 1985).

As in America, the level of suburb-to-suburb commuting also appears to be on the rise throughout Europe, synchronized with job dispersal. In Great Britain, for example, travel patterns have become more uniformly spread and less focused on city centers over the past ten years, with commute trips that occur wholly within outer areas of metropolises capturing an estimated 45 per cent of the growth in motorized travel during the 1970–84 period (Webster *et al.*, 1985). Anecdotal evidence also suggests that trip patterns are becoming increasingly dispersed and peripherally oriented. Greater London's M25 orbital beltloop, for instance, is today handling vehicular volumes that are nearly twice the level projected for the late-1980s only ten years earlier. In greater Paris, bumper-to-bumper traffic conditions plague motorists on the Boulevard Peripherique, the city's main circumferential, every bit as much as some of the busiest inner-city routes. Steadily worsening traffic snarls and unexpected volume gains have also been recorded on ring roads in greater Stockholm, Munich, and Rome.

Although the thrust of this book is devoted to the North American experience, the analysis and findings which follow clearly have policy relevance to both sides of the Atlantic. To the extent other industrialized nations of the world experience a suburban office boom similar to that taking place in the United States, many of the land use and transportation topics covered in this work will find much wider policy application than the boundaries of the United States. Indeed, an advantage other nations will have is that they will be in a position to learn from America's mistakes in grappling with suburban transportation problems while at the same time capitalizing on and emulating its success stories. The suburban congestion quandary and its relationship to contemporary land use planning practices is undeniably one which deserves serious policy attention on many fronts and in most post-industrializing nations of the world.

1.6   Study outline

In this study, both statistical and interpretative approaches are used in examining how the site and physical design characteristics of suburban workplaces influence travel behavior and local traffic conditions. Much of the empirical work is based on land use, employment, and travel data compiled for over 50 of America's largest suburban employment centers. This national scale analysis is supplemented by a more disaggregate study of worker travel behavior for employment centers in Pleasanton, California, one of the fast growing suburbs in the San Francisco Bay Area. The empirical phase of the study, moreover, is complemented by several case studies, based on the results of site visits, interviews with developers and public officials, and literature reviews. Various policy issues and competing theories related to land use and transportation in suburbia are interwoven throughout the analysis.

The book is divided into seven remaining chapters. Chapter 2 describes the research methodology and data sources in more detail and sets forth definitions for a number of terms applied throughout the analysis. In Chapter 3, the land use, site development, employment, and transportation characteristic of 57 of the largest suburban employment centers in the United States are summarized. This chapter also reviews the literature and cites empirical findings on the land use and development characteristics of suburban work centers. Various contemporary policy topics on land use and mobility are also discussed.

Chapters 4 and 5 are devoted to classifying these employment centers into one of six homogeneous groups based on clustering techniques and examining variations in site, land use, employment, and transportation characteristics among these groups. Chapter 4 reviews past work on metropolitan growth, presents the results of a cluster analysis, and describes several employment centers within each classification group. Threshold ranges on the size, density, site designs, and land use features of each group are also presented. Chapter 5 follows this with a detailed analysis of the degree to which site, employment, and travel characteristics vary among the groups, based on both statistical tests and a variety of charts and figures.

Chapter 6 subjects the hypotheses presented in section 1.3 to statistical tests. Specifically, the influences of various site, land use, and density characteristics on mode choice, average speeds, level of service, and other mobility indices are examined and empirically tested. Overall policy inferences are drawn from these test results.

Chapter 7 embellishes the empirical phase of the study by presenting an overview of land use, development, and mobility issues for suburban employment centers in the greater Chicago, Houston, and Seattle areas. Such topics as jobs-housing imbalances, site design practices, and growth management policies are covered.

The concluding chapter presents policy options for designing future suburban employment centers with mobility concerns in mind. Examples of higher density, mixed use projects that seem to be offering mobility payoffs are highlighted. Design practices which enhance mobility are presented as well. Institutional and legislative remedies that might be introduced for synchronizing job and residential growth in suburban areas are also discussed.

Notes

1. For a fuller discussion of this process, see Masotti & Hadden (1973) and Hartshorn & Muller (1986).
2. These statistics, it might be noted, stand in marked contrast to those cited by Liepman (1944) in the first systematic analysis of urban commutation profiles in America during the height of World War II. Liepman (1944) characterized metropolitan commuting as tide-like movements into central cities, involving a rhythmic convergence of trips into "zones of conflux" i.e., downtowns, in the morning and the return of these trips to "zones of dispersion" i.e., residences, in the evening. By the late 1950s, however, it was becoming increasingly apparent that commuting in America followed not only a centripetal and centrifugal pattern in the morning and evening, respectively, but also involved a complicated cross-current of movement streams. In a prophetic article, Schnore (1959, 203) warned that unless the steady flight of people and jobs to the suburbs was reversed, by the 1980s "a confusing and asymmetrical compound of variously oriented threads of traffic, overlaying the older (and perhaps rudimentary) center-oriented pattern" would emerge. Over time, a number of authors have confirmed Schnore's premonition, documenting the steady growth in lateral, cross- hauling, and peripheral commuting since the 1960s (Meyer *et al.*, 1965, Taaffee *et al.*, 1963, Vernon 1963, Catanese 1971, Hughes & James 1975).

2

Probing the suburban
land use – transportation link:
definitions and
research methodology

2.1 Defining terms

The proliferation of terms used to describe concentrations of suburban employment and activities has given rise to a rather loose jargon, found in the press and research literature alike. This section defines key terms used throughout this book. It is followed by a discussion of the methodologies and data sources used in carrying out the empirical phases of this research.

Suburban

The distinction between what is "suburban" and what is "urban" has blurred in recent years. In many cases, political boundaries are used to distinquish suburbs from central cities, even though activities on both sides of the boundary may be virtually identical. Some employment centers are on the metropolitan fringes and have distinct suburban characters, while others are in more mature, inner-tier areas. Perimeter Center (a mid-rise office complex and regional shopping center north of Atlanta) is an example of the former while Bethesda's cluster of offices around its Washington Metro rail station represents more of the latter. Still other clusters function more as satellites, straddled between two or more central cities. The Research Triangle, for instance, lies approximately 15 miles west of Raleigh, North Carolina and operates more as a satellite employment center than as a suburb of the Raleigh–Durham–Chapel Hill metropolitan area. Perhaps the common feature all of these centers share is that they are "Non-Central Business District," or "Non-CBD," locales. Partly for convenience, the term "suburban" is used in this book. It is used loosely, however, and is meant to suggest the location of any land activity outside of a regional CBD, generally at least five or more radial miles away.[1]

Centers versus corridors

Another distinguishing characteristic of suburban agglomerations is whether they are nodal clusters of development, i.e., centers, or linear strips, i.e., corridors, (Baerwald 1982). Clusters, or centers, tend to be well-defined, focused concentrations of development, often with relatively high densities and a mixture of land uses. They are generally surrounded by a traditional pattern of low-density, homogeneously zoned development, such as tract residential housing. Corridors, on the other hand, can generally be thought of as a series of pod-like developments that straddle one or more major thoroughfares, akin to a string of pearls, and that function independently of one another. Some concentrations are more or less hybrids of the two. Where possible, this book will refer to suburban developments as either centers[2] or corridors.

Employment centers

The phrase that has gained currency for describing a large-scale, mixed-use concentration of urban or suburban development is "activity center." To be considered a major activity center in the greater Washington, D.C. area, Christopher Leinberger used the following five-pronged criteria:

(a)   The area must have at least 5 million square feet of development;
(b)   The area must have at least 600,000 square feet of retail space;
(c)   The area must have more people commuting into it than out of it each morning;
(d)   The area must have more jobs than housing; and
(e)   The area must be perceived by the public as "having it all" – being an end destination for mixed use: entertainment, shopping, and jobs.

Based on these criteria, Leinberger identified 13 suburban activity centers in the greater Washington, D.C. area, with Tysons Corner, Rockville/Gaithersburg, Rosslyn/Ballston, and Crystal City forming the largest ones (Garreau 1987).

In the analysis of major growth centers in the Houston area, the Rice Center (1987, I–1) also adopted the phrase "activity center," which was defined as "major employment concentrations located outside of the Central Business District." Twenty-two activity centers were identified based on employment, density, land uses, and other factors. Centers ranged in size from 1 to 15 million square feet of building space, 900 to 7,500 acres of land area, and 60,000 to 100,000 residents. Outside of downtown, the three largest activity centers in the Houston area were Post Oak (purported to be the nation's largest non-CBD center), Greenway Plaza, and the West Houston Energy Corridor.

In another study, the Atlanta Regional Commission (1985, 5) defined activity centers as "areas with more than 7,500 jobs in contiguous census blocks that have an identifiable relationship." This simpler definition resulted in 17 activity centers (including downtown) being identified in the Atlanta region, ranging in size from 1,011 acres (CBD) to 48,536 acres (Fulton Industrial District) and in employment from 7,920 (South Lake Mall) to 94,135 (CBD).

While these and other studies have adopted the "activity center" naming convention, in this study the term "employment center" is used in order to convey the idea of a massing of workers. While most major centers support retail and other uses, it is their employment base, and more specifically office jobs, that are their dominant feature and that contribute most directly to peak-period traffic problems. Since congestion occurs principally in rush hours and is thus connected with the journey-to-work trip, using the term "employment" rather than "activity" in qualifying these centers seems preferable. As defined by the Institute of Transportation Engineers (1976), "activity centers" can also include regional shopping centers, university campuses, medical centers, airports, major recreation centers, and sports stadia. Travel to many of these centers generally occurs outside of traditional peak periods, even though roads leading to them are quite often congested. To use the more generic term "activity center," then, would encompass a wide range of places outside of CBDs and obfuscate the purpose of this study – to focus on mobility and land use relationships in areas of massive suburban employment growth.

In light of the above, the phrase "suburban employment center," abbreviated to SEC, is used throughout the remainder of this study. As noted above, distinctions should also be made between centers and corridors. Thus, the SEC abbreviation is used to represent both "suburban employment centers" and "suburban employment corridors."

The minimum thresholds used in selecting SEC case sites are described in the next section and in Chapters 3 and 4. All of the SECs examined in this study had at least 2,000 employees and 1 million square feet of office floorspace, which under this definition, would have included most of the "activity centers" selected for Washington, D.C., Houston, and Atlanta in the above cited studies.

Land use

Land use generally refers to "how land is put to use" – that is, whether it is employed for residential, commercial, industrial, open space, or some other purpose (Chapin & Kaiser 1979). Virtually all travel is inextricably tied to land use. With the exception of Sunday excursions and, perhaps, teenage joy-riding, few motorized trips occur for the simple pleasure of driving. Rather, people make trips to access places in order to satisfy personal and social objectives, be it earning wages, visiting a doctor, or attending a sports event. How these places are developed and designed – their densities, mixture of uses, site layout, parking provisions, and so on – sets the stage for virtually all commuting behavior.

In this book, the term "land use" is employed fairly liberally. It refers to all aspects of the built environment of a SEC – its density, composition of activities, scale, layout, and physical design. Thus, under this broader definition, the "land-use transportation link" is meant to convey how various site features, including density and design, influence mobility, not just the composition of land activities.

2.2 Methodology

Since many of America's SECs are relatively new, some having evolved only within the past ten years, land use and transportation data on them tend to be fairly sparse. Because most of the hypotheses tested in this study relied upon empirical data, a national data base of selected land use, employment, and transportation variables was built. In all, 57 SEC case sites were sampled. This and other data sources used in this study, along with the general research design, are described below.

Case selection and data sources

Because suburban traffic congestion is most acute around the largest SECs in the United States, the sample frame for this study was SECs: (a) of at least 1 million square feet of office floorspace; (b) with 2,000 or more workers; and (c) located at least 5 radial miles away from the regional CBD. Through an initial review of the literature and various publications available from the Urban Land Institute (1984, 1987), the Office Network (1987), and other primary sources, it was found that most SECs meeting these minimum thresholds were from Metropolitan Statistical Areas (MSAs) with 1980 populations exceeding 1 million, which numbered 39 in all. Because of the national prominence of some SECs, such as the Research Triangle in central North Carolina, as well as the availability of nearly complete data for these places, case sites from several smaller MSAs were also included. Thus, the sampling frame consisted of potential SECs in the 39 largest MSAs in the country plus several others from smaller MSAs that were known to have reasonably complete data.

The major factor constraining the choice of case sites was the availability of data on the travel characteristics of an SEC's workforce. In most cases, only 1980 journey-to-work census data were available for the tract or tracts most closely corresponding to an SEC. Data on land use and employment characteristics of SECs, however, were usually more recent, generally available for the 1985–87 time frame. Because many SECs were only in their embryonic stage of growth in 1980, and in order to ensure data were longitudinally consistent, cases were generally eliminated from consideration if only 1980 journey-to-work data were available. In several instances, regional transportation planning agencies had updated 1980 travel data to 1985 or later, enabling these cases to be included in the analysis.

One notable difficulty that was faced was defining the geographic boundary of each SEC. In some cases, such as for master-planned developments, newtowns, business parks, and planned urban developments (PUDs), boundaries were clear, corresponding to the property lines of the project. In other instances, in particular large-scale corridors, boundaries were not easily delineated. In these cases, the boundaries defined by local or regional planning authorities (often as a specific study area) and local business associations[3] were generally adopted. In general, the SEC boundaries corresponding to the territories for which relevant data were most readily available were used in this study.

The actual instruments and sources used to compile relevant data included a questionnaire, land use and transportation inventories maintained by both local agencies and by national associations, various published and unpublished documents and reports, and primary data collected locally through site visits and field surveys. Where not available from questionnaire responses, land use and employment data (e.g., floorspace, housing units, employment densities, and workforce composition) were obtained from inventories and publications provided by the Urban Land Institute[4], the Rice Center[5], the Office Network[6], local and national real estate firms, private developers, corridor and business associations, chambers of commerce, city and county planning agencies, and metropolitan planning organizations (MPOs). Land use data were also compiled from a number of monthly real estate publications, such as *National Real Estate Investor* (City Review section), *Real Estate Forum*, and *Real Estate News* (available for four different regions of the country).

Data on the travel characteristics of SEC workers were obtained from reports and summaries provided by developers, business and property owner associations, and local transportation planning agencies. Information on traffic volumes, average travel speeds, and levels of service for major arterials and freeways serving SECs was obtained from local traffic engineering departments. And most of the data collected on regional travel characteristics were obtained from various publications by the US Bureau of Census (1982) and the Federal Highway Administration (Briggs *et al.*, 1986, Klinger & Kusmyak 1986, and Rodriquez *et al.*, 1985).

Survey instrument

To supplement the data mentioned above, two different questionnaires were designed, pre-tested, and administered. Appendix I (see pp. 211–16) shows the questionnaire sent to "centers," in general well-defined, master-planned projects for which preliminary investigations revealed fairly extensive data were available. Another survey, a more abbreviated version of the former, went to "concentrations," in general clusters of several independent projects and defined corridors.[7]

After candidate sites within each metropolitan area were identified, a reconnaissance investigation was conducted to determine which agencies and individuals were best able to respond to the questionnaire. Individuals were queried over the telephone to find out the general availability of relevant data and to assess their willingness to participate in the study. In most instances, three or more individuals filled out a questionnaire for each SEC, providing information only for those questions for which reliable data were available. A typical case was a developer providing responses to questions on land use and employee travel characteristics for his or her project, staff of a business association furnishing information on density and square footage of a corridor, and local transportation planners completing the survey for those questions regarding areawide traffic conditions. By obtaining multiple responses from different informants and triangulating inputs, it was possible to cross check many responses for internal consistency.[8]

The questionnaire shown in Appendix I elicited the following basic information:

(a) *Scale and Locational Characteristics* – total acreage, square footage, miles to CBD;
(b) *Employment Characteristics* – current employment, workforce composition;
(c) *Density and Design Characteristics* – floor area ratios (FAR)[9], average building heights and lot sizes, and project design philosophy;
(d) *Land Use Characteristics* – composition of land uses, number of on-site housing units and retail centers, and mean single-family home purchase price within a three mile radius of the development;
(e) *Land Ownership Characteristics* – number of property owners and per centage of land owned by companies and firms;

(f) *Workforce Travel Characteristics* – mean travel time, modal splits, and time distributions of travel;

(g) *Site and Areawide Transportation Facilities, Services, and Conditions* – level of service of principal freeway serving the SEC, parking spaces per employee, and number of company–sponsored vanpools operating.

Questionnaires were sent out in mid August, 1987 and returned by mid October, 1987. Informants were asked to furnish information as of mid-1987 or for whatever time period the latest data were available. While some responses were for different years, in the vast majority of cases responses were for either 1986 or 1987, and in no case was there more than a three-year difference in the period of responses.

Data base cases

In all, questionnaires were mailed to informants from 88 different SECs which met the minimum size and locational threshold requirements and for which preliminary inquiries suggested fairly complete data might be available (most notably, the existence of recent employee travel data). Call-backs were made to clarify questions and increase the response rate. In all, at least one questionnaire was returned for 79 of the candidate sites, for an initial response rate of almost 90 per cent. However, reasonably complete, reliable data were obtained from 57 of the SECs, for a final response rate of 65 per cent. In general, the lack of sufficient data on the travel characteristics of an SEC's workforce resulted in the elimination of most of the 31 omitted candidate sites.

Table 2.1 lists the SECs that comprised the national data base used in this study and Figures 2.1 through 2.18 show the geographic locations of these sites, both nationally and within metropolitan areas. The 57 sites are spread among 21 different states and 26 metropolitan areas. The geographic diversity of these sites is evident in Figure 2.1. From a sampling standpoint, such variety is important since commuter attitudes and behavior, e.g., driver aggressiveness, tolerance for delay, perceptions of public transit, are not uniform across the country or within regions. Figures 2.2 through 2.18 also show that selected SECs lie at varying distances from regional CBDs, representing older, inner-tier suburban sites as well as newer, peripheral settings.

It should be noted that SECs from many older industrial cities, such as Buffalo and Pittsburgh, are not represented in this analysis. In general, these cities have not experienced massive-scale suburban employment growth, in large part because their transition from a "smokestack" to a service-based, postindustrial economy has been

Table 2.1 Listing of case sites by state, metropolitan area, and jurisdiction.

State	Metropolitan Area	Jurisdiction[1]	SEC Case Site	Map Figure
Arizona	Phoenix	Phoenix	Central Avenue Corridor	--
			Camelback Corridor	--
California	Los Angeles-Orange County	Los Angeles	Warner Center	Figure 2.2
		Santa Ana	South Coast Metro	Figure 2.2
	San Francisco-Oakland-San Jose	San Ramon	Bishop Ranch	Figure 2.3
		San Jose	Santa Clara Golden Triangle	Figure 2.3
		Pleasanton	Hacienda Business Park	Figure 2.3
		Walnut Creek	Central Walnut Creek	Figure 2.3
Colorado	Denver	Denver	Denver Technological Center	Figure 2.4
			Greenwood Plaza	Figure 2.4
			Inverness Business Park	Figure 2.4
Connecticut	New York	Stamford	Central Stamford	Figure 2.5
Florida	Miami-Ft. Lauderdale-Palm Beach	Boca Raton	Avida's Park of Commerce (APOC)	Figure 2.6
		Ft. Lauderdale	Central Ft. Lauderdale	Figure 2.6
			Cyprus Creek	Figure 2.6
			Plantation	Figure 2.6
	Orlando	Orlando	Maitland Center	--
Georgia	Atlanta	Gwinnett Cty.	Gwinnett Place	Figure 2.7
		DeKalb Cty.	North Lake	Figure 2.7
		DeKalb Cty.	Perimeter Center	Figure 2.7
		Gwinnett Cty.	Technology Park	Figure 2.7
Illinois	Chicago	Naperville	Naperville/I-88 Tollway	Figure 2.8
		Oak Brook	Oak Brook/I-88 Tollway	Figure 2.8
		Schaumburg	Schaumburg Village	Figure 2.8
Kansas	Kansas City	Overland Park	College Blvd. Corridor	--
			Corporate Woods	--
Maryland	Baltimore	Anne Ar. Cty.	BWI area	Figure 2.9
		Baltimore	Central Towson	Figure 2.9
			Hunt Valley	Figure 2.9
	Washington, D.C.	Montgomery Cty.	Rocksprings Park	Figure 2.10

Note:
1. City or county in which the SEC is located.

Table 2.1 (continued)   Listing of case sites by state, metropolitan area, and jurisdiction.

State	Metropolitan Area	Jurisdiction[1]	SEC Case Site	Map Figure

Massa-
  chusetts
	Boston	Lexington	New England
			  Executive Park
				Figure 2.11

		Middlesex Cty.	Route 9 Corridor	Figure 2.11
			Route 128 Corridor	Figure 2.11
			Route 495 Corridor	Figure 2.11
Michigan	Detroit	Dearborn	Fairlane Town Center	Figure 2.12
Minnesota	Minneapolis-St. Paul	St. Paul	3M Center	Figure 2.13
			Edina/I-494 Corridor	Figure 2.13
New Jersey	New York-Newark	Bergen Cty.	The Meadowlands	Figure 2.5
	Trenton-Princeton	Mercer Cty.	Route 1 "Zip Strip"	Figure 2.14
New York	New York-Newark	Garden City	E. Garden City/Rte. 25	Figure 2.5
		Farmingdale	E. Farmingdale/Rte. 110	Figure 2.5
North Carolina	Raleigh-Durham	Durham Cty.	Research Triangle Park	--
Ohio	Cleveland	Cuyahoga Cty.	Chagrin Blvd. Corridor	Figure 2.15
			I-77/Rockside Corridor	Figure 2.15
Oregon	Portland	Portland	I-5 Corridor	--
Pennsyl- vania	Philadelphia	Chester Cty.	Chesterbrook Center	Figure 2.14
Texas	Austin	Austin	3M Center - Austin	--
	Dallas	Dallas	North Dallas Parkway	Figure 2.16
	Houston	Montgomery City.	The Woodlands	Figure 2.17
		Houston	City Post Oak (Uptown)	Figure 2.17
			Greenway Plaza	Figure 2.17
			N. Houston North Belt	Figure 2.17
			West Houston Energy Corridor	Figure 2.17
Virginia	Washington, D.C.	Fairfax Cty.	Tysons Corner	Figure 2.10
Washington	Seattle	Bellevue	Central Bellevue	Figure 2.18
			Bell-Red Corridor	Figure 2.18

Note:
1. City or county in which the SEC is located.

Figure 2.1 Location of 57 case sites in the United States.

Figure 2.2 Los Angeles-Orange
County cases.

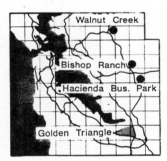

Figure 2.3 San Francisco-San
Jose cases.

Figure 2.4 Denver cases.

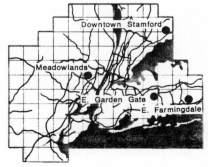

Figure 2.5 New York-New Jersey-
Connecticut cases.

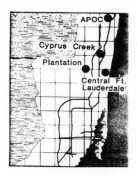

Figure 2.6 Miami-Ft. Lauderdale-Palm Beach cases.

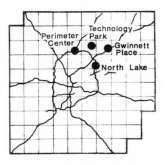

Figure 2.7 Atlanta cases.

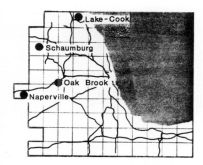

Figure 2.8 Chicago cases.

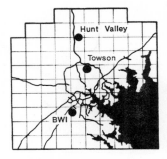

Figure 2.9 Baltimore cases.

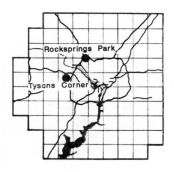

Figure 2.10 Washington, D.C. cases.

Figure 2.11 Boston cases.

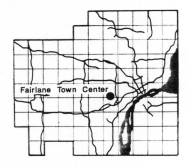

Figure 2.12 Detroit cases.

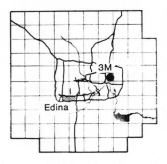

Figure 2.13 Minneapolis-St.Paul cases.

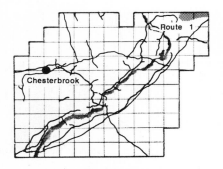

Figure 2.14 Philadelphia cases.

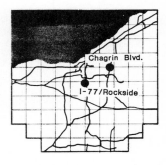

Figure 2.15 Cleveland cases.

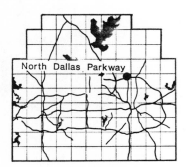

Figure 2.16 Dallas cases.

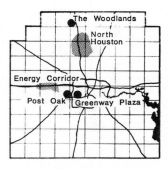

Figure 2.17 Houston cases.

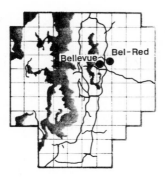

Figure 2.18 Seattle cases.

relatively slow (Hartshorn & Muller 1986, 124). There are some exceptions, however, such as Detroit, a metropolis with a strong tradition of
suburban business centers, owing largely to the early suburbanization of
automobile assembly plants. In this study, Detroit is represented by the
Fairlane Town Center, a massive office-retail complex being developed
by Ford Motor Land Development Corporation. Additionally, some
newer metropolises with fairly diversified economies that meet the 1
million population threshold, such as Columbus and San Diego, are
not represented among the SEC cases either. In these instances, none
of the candidate sites had sufficient data to allow inclusion.

Research methods

A combination of simple statistical tabulations, hypothesis tests, and
causal models are developed and presented in the next four chapters
in probing the relationship between the site and development characteristics of SECs and the travel choices and mobility levels of their
workforces. In addition to the more aggregate-level national-scale
analysis, a disaggregate study of commute choices among suburban
workers is carried out based on a 1986 travel survey of workers in
Pleasanton, California, one of the San Francisco Bay Area's fastest
growing suburbs. A variety of statistical techniques, including factor
analysis, cluster analysis, analysis of variance (ANOVA), regression
analysis, and logit analysis are employed in exploring patterns in
these two data sets and in carrying out specific hypothesis tests.
These empirical evaluations are supplemented by more qualitative
assessments based on literature reviews, site visits, and interviews.
Together, it is felt that empirical and interpretative techniques offer
a balanced perspective into the transportation–land use link among
America's SECs.

Notes

1. See Cervero (1986b, 17–18) for further discussions on locational dimensions of suburban growth.
2. Some observers make a further distinction between centers and clusters. Centers generally connote a well-defined, master-planned project, sometimes under single ownership. By comparison, clusters are sometimes thought of as amalgamations of independent projects – a nodal version of strip development, of sorts. In this book, the two terms are used interchangeably and are meant to connote a concentrated form of suburban growth.
3. Corridor and business associations, such as the West Houston Association and Warner Center Association in Los Angeles, have been formed by property-owners and major businesses in the largest SECs to take positions on public policy matters, to deal with common concerns such as traffic congestion, and to promote the collective interests of participants. These associations typically maintain the most recent land use, employment, and transportation data available for specific SECs. For more discussion on associations, see Orski (1986b).
4. In addition to such publications as *Development Trends* and *Market Profiles*, data were obtained from the *Project Reference File* series, the *Metropolitan Today* series, the *Land Use Digest* series, the *Urban Land* publication, the *Office Development Handbook*, and several technical memoranda and data listings made available by ULI, generally for the periods 1980 through 1987.
5. Information was obtained from a number of Rice Center publications from the past ten years, including various case study reports (e.g., *Houston's Major Activity Centers and Worker Travel Behavior* (1987), the *Research Brief* series, the *Private Sector Briefs* series, and other documents made available by the Rice Center.
6. The primary sources used were the *National Office Market Report* and monthly office inventory publications.
7. The original versions of both questionnaires were pre-tested and eventually redesigned to improve the wording and clarity of questions and to remove possible biases stemming from question phrasing and sequencing.
8. Cross-checking between responses and empirical data compiled from primary sources was also carried out. Questionnaires with two or more discrepancies were eliminated from consideration. In some cases, respondents furnished best "guestimates." In these instances, estimates were only used if they could be corroborated from other sources or informants.
9. Floor area ratio (FAR) represents the ratio of gross floorspace of all buildings divided by the total land area of the development. A ratio of one could represent either a one-story building that covers the full perimeter of a property, i.e., zero side, front, and back lot setbacks, or a four-story building covering only one-quarter of a lot.

3

Land use, employment and transportation characteristics of America's SECs

3.1 Characterizing SECs in the United States

This chapter introduces various suburban land use and transportation topics discussed throughout this study and characterizes the 57 SECs' case sites from across the United States. Summary statistics are interwoven into the more general discussion of land use planning principles for SECs. Particular attention is given to the topics of site design, mixed-use development, and jobs–housing balancing.

In the following sections, land use is expressed in terms of: (a) size and scale; (b) composition of land uses; (c) land and employment densities; (d) housing, retail, and other tenant-support provisions; (e) site organization; (f) lotting practices; (g) land ownership; and (h) SEC evolution. Employment is examined in terms of: (a) current and future workforce size; and (b) laborforce composition. Finally, transportation and mobility are summarized with respect to: (a) travel characteristics of workers for home–work trips, including travel times, speeds, and modes of commuting; (b) available transportation facilities and services, both within and near SECs, including roadway capacity, transit operations, van and ridesharing services, and parking provisions; and (c) level of service on nearby road facilities. Through a literature review, the characteristics of the case SECs are compared with empirical findings of other researchers.

3.2   Scale, locational, and employment characteristics of SECs

These factors – scale, location, and employment composition – provide a general context for describing SECs: how big they are, where they are situated, and what goes on in them.

Table 3.1 presents summary statistics on the size, location, and employment characteristics of the SECs studied in this book. On average, SECs cover an expansive territory, with a mean land size of 27,162 acres (42.4 square miles). This average, however, is skewed by the inclusion of some very large corridors. Acreage varies from as small as 82 to as large as 440,000 (Route 128 corridor outside of Boston). The standard deviation is also three times the size of the mean value, offering further evidence of the extreme variation in the size of SECs.[1] Excluding seven large corridors with acreage exceeding 20,000 (Routes 9, 128, and 495 in Boston; Route 1 in central New Jersey; Golden Triangle in Santa Clara County; Portland's I–5 corridor; and N. Houston Beltloop corridor), the mean acreage is much smaller – 3,068 (nearly 5 square miles), although the degree of variation still remains high. Still, the SECs examined in this study encompass a much larger territory than those studied previously. A 1970 study by the Urban Land Institute of suburban business parks found an average size of 70 acres (McKeever 1970), whereas a more recent analysis of suburban office parks by the author examined centers averaging 270 acres (Cervero 1986b). As discussed in the Chapter 5, the SECs comprising campus-style, business parks in this study compare favorably in size to those parks examined in the analysis several years previously.

From Table 3.1, the case sites appear to be fairly built up as well, with the amount of office, commercial, and industrial floorspace (exclusive of the seven large corridors) averaging 8.1 million square feet. Floorspace varied from 1 million to 31.28 million square feet (New Jersey's Meadowlands).

SECs also tend to be far removed from regional CBDs. The mean distance is 18 miles, with a high of 36 miles (East Farmingdale/110, whose approximate center is 36 miles from mid-town Manhattan). On average, the SECs examined in this study are much farther from their region's CBD than were the 120 large-scale office parks examined in the earlier study (which averaged a mean distance of 10.7 miles) (Cervero, 1986b). The inclusion of a number of large suburban employment clusters, agglomerations, and corridors on the peripheries of metropolises and large conurbations (such as New York–Newark) resulted in a ratcheting of the mean mileage statistic.

Table 3.1 further reveals that the SECs generally have extremely large employment bases, averaging 46,100 full-time workers, inclusive of all

Table 3.1 Size, locational, and workforce characteristics of 57 large SECs in the United States, as of 1987.

	Mean	Std. Dev.	Min.	Max.	No. Cases
SIZE AND SCALE					
Total land acreage (All Cases)	27,162	88,916	82	440,000	57
(Excluding Large[1] Corridors)	3,068	4,791	82	25,100	50
Square footage of floorspace in office, commercial, and industrial uses (millions) (All Cases)	10.35	13.07	1.00	85.00	57
(Excluding Large Corridors)	8.10	8.04	1.00	31.28	50
LOCATION					
Radial miles to regional CBD	18.0	9.9	5	36	57
EMPLOYMENT					
Size of workforce (thousands) (All Cases)	46.1	97.0	2.0	480.5	57
(Excluding Large Corridors)	19.3	17.3	2.0	67.7	50
Percent of workforce in management, professional, technical, and administrative occupations	47.2	17.6	2.0	70.0	57
SEC EXPANSION					
Expected Year of Build-out (Non-corridors only)	1999	--	1988	2026	20

Note:
1. Large corridors are SECs of over 40,000 acres.

cases. Ignoring the seven large corridors, however, the average SEC laborforce is 19,300 full-time workers. Table 3.1 indicates that there is tremendous variation in the size of employment bases as well.

The average occupational breakdown of SEC employees, shown in Figure 3.1, reveals the dominance of white-collar workers. The largest group is clerical staffs, comprising 22 per cent of the workforce. This

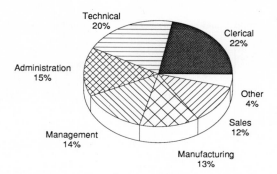

Figure 3.1 Distribution of job classifications in SECs.

share closely matches the national average, which was 19 per cent in 1982 and no doubt has risen since (Dowall 1987). The next highest occupational group is technical workers, e.g., engineers, programmers, researchers, followed by a fairly even split between administrative (finance officers and billing agents, for example), managerial, and manufacturing staffs. In all, nearly one-half of employees are in professional/administrative positions (Table 3.1) and over 70 per cent work in desk jobs that involve some form of information-processing. This large share reflects the assignment of many mid-management, clerical, and back-office business functions to the suburbs over the past decade (Dowall 1987, Urban Land Institute 1986). These findings are consistent with those from a recent study of SECs in the greater Houston area which found that suburban centers tend to have even larger shares of white-collar workers and a higher proportion of professional–administrative staffs than CBDs (Rice Center 1987).

Finally, Table 3.1 reveals the general time schedule planned for completing SECs. The "typical" SEC in the survey, excluding large corridors and non-master-planned centers, is projected to reach build-out in 1999. At build-out, these centers are expected to have, on average, 13.2 million square feet of office-commercial-industrial space and 21,000 full-time employees. Based on the ratio of current to expected future floorspace, on average, the surveyed SECs are approximately 57 per cent built out.

3.3   Density, site design, and property ownership characteristics

Density and design

The densities of land uses have been shown to be one of the most important determinants of travel behavior, perhaps influencing the modes people opt for as much as any single factor (Pushkarev & Zupan 1977). Over the past decade, the design emphasis of many suburban office projects has been on creating a spacious, comfortable, and aesthetically pleasing working environment (Cervero 1986b). Many projects aim to attract prestigious corporate tenants, offering first-floor atriums and courtyard space, high ceilings, and various ornamental design treatments, such as lawn sculptures and fountains. Such add-ons usually increase the amount of floorspace per worker. "Smart buildings" designed for high-tech and information-processing tenants also tend to enlarge the floor and ceiling area in order to accommodate cables, computers, and satellite dishes as well as to ensure proper ventilation. One study of the Routes 73/38/70 corridor in central New Jersey found atriums and other common space add-ons comprised 7 per cent of gross leasable space (Louis Berger & Associates 1986).

This tendency to expand building space per worker has often been coupled with design initiatives that vastly increase land area per worker as well, such as lavish and spacious landscaping and the provision of bountiful parking. Many campus-style office parks feature low-rise buildings that hug the landscape, surrounded by a sea of parking, jogging trails, and nicely contoured open spaces. At the usual standard of four parking spaces per 1,000 square feet of building space, with each stall measuring approximately 325 square feet in size, 1,300 square feet of asphalt is paved for every 1,000 square feet of office space (O'Mara & Casazza 1982, Leinburger & Lockwood 1986). Thus, typically more land is used for the unproductive purpose of housing cars than for the productive purpose of housing office workers. From a mobility standpoint, buildings are usually so widely separated and the overall scale of the project is so spread out that the automobile becomes almost indispensable for circulating within an SEC. What this means, of course, is that many workers are almost compelled to drive to work in order to have a vehicle available to move around within their work compound.

Table 3.2 summarizes some of the density features of the SEC case sites examined in this study. The average floor area ratio (FAR) is nearly one, quite high by suburban standards. The 1985 study of 120 US office parks (Cervero 1986b), for instance, found an average FAR of 0.29, while a recent study by Gruen Gruen & Associates (1986) of nine office developments in suburban Philadelphia and San Francisco found an average of 0.30. In this present study, FARs were found to vary tremendously, from a low of 0.09 (Research Triangle Park) to a high of 6.00 (downtown Bellevue).

Table 3.2 also reveals the average maximum FAR allowed by local zoning ordinances governing SECs. The mean is 2.34, skewed somewhat by the disproportionate share of higher density clusters

Table 3.2   Density, lotting, and land ownership characteristics of SECs.

	Mean	Std. Dev.	Min.	Max.	No. cases
Density					
Floor area ratio (FAR)[1]	0.98	1.10	0.09	6.00	55
Maximum allowable FAR[1]	2.34	3.68	0.25	15.00	35
Employees/acre[2]	19.9	25.5	0.25	134.5	50
Square footage of land/employee[2]	11,200	25,158	324	94,500	50
Square footage of floorspace/employee[2]	492	398	164	2,150	50
Coverage ratio[3]	0.31	0.20	0.10	0.90	52
Number of stories of:					
highest building	15.7	11.0	3	64	57
lowest building	1.3	1.1	1	8	57
"modal" building[4]	4.1	3.9	1	22	57
Building lines and lotting					
Acreage of:					
smallest lot	1.3	1.9	1.0	9.0	44
largest lot	71.4	110.7	1.0	509.0	44
"modal" lot[4]	8.4	12.2	1.0	57.0	44
"modal" lineal footage from:[4]					
side of building to property line	49.2	53.5	0	300.0	48
front of building to property line	64.4	57.0	0	300.0	48
Property ownership					
Number of property owners[2]	112	204	1	900	41
Proportion of land owned by developers[2]	0.66	0.24	0	1.0	41

[1] FAR = building square footage/lot size. Maximum FAR is what current zoning allows.
[2] Exclusive of seven large corridor cases (see Ch. 3, sec.3.2).
[3] Proportion of land covered by buildings – footprint of buildings to total land area.
[4] Modal represents most frequently occurring case. This reflects the "typical" building.

among the 35 cases (due to missing observations). On average, these 35 SECs are being built at 48 per cent of allowable density.[2] In some cases this "underdevelopment" is due to the relative infancy of the SEC and the lack of market demand, while in other cases growth control pressures have forced developers to settle for lower densities during the negotiation of site plans.

From Table 3.2, the average amount of land area per worker for the case SECs is also exceptionally high – 11,200 square feet. This far exceeds the average ratio found in the 1985 study of 120 office parks, which was 1,410 square feet of land per employee (Cervero 1986b). In that 18 of the case sites in the current study have ratios below 1,000, it is clear that tremendous variation exists in land-to-employee intensity levels among the SECs. In some cases, bloated figures are due to

Photo 3.1 Horizontal skyscraper. Building in background houses over 5,000 workers. The structure would be scaled vertically if in a central city. In surbuban San Ramon, California, where land costs are comparatively low, developers opted to scale it horizontally instead. (Photo by the author.)

Photo 3.2 Typical suburban office buildings. SEC buildings with coverage rates of 0.30 and FARs of 1.0 in Pleasanton, California. (Photo by the author.)

the preponderance of retail and residential land uses within an SEC, resulting in a relatively low denominator. In other cases the high figure can be attributed to the existence of vast expanses of open space within the SEC boundaries. If data were available on net usable land area for only office and industrial uses, the mean ratio would be much lower.

Within buildings themselves, SEC employees working in the case sites appear to enjoy considerable elbow room. The fifth row of Table 3.2 indicates that the average amount of gross floorspace per worker is nearly 500 square feet. This figure generally falls in the range found by other researchers. The 1985 study of low-density office parks found an average of 380 gross square feet of floor area per worker (Cervero 1986b). In their study of business parks, Gruen Gruen & Associates (1986) found an average of 347, 485, and 724 square feet per worker for office, research and development (R&D), and industrial-services land uses, respectively. A prior study by Gruen Gruen & Associates (1985) found slightly lower average figures – 360 square feet for R&D and 490 square feet for commercial services.

In general, the trend has been toward roomier work environments for suburban workers. As Dowall (1987) notes, clerical and information-processing work pools typically need large expanses of floor area on one level. Most back office facilities have floorplates (the square footage of a single floor of a building) exceeding 20,000 square feet. With this amount of space, "bullpen" clerical areas and computer networks can be more efficiently laid out than would be the case for multi-story installations. Thus, this trend has not only increased workspace area but has encouraged the construction of low-lying, squatty office buildings as well – what some refer to as "horizontal skyscrapers."

In sum, when compared with traditional downtown work settings, suburban office structures are not only much closer to the ground, they are also more spacious and physically isolated. Increasingly, the office workplace of tomorrow is heading in the direction of a low-lying building with plenty of room per worker and vast expanses of land separating buildings. All of which adds up, of course, to extremely low project employment densities.

Building coverage and heights

Table 3.2 also summarizes statistics on the average lot coverage and number of stories of buildings within SECs. The mean coverage ratio (footprint of a building divided by land area) is 0.31. In no instance could buildings consume more than 90 per cent of a lot, and in most cases footprints were required to be far less land-enveloping. The 0.31 average closely matches the coverage restrictions found in land covenants of most office parks, with the total impervious coverage

Photo 3.3 Transco Tower in Post Oak, Houston. Ten-story parking garage, far taller than most suburban structures, abuts the 65-story tower, purportedly the tallest suburban building in the world outside of a central business district. (Photo by the author.)

normally limited to 60 per cent in order to maintain an open, park-like atmosphere (Cervero 1986b).

With an average FAR of 0.98 and an average coverage rate of 0.31, one could infer that the "average" height of building in the SECs is slightly over three stories.[3] On average, the most frequently occurring building height, i.e., the "mode," is around four stories. This figure is no doubt skewed by the inclusion of some fairly highrise developments, such as Post Oak and Greenway Plaza in Houston, in the data base. On average, each SEC's lowest building is around one story and its highest building reaches nearly 16 stories in height (equivalent to around a 210 foot elevation). The highest building within any of the SECs is the 65-story Transco Tower in Post Oak, the world's tallest skyscraper outside of a downtown. Overall, the buildings within the SECs of this study appear to dwarf most of their suburban counterparts – in 1983, 43 per cent of all suburban office structures were one or two stories high, and only 8.9 per cent exceeded ten stories (Institute of Real Estate Management 1984). Lastly, the majority of buildings of the master planned SECs included in this study could be classified as "Class A" structures, typically featuring all glass exteriors and tilt up or steel frame construction.[4] Typical tenants of Class A office space are law firms, advertising companies, stockbrokers, and professional consultants.

Building lines, lotting practices, and site organization

Besides land area, the dimensions and shapes of office compounds, as well as the configuration of individual parcels within them, can exert a strong influence on circulation patterns, and in particular on people's willingness to travel by foot. Take a 500 acre tract, for instance. If square, the diagonal distance (from corner to corner) is about 1.2 miles (Fig. 3.2). If rectangular, the distance increases to 2 miles, two-thirds

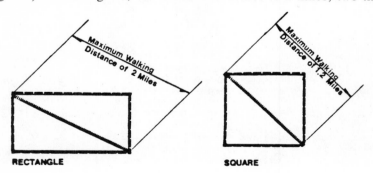

Figure 3.2 Alternative configurations of a 500 acre parcel.
Source: Anderson [1986].

farther. To span such a distance would require a one-half hour walk (assuming a 3 m.p.h. walking speed), far more than the maximum threshold of ten minutes most suburban workers and residents are generally willing to invest in a walk (Untermann 1984).

Lotting patterns of suburban technology parks typically consist of five-acre tracts that can be assembled into 25-acre tracts, or larger (Reimer 1983). From Table 3.2, the most frequently occurring lot size was eight acres for 44 of the case sites in this study. Within the SECs, the smallest lot tended to be 1.3 acres whereas the largest one averaged 71.4 acres, with considerable variation among cases. On average, the smallest lot within an SEC is one-twentieth the size of its largest lot.

Based on site inspections and survey responses, around 60 per cent of the SECs are comprised of lots of varying shapes and sizes, whereas 40 per cent have lots of fairly uniform dimensions. In the latter cases, lots tended to be rectangular in shape. A number of the denser suburban clusters, such as Post Oak, Bellevue, and Denver Tech Center, were originally platted on a superblock schema, with block faces of 1,000 feet or more not uncommon.

The way buildings are organized on a tract can also have a strong bearing on circulation patterns and travel choices. Some sites feature clusters of buildings fronting on sidewalks and common spaces that invite foot travel. Others host a single "signature" building that is sited thousands of feet from its nearest neighbor. Such inwardly focused buildings have been criticized for not only discouraging walk trips but also for their "egocentricity" and "detachedness" (Galehouse 1984, Lynch & Hack 1984).

The notion of site organization is difficult to express in quantitative terms. Measures such as inter-building distances and building lines are sometimes used. Building lines are usually expressed in terms of front, rear, and side setbacks. Setbacks reserve areas of open space between structures and the edges of individual properties. They generally serve aesthetic purposes, providing a landscaped buffer between buildings and roadways. In his study of campus-style office projects in the US, Anderson (1986) found typical setback of 50 feet for sidelots and 75 feet in the front. For 48 of the case SEC sites in this study, the most frequently occurring setbacks matched Anderson's findings fairly closely – averaging nearly 50 feet on the sides and 64 feet in the front (see Table 3.2).

Overall, setback regulations tend to push buildings toward the center of parcels, thereby discouraging a clustered development pattern within SECs that might be more favorable to transit and pedestrians. The general influence of site designs on the propensity of suburban workers to walk and choose travel options to the automobile are discussed in more detail in Chapters 5 and 6.

Property ownership

How many parties hold title to land and the degree of developer control over site decisions can exert a strong influence on the character, style, and evolution of an SEC. With fewer property owners, there tends to be more centralized control over design decisions. The potential for more systematic, coordinated site plans might also be expected to increase with fewer deed-holders.

Table 3.2 reveals that the SECs included in this study average over 100 different property owners, with tremendous variation, from as few as one to nearly one thousand. On average, around two-thirds of land is owned by private developers and real estate syndicates, generally in the form of speculative rental space, with the remaining one-third owned outright by private businesses and firms.

How ownership influences the density, site design, and evolution of SECs is examined in Chapter 6. Based on interviews and questionnaire responses, it appears that around 29 per cent of the SECs studied have evolved over the years as centrally controlled, master-planned projects (Fig. 3.3). Another 29 per cent have evolved on the basis of periodic, sometimes year-by-year, revisions to master plans, more or less a hybrid of planned versus *ad hoc* evolution. The remaining 42 per cent of SECs appear to have evolved in a more incremental, atomistic fashion.

3.4   Land uses and mixed-use activities

The advantages of mixed-use developments

The variety of land uses can have a profound influence on the travel choices of suburban workers. In many single-use environments, such as business parks with exclusively office functions, an automobile becomes almost indispensable for circulating within a project and

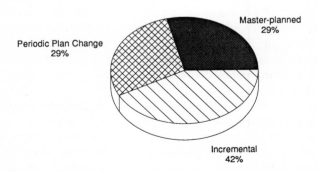

Figure 3.3   Percentage of SECs in three growth categories, exclusive of corridors.

accessing restaurants, banks, and other consumer services that are off site. A SEC with a lively mixture of activities, on the other hand, can internalize trips that otherwise would be made on areawide roads. Notably, significant shares of trips end up as foot traffic within individual buildings or between groups of buildings in mixed-use environments (Cervero 1986b).

Mixed-use developments (MXD)[5] can potentially reduce motorized travel and congestion levels in several key ways:

(a) Since land uses have different trip generation rates, a given amount of floorspace spread among multiple activities will normally produce fewer trips than the same floorspace devoted to a single, more intensive use, such as office;

(b) More travel is made by foot and bicycle, particularly during the noon hour, and to the extent workers are able to reside on-site or nearby, some motorized travel during morning and evening peak periods will also be replaced by walk and cycle trips; and

(c) With a combination of office, retail, recreational, and other land uses, trips tend to be spread more evenly throughout the day and week; in contrast, with a single function, such as office enterprises, many trips are concentrated in the morning and evening peak hours.

Take a 100,000 square feet office development, for example. Using a trip generation rate of 12.3 weekday trips per 1,000 gross square feet of general office space from the Institute of Transportation Engineers' *Trip Generation* manual (Institute of Transportation Engineers 1987), this project could be expected to produce 1,230 daily trips, many of which would occur within a concentrated peak period. If this same floor area was split into 25,000 square feet of general office space, 25,000 square feet of R&D space, 40,000 square feet of multi-family apartments (assuming an average of 1,600 square feet per unit), and 10,000 square feet of specialty retail, based again on ITE rates, the daily trips would fall to 1,000, spread much more evenly throughout the day.[6] That is a 18.7 per cent drop in daily traffic volume. Peak hour volumes would likely fall even more since many retail trips occur throughout the day.

While retail, hotel, restaurant, and other consumer land uses average far higher daily trip generation rates than office functions do on a square footage basis, most trips to such establishments occur in the evening, on weekends, and during lunch time when capacity is readily available. Thus, adding such activities into a development will normally add hardly any traffic to the morning rush hour and far less to the evening rush period than a comparable amount of office space would.

By spreading out trip-making, MXDs in a way accomplish what flex-time and staggered work hour programs accomplish without disrupting the work schedules of a private business. Moreover, by spreading out demand, MXDs allow available infrastructure to be used efficiently throughout the day, thus tempering the need to expand roads serving suburban job centers.

By allowing people to walk between nearby activities, MXDs also reduce vehicular traffic. For instance, workers in a mixed-use setting are more likely to spend their lunch hour at shops and restaurants within the development than to drive to an off-site shopping center. One study of MXDs in the greater Denver area, for instance, concluded that mixed uses could reduce trip generation rates of individual uses within the development by as much as 25 per cent (Institute of Transportation Engineers 1987).

MXDs offer two other noteworthy transportation advantages. One, they can be a boon to ridesharing. Unless restaurants, shops, and banks are nearby, most suburban workers will find it necessary to drive their own cars in order to reach lunchtime destinations and run midday and after-work errands. From a mobility standpoint, the addition of noon hour traffic poses few problems. Rather, problems are encountered during the peak hours because of the surfeit of automobiles with a single occupant who drives in order to have a car available during the day and after work. Several recent surveys reveal how important an automobile can be to suburban workers for taking care of personal business. The top two reasons given by 17,000 surveyed employees of the Warner Center in Los Angeles's San Fernando Valley for commuting alone were the need for a car after work (36 per cent of respondents) or for running midday errands (32 per cent of respondents) (Commuter Transportation Services 1987). Another survey of employees working at Orange County's South Coast Metro found that 83 per cent felt they needed their cars at least once a week for personal business and 44 per cent needed them at least three times a week (Ruth and Going 1983). Lastly, a recent study of SECs in the greater Houston area found that suburban employees were 1.6 times more likely to leave the area for lunch than their CBD counterparts, in large part because of the dearth of on-site eateries and other consumer services near most suburban workplaces (Rice Center 1987).[7]

A second additional advantage of MXDs is that they create opportunities for shared parking arrangements which can reduce the scale of a project and, accordingly, create a more pedestrian-friendly environment. In most instances, the parking demands of different land uses normally peak at different time periods (Barton-Aschman 1983). The same parking facility used by office workers from 8am to 5pm on Mondays through Fridays can serve restaurant and movie goers during the evening and on weekends. It could serve as overflow parking for weekend shoppers as well. For multi-purpose trips, such as a work-shop-movie trip, only one parking space might be necessary if offices, stores, and theaters lie in reasonable proximity to one another.[8] One study, for instance, found 28 per cent of employees of MXDs patronized the same or nearby development while only 19 per cent of workers from single use sites did so (Barton-Aschman 1983).

An often overlooked mobility benefit of MXDs is that they lower the total parking requirements for a site far below what would be the sum of individual office, retail, and recreational uses. Developers of Los Angeles's Warner Center, for instance, were able to reduce parking in a central garage from 1,400 to 1,100 spaces because of land use mixing, saving over $3 million in the process (1980 dollars) (Barton-Aschman 1983). Such a reduction in parking area can dramatically shrink the scale of a project and reduce the separation of buildings, thus inviting more foot travel. As noted earlier, many office parks today devote more space to parking than they do to buildings. To the extent that mixed-use projects allow the number of parking spaces to be reduced from 20 to 30 per cent, the overall dimensions of a project might be scaled down at a commensurate level, thus helping to contain sprawl and encourage more walk trips.

Besides these many transportation benefits, MXDs also add life to what sometimes are rather sterile and undistinguishable suburban work environments. By replacing vehicle trips with people trips, a far more active and socially interesting milieu can be created. A setting with an after-work night life can also entice more employees to live near their workplace, thus further cutting down on vehicular traffic. A common complaint voiced by suburban businesses today is that their employees, especially those who have been reassigned from CBDs, are disenchanted with the barrenness and lack of urban amenities around their workplaces. For this and other reasons, MXDs are becoming increasingly attractive to high-end tenants and are perceived by many developers as providing a competitive market advantage. Based on a recent Urban Land Institute report, MXDs appear to be gaining in popularity – 61 per cent of the more than 200 MXDs in the US that were studied had broken ground since 1980 (Schwanke *et al.* 1986).

Land use composition and consumer services within SECs

How mixed are today's SECs? Based on survey results, the answer would seem to be only moderately and far less than their CBD counterparts. Among the 57 sites surveyed, the highest proportion of floorspace is being devoted to office uses (Fig. 3.4 and Table 3.3). Retail is the second most prevalent activity, followed by housing, manufacturing, warehousing, and other uses, e.g., restaurants, hotels, and banks. Looking at the minimum and maximum ranges for shares of office and retail space in Table 3.3, it is apparent that the surveyed job centers vary considerably in their degree of land use mixture, a topic which is examined more closely in Chapter 5.

Table 3.3 also reveals the average number of restaurants and banks – important ingredients of any suburban mixed-use environments – within those SECs which are either master-planned or highly clustered, or both.[9] Among the 18 cases for which data were available, there is, on average, approximately twenty eateries (ranging from restaurants to private delis, but excluding company cafeterias) and four to five banks or other savings institutions. The South Coast Metro in Orange County holds the distinction of having the most of both among the case sites – 89 restaurants and 29 banks.

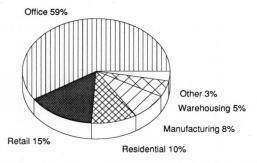

Figure 3.4   Percentage of floorspace in land use categories.

A larger subsample of 50 cases was available for studying the number of distinct retail centers within SECs.[10] The average is in the four to five range, with the 2,600 acre Schaumburg Village, northwest of Chicago, featuring the most with 47 centers. Additionally, the average number of shopping centers with over 100,000 square feet of gross floorspace within three radial miles of an SEC was found to be 3.6. These nearby shopping centers averaged around 170,000 square feet of space – an area comparable to a supermarket connected by around ten specialty stores.

Of course, the number of consumer establishments within an SEC is most relevant when compared to the number of on-site employees. Table 3.3 also summarizes several retail intensity statistics. For the subsample of 18 SECs, on average there are around 3,700 employees per eatery and 6,800 employees per bank, with considerable variation among sites. South Coast Metro again earns top honors for having the highest level of retail intensity among suburban job centers, featuring a restaurant and a bank for every 281 and 862 employees, respectively.[11]

Table 3.3 Land Use and Mixed-Use Characteristics of SECs

	Mean	Std. Dev.	Min.	Max.	No. Cases
LAND USE COMPOSITION					
Percent of Floorspace in:					
Office Use	59	23	10	99	56
Retail Use	15	11	1	40	56
CONSUMER SERVICES					
Number of On-Site:					
Restaurants/Eateries[1]	19.6	27.3	0	89	18
Banks[1]	4.5	6.6	0	29	18
Shopping clusters and retail centers[2]	4.4	8.0	0	47	50
Employees/On-Site Restaurant[1]	3,715	7,335	281	30,000	18
Employees/On-Site Bank[1]	6,784	9,273	862	41,000	18
Employees/On-Site Retail Center[2]	8,640	11,097	550	64,700	50
Square Footage of Retail Space (millions) within 3 radial miles of SEC[2]	1.92	2.10	0.02	8.0	45
Square Footage of Nearby Retail Space/Employee[2]	170	329	12	2,215	45

Notes:
1. Exclusive of corridors, consisting mainly of master-planned projects.
2. Exclusive of corridors, consiting mainly of well-defined clusters.

Additionally, the SECs were found to average around 8,600 workers for every on-site retail center and 170 square feet of areawide shopping center space per employee.

Overall, it is apparent that the nation's largest suburban employment centers vary considerably in their degree of land use mixture. While many have over 90 per cent of floorspace devoted exclusively to office use, others feature a balance of office, commercial, and institutional activities. It is because of such variation that one could expect appeciable differences in the commuting behavior of workers among the study sites.

3.5   Jobs-housing balancing and on-site housing provisions

Jobs-housing balancing

Among the benefits that might be expected from the suburbanization of office employment over the past decade are the transformation of America's suburbs into more "balanced" communities, a shortening of journeys to work, and generally less traffic. Evidence is somewhat mixed on this, however. In 1980, suburb-to-suburb work trips in the US were, on average, 50 per cent shorter than suburb to central city trips – 8.2 miles versus 12.2 miles (Pisarski 1987). However, inter-suburban trips, the fast growing commuting market, increased in length by around 15 per cent during the seventies. In addition, jobs don't appear to be getting closer to suburban residents. From 1977 to 1983, the mean journey-to-work for Americans residing outside of a central city (but within an urbanized area) increased from 10.6 miles in length to 11.1 miles (Klinger & Kusmyak 1986). Indeed, most Americans continue to live in one community and work in another. According to the 1980 census, the majority of Americans do not work in the community where they live (US Bureau of Census 1984).

A similar mismatch in the location of people and jobs exists in Great Britain. With the reindustrialization of Britain's economy, higher than average concentrations of the unskilled and semi skilled workforce have been left in inner city areas with diminishing access to the type of manufacturing jobs they traditionally held (Fothergill & Gudgin 1982, Castles & Kosack 1985). Webster *et al.* (1985, p. 10) note that "in Britain, the inner areas house concentrations of the relatively unskilled, who must travel to the peripheral areas for the type of job they need, while more central jobs are occupied by white collar suburban residents". According to one account, Britain's spatial mismatch of jobs and homes has contributed to work trips lengthening by an average of around 1 per cent per year between 1921 and 1966 (Warner 1972).

A "balanced" community is generally thought of as a self-contained, self-reliant one, where people live, work, and enjoy their recreation (Burby & Weiss 1976). "Balance," however, is a fairly abstract notion that resists measurement. Margolis (1973) adopted the rule-of-thumb that communities are "balanced" when the ratio of jobs to housing units lies within the range of 0.75 to 1.25. With today's demographics of two wage-earner households, the upper end of Margolis's range is likely to be too low. With two working people living together, potentially fewer nearby houses are needed to accommodate a local workforce, especially when one of the persons is a secondary wage-earner – stereotypically, a married woman entering the laborforce. Nationwide, the percentage of households with two or more wage earners rose from 42.7 per cent in 1960 to 68.5 per cent in 1984, confirming the on-going feminization of America's workforce (US Bureau of Census 1984). Assuming that 90 per cent of working adult Americans live in cohabitant households and that 70 per cent of these are made up of two or more wage earners, a more reasonable ceiling for signifying "balance" is around 1.5.[12] Any jobs–housing ratio above this means there is an insufficient supply of available housing to meet the needs of the local workforce, resulting in a predominant pattern of in-commuting of workers in the morning and out-commuting in the evening.

Many of the fastest growing suburban communities have jobs–housing ratios that far exceed this 1.5 threshold. For instance, the Golden Triangle area of Santa Clara County, California, known more popularly as the Silicon Valley, epitomizes a jobs-rich/housing-poor environment. The Silicon Valley communities of Santa Clara, Sunnyvale, and Palo Alto, for instance, have jobs–housing ratios of 3.13, 3.16, and 3.08, respectively (Association of Bay Area Governments 1985). Along central New Jersey's booming Route 1 corridor, disparities are even greater. Two of the fastest growing municipalities along Route 1, Cranbury and Lawrence, have jobs/housing ratios exceeding 3.5 (Delaware Valley Regional Planning Commission 1986). In greater Atlanta, the two hottest office markets, Midtown and Perimeter Center, have more than five times as many jobs as housing units among census tracts

Photo 3.4 Jobs–housing integration in suburbia. Moderately priced rental units are interspersed among mid-rise towers in the Galleria area of the North Dallas Parkway corridor in Texas. (Photo by the author.)

encompassing both centers as well as tracts within a two mile radius of both (Atlanta Regional Commission 1986).

Jobs–housing ratios only indicate the potential for greater balance. The degree to which that potential is realized is reflected by the share of jobs in a community actually filled by residents, and conversely the share of workers finding a place to live in that community. What this means is that besides numerical parity in jobs and housing, there must also be a match-up between the skill levels of local residents and local job opportunities as well as between the earnings of workers and the cost of local housing.

In many of the nation's largest suburban work centers, a fairly small share of workers reside locally. In the Bay Area suburbs of Walnut Creek, Mountain View, Palo Alto, and Santa Clara, for instance, less than one-fifth of all local workers reside in those communities (Cervero 1986a).[13] And in the Chicago area, only 18.1 per cent of Schaumburg workers reside in that community while in Oak Brook and Oakbrook Terrace under 3 per cent of workers find a place to live locally. In the study of Schaumburg's workforce, it was found that those finding local housing tended to work in the higher-salaried FIRE occupations (Sachs 1986).

A shorthand reason for jobs–housing mismatches in the US is that *ad hoc*, market forces have largely shaped suburban growth in most US metropolitan areas. Localities, critics argue, typically make decisions to accept or reject housing and employment with little regard to the

Photo 3.5 Jobs–housing segregation in suburbia. Quarter-acre lot ranch estates surround the Greenwood Plaza complex southeast of Denver, Colorado. (Photo by the author.)

regional consequences of their decisions. The lack of regional land use planning, however, is only partly to blame. Underlying this are at least five powerful economic and demographic forces that have impeded the ability of Americans to reside in the community where they work. These are:

(a) *Fiscal zoning*: The practice of zoning land predominantly for high revenue-generating uses, such as commercial and industrial development, has generally limited the supply of housing and driven housing prices upward (Windsor 1979, Rolleston 1987). Because of fiscal pressures, more and more communities are competing actively for attractive high-tech developments and the tax dollars they generate (Wasylenko 1980). At the same time, many are snubbing housing proposals, viewing the demands housing additions place on schools and public services as drains on already strained public treasuries. A prime example of such fiscal zoning in the US is in Santa Clara County, California, home of the Silicon Valley, where the General Plan calls for 250,000 new jobs yet only 78,500 new housing units (Dowall 1984). The spatial consequences of jurisdictions actively vying for high-tech projects has been an uneven distribution of industrial and residential growth. The "winners" of the competition have frequently become prosperous corporate centers (i.e., with high jobs–housing ratios) while the "losers" have ended up as dormitory communities, left to housing the workers of these well-to-do places.

(b) *Growth restrictions*: Moratoria on building permits and down-zoning have also depressed housing supplies in many suburbs. In response to mounting growth pressures, for instance, Nassau and Suffolk Counties east of New York City placed a minimum one acre restriction on new housing permits in 1982. More recently, at least a dozen communities along Boston's Route 495 corridor have taken steps to halt new housing construction by capping building permits, increasing minimum lot sizes, or imposing growth moratoria. Within SECs themselves, there are at least two precedents where new housing starts were either restricted or banned. At Bishop Ranch east of Oakland, developers originally intended to transform their entire 585-acre vacant parcel into a planned unit development (PUD) with a mixture of office, industrial, and housing components. A groundswell of citizen opposition to commingling uses forced the developers to eliminate the residential portion of their plan (Cervero 1986b). Just six miles to the south at the 860-acre Hacienda Business Park, developers initially proposed building 3,500 rental housing units on-site, however citizen complaints forced this to be lowered to 650 units.

(c)   *Worker earnings/housing cost mismatches*: By restricting housing
      supplies, fiscal zoning and growth restrictions have unavoidably
      increased suburban housing prices (Dowall 1984, Ley 1985). Many
      moderate-salaried clerical and service-industry staff cannot afford
      the executive-priced, single-family homes and townhouses near
      many SECs. In California's two fastest growing non-rural counties,
      Contra Costa and Orange Counties, average home prices exceed
      $170,000; to finance this an income of roughly $55,000 per annum
      would be needed, yet the average worker in both counties earns
      less than $27,000 (1986 dollars). Forced to live in other counties,
      one-way commutes of 50 miles are becoming more and more com-
      mon among displaced workers. Many suburban areas, moreover,
      are experiencing serious labor shortages, forcing some businesses
      to operate special shuttles that transport inner-city residents to
      such job sites as hotels and fast-food restaurants. Class segregation
      has also been compounded by these mismatches. At Atlanta's
      booming Perimeter Center, note Leinberger & Lockwood (1986),
      many black employees can be seen walking through parking lots
      on their way to bus stops every evening. Most live 15-20 miles to
      the south of the Center and must endure one to two hour bus
      rides, twice a day.

(d)   *Two wage-earner households*: The trend toward multiple wage-
      earners has also contributed to jobs-housing imbalances. Where
      there is a clear distinction between primary and secondary wage-
      earners, most families could be expected to locate with reference to
      the breadwinner's workplace, with the other partner finding work
      close by. Where couples earn comparable salaries, however, the
      residential location choice is less likely to be one-sided in favor of
      a single partner. In such households, familes could be expected to
      live somewhere in between the workplaces of both wage-earners
      in order to balance out commuting distances. Unless a region
      has a large share of households where both wage-earners work
      in the same vicinity, a certain degree of jobs–housing imbalances
      will be inevitable. In the case of California's Silicon Valley, most
      members of two wage-earner households do not work near each
      other – 57 per cent work in different cities (Communications
      Technologies 1987).

(e)   *Job turnover*: A second demographic trend influencing
      jobs–housing relationships is increasing rates of job turnover.
      Today's workers are changing jobs and careers more frequently
      than in years past, for a host of reasons, including the career-shifting
      affects of post-industrialization, increased corporate mergers, and
      continuing plant closings. For example, in fast-growing Naperville
      on the western edge of the Chicago area's Interstate 88 corridor, a

recent survey found that corporate executives average a job change
every three years.[14] Thus, even if a person is able to buy a home
within walking distance of his office, he may end up commuting
long distances if he switches jobs, particularly given today's high
cost of financing new home mortgages.

Clearly, market and demographic forces are giving rise to a situation
where job–housing imbalances in suburban labor markets could reach
serious levels in coming years. What benefits might be attained from
reversing this trend? For one, closer jobs–housing balancing can shorten
commute distances and increase the share of non motorized trips (i.e.,
walking and cycling to work). This not only reduces the number of
potential miles workers log on roads, but reduces energy consumption
as well. Perhaps equally important, jobs–housing balancing helps to
rationalize commutersheds by segregating local and through traffic.
Around many SECs today, through travel conflicts with SEC-oriented
travel because centers often straddle major arterials and freeway interchanges. Thus, the same high-volume facilities that provide regional
access to outlying centers must also carry traffic not related to SECs.
Bringing people closer to their jobs would reduce the need of many
workers to use line-haul freeways, thus moderating the clash between
local and through travel.

With a jobs–housing balance, local streets and collectors can also
be used more efficiently. Local streets have considerable untapped
capacity, constituting around 85 per cent of lane miles of roadway
nationwide, yet carrying only about 15 per cent of vehicle mileage
(Federal Highway Administration 1986, Levinson 1976). By shortening
trips, jobs–housing linkages would allow local streets to be utilized more
fully (whether by foot, bicycle, or car) while deflecting cars from already
over-burdened freeways.

On-site and off-site housing provisions

Table 3.4 reveals some of the characteristics of housing within and near
the SECs surveyed in this study. On average, the non corridor SECs
had around 1,400 on-site units, with a substantial degree of variation
among cases. The master-planned SEC with the largest on-site housing
component is the Woodlands, a new town north of Houston, which has
9,600 units (and is still growing). Other surveyed SECs with sizeable
on-site housing offerings include the South Coast Metro, Chesterbrook,
the Meadowlands, and the North Dallas Parkway.

Of the on-site housing units, on average, around 70 per cent are
multi-family townhouses, condominiums, and apartments. SECs such
as the Perimeter Center in Atlanta, Greenway Plaza in Houston, and

Table 3.4 Housing Provisions Within and Near SECs

	Mean	Std. Dev.	Min.	Max.	No. Cases
ON-SITE HOUSING PROVISIONS					
No. of On-Site Housing Units[1]	1,408	2,377	0	9,600	42
Percent of Units Multi-Family[1]	69	65	0	100	42
Employees/On-Site Housing Unit[1,2]	30.9	35.8	3.6	113.3	28
OFF-SITE HOUSING PROVISIONS					
Approximate number of Housing Units within a three mile radius of SEC[1,3]	11,100	18,400	0	83,100	41
Percent of Housing Units within a three mile radius that are multi-family[1,3]	35.0	25.0	0	99	41
Estimated Purchase Price of Single-Family Unit within a three mile radius ($1,000s)[1,3,4]	148.4	56.6	65	300	41
Esimated Monthly Rent of Multi-Family Unit within a three mile radius ($)[1,3,4]	593.5	143.5	325	900	41

Notes:
1. Exclusive of corridors, consisting mainly of master-planned projects and well-defined clusters.
2. This ratio is only for the 28 cases with some (at least one) housing units on-site (i.e., cases with zero values in the denominator were excluded).
3. Includes the housing units within the SEC.
4. In 1987 dollars.

the Hacienda Business Park in the Bay Area have multi-family units exclusively. In most cases these units are inhabited by families who do not work in the complex. In several cases, on-site housing units were found to serve mainly as company condominiums for out-of-town visitors and business entertainment. Company condominiums obviously do little to provide workers with nearby housing opportunities.

The average ratio of on-site jobs to housing for the 28 surveyed SECs with some housing provisions was very high at 30.9. Around half of these SECs fell within the range of 20 to 28 workers for every on-site housing unit. Only the Woodlands and Chesterbrook had more housing units than jobs in 1987, whereas the rest of the SECs had ratios that exceeded the 1.5 threshold of jobs–housing balance.[15] Both the Woodlands and Chesterbrook, however, were consciously designed as "balanced" communities whereas, almost by definition, the other SECs have evolved more as employment concentrations, so fairly high ratios could have well been expected. Regardless, it is apparent that the vast majority of SECs today offer their tenants' employees relatively few on-site housing opportunities.

As noted earlier, more important than the ratio of jobs-to-housing is the share of workers who actually live in on-site units. Unfortunately, data were not available in most cases to assess this. From interviews, most developers and property managers of SECs with substantial residential components estimated that somewhere in the neighborhood of 5 to 10 per cent of workers lived in those units. For the Warner Center in suburban Los Angeles, a 1985 survey of the tenants of on-site townhouses and condominiums indicated that 8 per cent of the heads of households worked within the SEC (Cervero 1986b). Thus, even where there are on-site housing provisions, it is apparent that in at least some cases, relatively few workers are residing in them, ostensibly because they either cannot afford the units or they choose to live elsewhere.

Of course, it is not imperative that suburban employees live actually on a site to achieve the benefits of jobs-housing balance. More important is the match-up of housing with employees within a small subregion, say, within a three to five mile radius of the workplace. Table 3.4 indicates that for non-corridor SECs, the estimated amount of housing within three miles of the workplace averages around 11,000 units, with substantial variation among cases. Of these areawide units, only around 35 per cent are multi-family. From site visits, a number of the SECs were found to be encircled by secluded ranch estates and exclusive neighborhoods with guards and gated security control. In most of these cases, the largest class of SEC employees worked in clerical positions, earning wages far below what would be required to purchase or rent nearby homes.[16]

From Table 3.4, the upscale character of nearby residences is further suggested by the high average estimated purchase price ($148,000) and monthly rent ($600) of units within a three mile radius of SECs. In every instance, estimated mean purchase prices and rents were higher than metropolitan averages. That many workers are unable to live within three or so miles of these SECs seems inescapable, particularly in light of the fact that, as shown earlier, over 40 per cent of SEC employees have clerical, manufacturing, and other non-professional positions. This inference is further supported by the findings of other researchers that show clerical and manufacturing employees in SECs in the Atlanta and Chicago areas commute farther to work than any other class of employees (Hartshorn & Muller 1987, Sachs 1986). The mismatch between the earnings of employees and the cost of nearby housing at many of the nation's largest SECs no doubt bears some responsibility for jobs–housing imbalances and declining regional mobility.

3.6   Transportation facilities and services in SECs

In addition to land use features and jobs–housing relationships, of course, the amount and quality of both on-site and off-site transportation facilities and services influence the travel behavior of SEC workers. In particular, roadway capacity, parking provisions, and the availability of commute alternatives, such as vans and buses, can have a powerful influence on the modal choices of SEC workers.

On- and off-site roadway facilities

Table 3.5 summarizes some of the transportation facilities and services of the surveyed SECs. Among the 18 master-planned SECs for which data were available, there are, on average, around nine directional miles of roadway within each site. This averages out to around 2,600 employees per directional mile. Most road networks within suburban office parks consist of a system of curvilinear streets that interconnect in a grid-like manner (O'Mara & Casazza 1982, Cervero 1986b). Some feature a main spinal road that penetrates the core of the project, flanked by minor loops that provide direct site access.

In many master-planned business parks, individual parcels have their own access roads. This enables main roads to function as through channels, with access and frontage roads providing direct ingress and egress to sites. Where buildings are far apart, those relying on their vehicles for on-site circulation must exit from one development on to a collector or arterial and promptly turn into the next development's autonomous entry road and parking lot. Such movements can interrupt traffic flows on main thoroughfares and create fairly circuitous travel patterns.

Of course, freeways play a vital role in linking many suburban workers to their residences. Over 90 per cent of the non-corridor SECs are served by controlled-access freeways. On average, these SECs have 7.3 directional miles of freeway and 5.6 grade-separated interchanges within a five mile radius. This averages out to around 3,800 employees per directional freeway mile and 6,400 employees per interchange. The average spacing between interchanges is 2.5 miles (directional miles/interchanges).

On-site parking provisions

The availability and price of parking are two of the most significant determinants of the modes commuters choose (Shoup, 1982). In most

Table 3.5 Transportation Facilities and Services

	Mean	Std. Dev.	Min.	Max.	No. Cases
ON-SITE ROAD FACILITIES[1]					
Directional roadway miles[2]	8.9	6.6	2.0	23.0	18
Employees/Roadway mile	2,584	2,194	400	8,333	18
OFF-SITE ROAD FACILITIES					
Freeway directional miles within 5 mile radius[2]	7.3	5.3	0	20	47
Employees/Freeway mile	3,827	4,420	157	20,000	46
Freeway Interchanges within 5 mile radius	5.6	9.7	0	11	56
Employees/Interchange	6,431	5,247	457	20,500	56
Freeway directional miles/Interchange[2]	2.5	1.5	0.6	9.0	47
ON-SITE PARKING PROVISIONS					
Parking Spaces/1,000 gross square feet of Floorspace	3.85	0.68	2.0	5.5	55
Parking Spaces/Employee	1.04	0.18	0.6	1.4	55
"Modal" daily Parking Price ($)[3]	0.60	0.90	0.0	3.50	48
TRANSIT AND RIDESHARING SERVICES[4]					
No. peak hour public Bus Runs:					
On-Site[5]	4.8	4.5	1	15	18
Within 3 mile radius	12.0	13.6	1	61	48
No. daily private Commuter Buses[5]	3.8	7.3	1	30	41
No. Firms sponsoring Vanpools[5]	2.5	3.9	1	20	41
No. Company Vans operating[5]	14.1	22.8	1	115	41

Notes:
1. Statistics only for well-defined, master-planned SECs, exclusive of all corridors.
2. Directional miles measure lineal distance in one direction.
3. Most frequently occurring daily price for parking.
4. Exclusive of corridors.
5. Statistics only for SECs with some bus or van services. Minimum values are one.

suburban work environments, parking is closely controlled, with zoning ordinances and site covenants usually governing the minimum number of spaces provided, the location of lots, and the permissibility of on-street parking.

From Table 3.5, the surveyed SECs average around 3.85 parking spaces per 1,000 gross square feet of floorspace, which comes out to a little over one space per worker. For developments with a large retail component, rates tend to be higher whereas the rates for centers dominated by office uses are generally somewhat lower. Still, compared to many of the other statistics cited, there is relatively little variation across sites in the parking rates. Other surveys of suburban office parks and activity centers across the country also show surprisingly little variation, with averages consistently falling in the range of 3.5 to 4.0 spaces per 1,000 square feet of floorspace (Lea, Elliott, McLean & Co. 1985, Gruen Gruen & Associates 1986, Cervero 1986b). In general, the provision of roughly one parking space per office worker has become a universally accepted standard in the real estate industry (O'Mara & Casazza 1982, Lenny 1984). Zoning codes which require ample parking as a hedge against vehicles spilling over into surrounding streets, pressures from financial lenders to exceed minimum parking standards in order to improve a project's marketability, and fears that a project will only be competitive if excess parking is provided have frequently combined to inflate parking supply in SECs.[17]

Several studies suggest that many suburban office centers have in the range of 60–70 per cent excess capacity. A survey of actual usage rates in California and Texas found suburban office workers only required around 2.2 spaces per 1,000 square feet, even though 3.7 spaces per 1,000 square feet were being provided (Lea, Elliot, McClean & Company 1985). Gruen Gruen & Associates', (1986) study of nine business parks in suburban Philadelphia and San Francisco revealed that the highest occupancy rate during the peak period of parking was 60.6 per cent. The researchers concluded that "the business parks surveyed appear to be allocating too much space for parking as an inducement to attract tenants from more congested urban locations. The data suggest that a 2.0 parking ratio would be sufficient to take care of the parking needs of most business parks" (Gruen Gruen & Associates 1986, 14). Besides inducing workers to drive, an overabundance of parking, particularly when it is laid out as surface lots, can also space buildings so far apart as effectively to discourage walking between buildings.

A number of suburban developers and communities are beginning to recognize the wastefulness and high cost of excess parking and have acted to remedy the situation. The developers of the Galleria office–retail complex in suburban Atlanta, for instance, provided the usual 4.5 spaces per 1,000 square feet for the original 20 story building of the multi-phase project. After noticing that many spaces were empty around the clock, they lowered the rate to 4 spaces for the second office tower and eventually down to 3.3 spaces for the third phase of the project, saving millions of dollars in the process (Hartshorn & Muller 1986). Developers of the high-rise Howard Hughes Center in western Los Angeles chose the opposite approach, providing below-standard parking for the initial phase of the project and adjusting the amount of parking

Photo 3.6 Massive surface parking lot. Zoned at 3.8 spaces per 1,000 gross square feet of floorspace, this parking lot in suburban San Ramon, California, consumes over three times as much land as the building it serves. (Photo by the author.)

in subsequent stages according to how full garages were and the success of company-sponsored ridesharing programs (Cervero 1986b). Moreover, several suburbs with large employment bases, notably Bellevue, Washington, and Palo Alto, California, have recently lowered minimum parking requirements to 2.0 spaces per 1,000 square feet. In the case of Bellevue, a maximum ceiling of 2.7 spaces per 1,000 square feet has been established for the downtown core (Freeman *et al.*, 1987, Kenyon 1984).

Besides supply, there are several other distinguishing features of parking in SECs that deserve mention. Around three-quarters of SEC parking is in the form of surface space. Unlike CBDs, moreover, most SEC parking is associated with a specific building or property (Rice Center 1987). Multilevel, joint-tenant structures are generally limited to higher density clusters where land prices exceed $8 per square foot (1982 dollars) (O'Mara & Casazza, 1982). A number of SECs around the country are dotted throughout with decked structures; these include Tysons Corner, Perimeter Center, South Coast Metro, Greenway Plaza, and the Denver Tech Center.[18]

Another prominent feature of SEC parking is its relative convenience. In many business parks, buildings are enveloped 360° by asphalt parking, offering a short trek from one's car to one's desk. A Houston study found that SEC parkers walked, on average, one-half of a downtown-size block from their parking spot to their office, roughly half the distance of the typical downtown office worker. Moreover, around 80 per cent of SEC parkers walked "zero blocks" to their offices, enjoying virtually front-door parking privileges. Another study of 32 office parks around the country found a mean walking distance of 116 feet between main building entrances and the middle of the closest parking lot; by comparison, the nearest on-site bus stop was, on average, 480 feet away – approximately four times as far (Cervero 1986b).[19] The same study found that around 7 per cent of parking stalls in business parks are reserved for carpools and vanpools; these stalls were generally within 50 feet of building entrances. Preferential parking, however, can only be expected to influence mode choice in congested locales where it is difficult to find parking; in the vast majority of SECs, this is not the case.

Not only do most suburban workers enjoy a guaranteed, convenient parking space, but in the vast majority of cases, the space is also free. Table 3.5 shows that the most frequently paid daily parking fee for long-term parking averaged out to 60 cents. This average, however, is skewed by several large centers where parking fees are generally collected, such as the South Coast Metro and central Stamford. At most SECs, free parking is provided as a marketing ploy. Even in several high-density centers, free parking is the norm. At Warner Center, for instance, 93 per cent of workers have their parking expenses paid entirely by their employers (Commuter Transportation Services 1987). Moreover, the Rice Center (1987) found that only 3.2 per cent of Post Oak's workforce pay for parking, even though its office inventory exceeds that of downtown Atlanta.

Parking charges and restraints on supply have been shown to have a significant effect on mode choice (Shoup 1982). Following the passage of Bellevue's landmark parking ordinance, for instance, one of the city's largest employers succeeded in getting 77 per cent of its 900 workers into carpools and buses by limiting parking to 410 stalls and charging $60 per month per space (Kenyon 1984). The majority of suburban employers are reluctant to charge for parking, however, since free parking represents an in-kind, tax-free benefit to their workers and is often looked upon as a "good will" gesture. Unless such hidden subsidies to motorists are eliminated, however, many SECs will be hard pressed to entice their tenants' employees into buses and vanpools.

In general, the practice of providing a free parking space per employee in the suburbs has become a self-fulfilling prophecy – to no surprise, most workers fill their allotted parking spot by driving. Transportation planners often point out that "auto disincentives" such as parking controls are more effective at relieving congestion than "transit incentives" such as subsidized bus fares. Calling these programs "auto disincentives" is a misnomer, however. More accurately, they are "auto equalizers" – that is, they aim to level the playing field by removing many of the built-in biases that favor solo auto commuting, thereby placing vanpools, bus transit, and other travel options on more equal footing.

Transit and ridesharing services

Historically, mass transit has played a minor role in suburban labor markets because of low employment densities as well as the prevalence of abundant, free parking (Orski 1986a, Cervero 1984). Table 3.5 shows that for the 18 non-corridor case sites with on-site public transit services, the average number of peak hour bus runs is around five. Within a three-mile radius of SECs, there is an average of 12 bus runs during the peak. On a daily basis, the surveyed SECs have, on average, nearly four private commuter buses operating on their premises. The two surveyed sites with the highest incidences of subscription bus operations are the Woodlands and the Meadowlands, where on an average weekday over 25 privately operated commuter buses serve their respective residents and employees. Successful private suburban bus operations can also be found in the greater Los Angeles and Norfolk–Virginia Beach regions, where thousands of suburban employees travel to work sites scattered throughout each metropolitan area every day in comfortable coaches offering headrests and guaranteed seats (Giuliano & Teal 1985).

Only six of the surveyed SECs were found to have on-site shuttle operations.[20] Most are noon-hour circulators, interconnecting major office towers with nearby restaurants and retail centers. In the cases of Bishop Ranch and Hacienda Business Park in the Bay Area, shuttles also operate to and from Bay Area Rapid Transit (BART) stations.

From Table 3.5, each surveyed SEC averages between two and three tenants who sponsor vanpools for their employees. The mean number of vans operating among these firms is 14. The 3M Park in suburban St. Paul has 110 company vans – the largest number in operation among the surveyed sites. Nationwide, large-scale vanpool programs also thrive in several other SECs, notably Lawrence Livermore Laboratory in suburban Alameda County, California, the Rockwell International headquarters in Golden, Colorado, and the Tennessee Valley Authority outside of Knoxville (Dingle Associates Inc. 1982).

Most of the surveyed SECs appear quite committed to ridesharing. Nearly one half have a staff member whose job assignment includes ridesharing coordination and promotion, and 56 per cent of the sites have an office or location devoted to ridematching and the dissemination of information on commute alternatives. In the majority of cases, ridesharing is somewhat incidental to the staff person's chief job assignment. The on-site rideshare office also usually consists essentially of a kiosk with bus schedules and other literature promoting the virtues of carpooling and vanpooling. Several centers, such as Tysons Corner and Bishop Ranch, do also have highly visible on-site transportation offices which are staffed with full-time rideshare coordinators who maintain active computerized ridematch listings and run carpool promotional efforts.

Cycling and pedestrian facilities

In order to promote cycling, around one-quarter of the surveyed SECs were found to have some on-site bike trails and other cycling amenities. Most bikepaths in suburban work settings are used for recreational rather than commuting purposes, however. Several large office parks, such as the Bay Area's Bishop Ranch, have also introduced covenants specifically requiring all buildings with large concentrations of employees to contain showers and lockers for cyclists and other recreationists.

Walkways are an essential ingredient of any work environment. While all SECs feature sidewalks, the overall quality of pedestrian facilities varies considerably. Many office parks and planned unit developments have nicely groomed, curvilinear footpaths, dotted with plantings, sculptures and other displays that not only enhance the site but also make walking pleasurable. At more congested SECs, grade-separated skybridges and underpasses can be found. In contrast, many unplanned, high-density SECs have a discontinuous, seemingly *ad hoc* system of sidewalks. In these settings, footpaths sometime end at property lines and all too often are lined by blank walls, vacant lots, and other indistinguishable spaces. Sometimes pedestrians are forced to search for a passable route around shrubbery and curbs to reach roadways; the sight of office workers crossing busy roadways, dodging cars, and scurrying to find refuge at mid-block traffic medians has become commonplace in and around many SECs.

Besides the provision of sidewalks, the distances between buildings within SECs and the proximity of nearby commercial and residential activities strongly influence the amount of walking that takes place. In many office parks, pedestrians frequently face long walks across parking lots and open lawns to get between buildings. Even high density SECs pose challenging distances to many pedestrians. In Houston, the nearest high-rise office tower to the Galleria, Post Oak's premier retail center, is 2,000 feet away (Rice Center 1987). Studies show, however, that only around 15 per cent of Americans are willing to walk 2,000 feet for non-leisure trips (Untermann 1986), and that the maximum acceptable walking distance for suburban areas is perhaps under 1,000 feet (Lynch & Hack 1984). Consequently, pedestrian activity in places like Post Oak is infrequent, with the preponderance of on-site trips made instead behind a steering wheel.

3.7 SEC commuting and traffic conditions

This section summarizes the characteristics of the journey-to-work trips of the employees of surveyed SECs as well as areawide traffic conditions on facilities serving SECs.

Time, speed, and distance of journey to work

The mean one-way travel times, distances, and speeds for journeys to work made by employees of the surveyed SECs are shown in Table 3.6.[21] Averaging across the SECs, employees commute around 11 miles one-way, at speeds of approximately 28 m.p.h. and taking around 24 minutes, with only a moderate degree of variation across sites. This is farther, slower, and longer, time-wise, than journeys to work made by the "typical" suburban employee in 1980. That worker traveled, on average, around 9 miles in a little over 18 minutes at speeds of roughly 30 m.p.h. (Pisarksi 1987). The differences are surely linked to the increase in congestion and the widening jobs–housing imbalance found around suburban employment areas since 1980.

The average one way distance of 11 miles for work trips made by SEC employees, it should be noted, is actually farther than the ten mile average for all work trips made within US metropolitan areas in 1980 (Pisarski 1987). With the relocation of office jobs to traditionally residential suburbs, one might expect SEC work trips to be relatively short. As noted in section 3.4, this discrepancy is likely due to the displacing effects of jobs–housing imbalances and, perhaps more directly, the mismatch between SEC employee earnings and the cost of nearby housing. More disaggregate surveys of commuting distances of individual SEC employees have also found comparatively long commutes being made. Of the greater Houston area's 11 SECs, the Rice Center (1987) found that workers in West Houston's Energy Corridor, the farthest SEC from downtown, averaged longer commutes than workers from any other SEC – 9.8 miles (even further than the 9.2 mile average for CBD workers). For two of the San Francisco Bay Area's largest and fastest-growing suburban employment markets, Pleasanton and the Golden Triangle of Santa Clara County, average one-way employee commutes exceed 15 miles, over one-quarter longer than the regional average (Cervero 1986b, Cervero & Griesenbeck 1988).

Table 3.6 Travel Characteristics of Workforce and Areawide Traffic Conditions

	Mean	Std. Dev.	Min.	Max.	No. Cases
JOURNEY-TO-WORK TRIP					
Average One-way Travel Time (minutes)	24.3	6.7	14	48	56
Average One-way Travel Distance (miles)[1]	11.1	3.6	7	22	12
Average Travel Speed (mph)[2]	28.5	8.9	8.5	48.5	56
Percent of Trips:					
Drive Alone	83	9	58	95	56
Rideshare	13	7	3	34	56
Average daily ridership of all bus runs serving SEC[3]	1,254	2,249	25	9.600	41
"Modal" Arrival Time (a.m.)[4]	8:16	--	7:30	8:45	55
"Modal" Departure Time (p.m.)[4]	4:56	--	4:30	5:30	55
AREAWIDE TRAFFIC CONDITIONS					
Average daily directional traffic volume on principal freeway or arterial serving SEC on typical weekday (thousands)[5,6]	67.9	46.7	6.0	215.0	48
Freeway miles per million population for region[7]	89.9	32.3	24.3	158.0	57

Notes:
1. Averages from worker travel surveys, representing a combination of straightline and elapsed distances.
2. For 35 cases with missing distance data, the average distance was assumed to be 11.1 miles, the average for the 12 SECs with available employee travel distance data.
3. Only for cases with at least one public or private bus run operating within the SEC.
4. Most frequently occurring time of arrival or departure.
5. Directional volumes are oneway traffic counts.
6. Exclusive of corridor cases.
7. Sources: Rodriquez, et al. [1985], Federal Highway Administration [1986].

It is apparent that bringing jobs closer to population masses does not guarantee shorter, or even easier, commutes.

Mode splits for SEC work trips

As mentioned earlier, the low-lying, spread out profile of many SECs, combined with their single-use nature and abundance of free parking, likely encourages many employees to drive to work. Among surveyed

SECs, on average 83 per cent of the workforce solo-commutes and 13 per cent either carpool or vanpool (Table 3.6 and Fig. 3.5). These percentages closely match those for the nation as a whole in 1980 (Pisarski 1987).[22] These national figures, however, include small and large metropolitan areas alike while the SECs surveyed were predominantly from regions with populations exceeding 1 million. For the 26 metropolitan areas in which the surveyed SECs are located, the share of drive-alone commute trips was 68 per cent in 1980.[23] Thus, on average, the share of SEC employees in these surveyed regions who relied on their cars for commuting to work exceeded that of the typical worker by 15 per centage points. Clearly, SEC workers are far more dependent on their automobiles than their inner-city counterparts.

Among the surveyed SECs, there tended to be the most variation in the shares of employees who carpool or vanpool (Table 3.6).[24] SECs with market shares of carpoolers/vanpoolers exceeding 20 per cent are Bellevue, Bishop Ranch, BWI, Cyprus Creek, East Farmingdale, Hunt Valley, the Meadowlands, Greenway Plaza, Post Oak, Stamford, and the 3M Park.[25] While these SECs vary in density and character, in all cases there is an active ridematching campaign under way and at least one major tenant underwrites the costs of employee vanpool services. In general, suburban areas average relatively high levels of ridesharing because of the absence of suitable public transit services in many cases (Briggs *et al.*, 1986). In many business parks, however, the dispersal of thousands of employees over several square miles, coupled with the usual absence of internal circulators and the multitude of parking options, stack the odds heavily against ridesharing. Where employee residences are widely scattered, ridematching can be next to impossible. As discussed in chapter 6, in places with few larger employers there might not be enough of a critical mass to sustain a ridesharing program. Despite active promotion, for example, the Denver Tech Center has been able to entice only around 10 per cent of its laborforce into carpools and vanpools, in part because over 400 individual tenants account for the development's 16,000 workers.

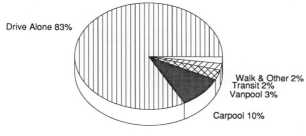

Drive Alone 83%

Walk & Other 2%
Transit 2%
Vanpool 3%

Carpool 10%

* weighted average by employment size

Figure 3.5 Percentage of work trips to SECs, by mode.

Figure 3.5 also reveals that public and private transit serve, on average, only 2 per cent of SEC employees.[26] This matches the nationwide average for work trips destined to suburbs (Fulton W. 1986b). Among the surveyed SECs, only Bellevue, Bishop Ranch, Hacienda Business Park, and the Meadowlands had transit mode splits exceeding the national average of 7 per cent for metropolitan areas. In addition to its parking containment program, Bellevue's success can be attributable to its superb transit services. Notably, a transit center in the heart of downtown Bellevue functions as a major transfer point for the region and is served by 17 Seattle Metro routes (136 buses during the 3 p.m.–6 p.m. peak). The sponsorship of premium-type coach services for tenants' employees by the developers of Bishop Ranch and Hacienda Business Park east of San Francisco likely accounts for much of mass transit's success at these two projects.

Other SECs have had less success at enticing workers into buses. At mixed-use complexes, such as the Denver Tech Center, Post Oak, and South Coast Metro, fewer than 5 per cent of employees commute by bus despite the fact that these centers serve as major transfer points, with, in the case of the South Coast Metro, as many as 12 bus routes converging into the premises during peak hours. Low densities at the residential end of work trips likely account for transit's low market shares in these cases (Cervero 1986b, Reichert 1979). Even SECs with direct rail transit connections tend to have low ridership levels. Travel surveys show that fewer than 5 per cent of employees in office towers circling rail stations in the suburban San Francisco–Oakland (BART) and suburban Washington, D.C. (WMATA) areas patronize transit (Baker 1983, Orski 1985, Knack 1986). Low ridership levels can be attributed to low residential densities and free employee parking in many of these cases (Cervero 1986b).

Lastly, Figure 3.5 reveals that walk and other (e.g., cycling, drop-off) trips comprise only some 2 per cent of work journeys made to SECs. This is less than the 4 per cent national share of work trips made on foot among suburban workers (Pisarski 1987). Again, the built-in design pressures to solo-commute and the lack of integrated sidewalk systems in many SECs discourage many employees from walking or cycling. In general, walk trips are more common for non-work purposes in SECs. The Rice Center (1987) study, for instance, found 19.5 per cent of all trips in Houston area SECs were made on foot (0.7 walk trips/per employee daily), one-third of which were made between 11 a.m.–2 p.m. However, of non-work trips within SECs, walking made up only 21.5 per cent of the total. In centers like Post Oak, disconnected sidewalks, long block faces, and limited mid-block cross-walk opportunities have discouraged foot travel. Lunchtime walk trips of as long as one-half mile are most likely to occur in mixed-use environments. Workers are more apt to walk along avenues with shops, parks, and other interesting places to go since a number of trip purposes can be accomplished along the way (Rice Center 1987). Along Bellevue's main pedestrian axis, for instance, walk trips comprise 32 per cent of midday travel, in large part because the street is lined with interesting shops and eateries (DKS Associates 1987).

Vehicle occupancy

Suburban workplaces generally enjoy high vehicle occupancy levels because of the relatively high incidence of vehicle pooling (Briggs *et al.*, 1986). Although occupancy data were not compiled for SECs in this study, travel surveys for several case sites documented the following rates, expressed in persons per vehicle during the peak period: Bellevue (1.21); Bel-Red Corridor (1.10); Denver Tech Center (1.13); Greenway Plaza (1.19); Hacienda Business Park (1.17); Tysons Corner (1.06); Post Oak (1.15); and West Houston Energy Corridor (1.13). These rates hover around the 1980 average occupancy level for all U.S. metropolitan areas of 1.15 persons per vehicle (US Bureau of Census 1982). Because of declining real gasoline prices and demographic trends (e.g., increases in single-headed households), however, national occupany rates have likely slipped somewhat during the 1980s.

Time period of travel

Suburban work settings have a number of distinct peaking characteristics. The afternoon peak is usually longer and more pronounced than the morning peak since late afternoon traffic usually includes a broad mix of work-commuters, business and delivery vehicles, shoppers, and other personal trips. In the Seattle area, for instance, 57.7 per cent of downtown trips from 4:30 p.m–5:30 p.m. are work trips, compared to a work trip share in the suburbs during this period of only 38.8 per cent (Puget Sound Council of Governments 1984). Afternoon peaks in the suburbs tend to be elongated since most suburban retail outlets stay open late whereas most downtown shops close at 5 p.m. Moreover, suburban work areas tend to have distinct midday peaks, mainly due to vehicular lunch-hour traffic. At Tysons Corner, the midday peak actually exceeds both the morning and the evening peak on the basis of the highest 15 minute traffic count. Viewed over time, the hourly distribution of vehicle trips in many SECs looks more like the profile of a camel with three rather than two humps.

The most frequently occurring time of arrival among the employees of surveyed SECs averaged out to 8:16 a.m. (Table 3.6); the modal departure time was just before 5 p.m. Those SECs with large shares of investment brokers, accountants, and other financial positions tended to have earlier average arrival and departure times since these workers usually are 'on-board' at the opening bell of the east-coast stock exchanges. Finally, among survey respondents, 65 per cent associated the morning peak hour for SEC work trips with the 7:30 a.m.–8:30 a.m. period; 70 per cent defined the 4.30 p.m.–5.30 p.m. period as the afternoon peak. In general, then, the heaviest hour of SEC-oriented commuting appears to coincide more or less with the peak hours of other work locales.

Trip generation

Although trip generation rates were not measured directly in this study, several SECs reported rates empirically derived for trips made by office workers. The Institute of Transportation Engineers (1987) *Trip Generation* manual presents the following rates, defined in terms of weekday trip ends per 1,000 gross square feet, for each of the below uses:

(a)   General Office – 12.3
      Buildings < 100,000 sq. ft. – 17.7
      Buildings 100,000–200,000 sq. ft. – 14.3
      Buildings > 200,000 sq. ft. – 10.9
(b)   Office Park – 20.6
(c)   Research Centers – 5.3.

Thus, office parks average almost twice as many vehicular trips per square foot as large general office buildings, reflecting the effects of low densities, single-use activities, and excess parking on vehicle usage.

For several SECs, the below-listed weekday trip generation rates for office uses have been estimated (also on a square footage basis):[27]

(a)   Bellevue – 18.1
(b)   Lake-Cook Corridor –19.98
(c)   Naperville – (single tenant – 5.17; multi tenant – 12.97)
(d)   Oak Brook – (single tenant – 9.48; multi tenant – 15.20)

With the exception of Bellevue, all of these SECs are located in the Chicago region. In general, these rates fall within the range of values found in the Institute of Transportation Engineers' manual. The wide variations suggest that a number of factors, including land use variables such as density and the variations in uses, influence office trip generation rates. From the Chicago data, it is apparent that tenancy is one influential variable – multi-tenant rates were far higher than those of single tenants. Multi-tenant buildings tend to be taller and more intensely used, producing higher trip rates. If all of these trips are made by automobile, then denser office areas can be expected to be more congested. If, on the other hand, significant shares of these trips are diverted to vehicle-pools, transit, cycling, and foot travel, then denser workplaces might be less congested. The relationship between density and mode choices for SECs is explored in chapter 6.

Areawide traffic conditions

Traffic congestion around America's SECs has been referred to as a "looming crisis" (Orski 1985). Just how bad have conditions become? For 57 surveyed SECs, level of service information was obtained for the primary arterial and freeway serving each SEC, based on both survey responses and local engineering records.[28] Figure 3.6 shows the distribution of peak hour levels of service for the main arterial serving SECs. In one-third of the cases, arterials operate at level of service D (80–89 per cent of capacity), a service quality generally associated with congested conditions in suburban settings. And in around 30 per cent of the cases, level of service falls below D during the peak (whereby volumes exceed 90 per cent of capacity and most motorists require two or more light changes to pass through a signalized intersection).

Comparing the righthand side of Figure 3.6, service conditions appear even worse along the principal freeway serving the surveyed SECs. In

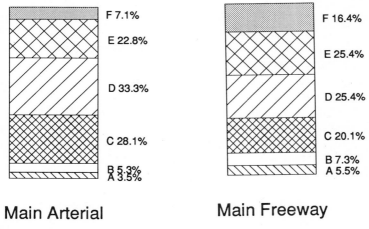

Main Arterial   **Main Freeway**

Figure 3.6   Percentage breakdown of average level of service on main roadways serving SECs.

over 40 per cent of the cases,[29] peak hour traffic flowed at the level of service E or worse (which for restricted-access, non-signalized facilities such as freeways means forced flows with no ability for the drivers to select lanes or speeds). This high incidence of freeway congestion suggests that many SECs are indeed approaching serious traffic conditions that rival those of many downtowns and inner-city corridors.

Examining the data for areawide traffic conditions in Table 3.6, the daily volumes on these connecting freeways are, on average, rather high – nearly 70,000 vehicles per day. SECs with the highest freeway traffic counts, in some cases exceeding 200,000 vehicles per day, are the Golden Triangle in Santa Clara County (Route 101, Bayshore Freeway), the North Dallas Parkway, South Coast Metro (Interstate 405), Cyprus Creek (Interstate 95), and Warner Center (Route 101, Ventura Freeway). Around 52 per cent of the surveyed SECs are in metropolitan areas with predominantly radial-ring freeway networks, 14 per cent are in regions with grid-like networks, and the remaining one-third are situated in areas with more or less irregular networks.[30] On average, the metropolitan areas with SECs that were surveyed have around 90 freeway miles per million population, which is slightly above the average of 84.7 miles for the 20 largest US metropolitan regions.[31] On the whole, then, the surveyed SECs appear to have reasonably good freeway provisions.

3.8   Summary

This chapter has discussed a range of transportation and land-use issues affecting SECs by both reviewing the literature and summarizing general statistics on the 57 centers and corridors surveyed for this study. The SECs were found to be diverse in many ways, so making generalizations about them can be hazardous. On the whole, however, they tend to be quite large, encompassing several square miles, with millions of square feet of floorspace and well over 10,000 employees. The workforces of SECs tend to be equally diverse, with clerical workers forming the largest single occupational group.

Most SECs have low floorspace and employment densities, generally with FARs below 2.0 and fewer than 20 workers per acre. Many master-planned, campus-style projects cover less than a third of land with structures, producing long setbacks and segregating buildings. When surrounded by surface parking, walking distances can become excessively long.

SECs were also found to vary considerably in their degree of land use mixture. Some have over 90 per cent of floorspace devoted solely to office use. Mixed-use environments, it has been argued, could reduce trip generation levels, encourage walking and ridesharing, spread trip-making more evenly throughout the day, and allow parking facilities to be shared. Equally important, the provision of more affordable housing near SECs could shorten commute distances and help segregate local and through traffic. Around many SECs there appears to be a wide disparity between the earnings of workers and the cost of nearby housing, setting the stage for long commutes and traffic tie-ups along connecting arteries.

Another prominent feature of SECs is the abundance of free, convenient parking. Most offer around one parking space per employee. This becomes a self-fulfilling prophecy of sorts, with most workers filling their allotted parking spot by driving. While most SECs are connected by buslines and have an assortment of ridesharing services, five out of six work trips nonetheless normally involve an employee commuting alone. SEC commuters generally average speeds under 30 m.p.h. on connecting freeways and arterials that are approaching unstable flow conditions.

It bears repeating, however, that SECs come in all shapes and sizes. Perhaps only by classifying centers into homogeneous groups and comparing differences among groups can one gain an appreciation of their distinguishing features as well as some insight into how varying land uses and site designs influence travel behavior. The following two chapters attempt to do this, first by grouping the cases into one of six different SEC classifications and then by studying differences among the groups.

Notes

1. The ratio of standard deviation to mean is sometimes called the coefficient of variation. Coefficients exceeding one signify a fairly dispersed distribution of values.
2. This average is based on the mean of the ratio of current FAR to allowable FAR for the 35 cases. This is higher than the "average of the average," which would be $0.98/2.34 = 0.42$, or 42 per cent.
3. FAR/Coverage Ratio $= 0.98/0.31 = 3.16$.
4. Class A space is a general term used to connote the highest quality of office building. The Urban Land Institute defines it as "buildings which have excellent location and access, attract high quality tenants, and are managed professionally. Building materials are high quality and rents are competitive with other new buildings" (O'Mara & Casazza 1982, 18–19).
5. The abbreviation MXD has been adopted by the Urban Land Institute (1986) and is used throughout the remainder of this book.
6. ITE (1987) daily trip rates are: 5.3 weekday trips per 1,000 gross square feet of R&D, 6.1 trips per apartment unit, and 40.7 trips per 1,000 gross square feet of specialty retail. Thus, for this scenario, the trip volume can

be calculated as: {[25,000 office sq. ft. * (12.3 trips/1,000 office sq.ft.)] + [10,000 R&D sq. ft. * (5.3 trips/1,000 sq. ft. R&D)] + [(40,000 sq. ft. apartments/(1600 sq. ft./apartment unit)) * (6.1 trips/apartment unit)] + [10,000 sq. ft. specialty retail * (40.7 trips/1,000 sq. ft. specialty retail)]} = 999.5.

7. Among CBD employees, 46.3 per cent ate lunch in the immediate area (but away from their office) while 4.3 per cent ate outside the immediate area. For SECs, 37 per cent of employees had lunch on-site (but away from their office) while 6.7 per cent left the premises for lunch.

8. The Barton-Aschman (1983) study, for instance, found 28 per cent of employees of MXDs patronized the same or nearby development, while only 19 per cent of workers from single-use sites did so.

9. Reliable data could only be obtained from 18 of the SECs which are either master-planned or clustered, or both.

10. Exclusive of corridors.

11. A high retail intensity level means a low value for the ratio of employees to retail establishments.

12. This normative ceiling for "balance" is based on: [(1.7 jobs/cohabitant household) * (0.9 cohabitant households)]/households = 1.53, or approximately 1.5 jobs/household.

13. In 1985, the shares of workers residing locally were: Walnut Creek (19.9 per cent); Mountain View (19.7 per cent); Palo Alto (19.7 per cent); and Santa Clara (16.8 per cent) (Cervero, 1986a).

14. For further discussion on job turnover rates in the Chicago area, see Church (1987).

15. It should be noted, however, that this threshold is most relevant when comparing jobs to housing at the community, rather than SEC, level.

16. Of course, one's ability to purchase a close-by home depends to a large degree on whether a person is the sole wage-earner in a household or not. The ability to purchase more expensive homes obviously increases with the number of wage-earners in a household, all else equal.

17. From the survey of 50 non-corridor SECs, respondents from 41 of the developments considered their parking rates to be at or above the rates of comparable developments in the region. Additionally, 84 per cent of the respondents indicated that parking exceeded the minimum parking requirements.

18. Decked structures generally cost $18 to $20 per square foot (1985 dollars), or roughly twice the footage cost of typical suburban land (Lea, Elliot, McLean & Co. 1985).

19. The study found that walking distances to on-site parking lots increased with the size of a project. The correlation between acreage of a project and average walking distance to on-site parking was 0.33.

20. This is about the same proportion – approximately ten per cent of studied sites–with on-site shuttle services that was found in an earlier study of office developments in the US (Cervero 1986b).

21. These statistics are actually "means of means". That is, they are the averages of the "average" travel time, distance, and speed of SEC employees. Reliable distance data were available only for 12 of the surveyed sites (see Table 3.6, n. 2).

22. These shares also match the modal distributions of work trips from the 1985 survey of 120 US office parks (Cervero 1986b).

23. Sources: Briggs *et al.* 1986, Rodriquez *et al.* 1985.

24. The standard deviation relative to the mean is much higher for ridesharing than drive-alone commuting.
25. Non-corridor cases only.
26. From Table 3.6 one sees that transit trips were made on bus runs serving around 1,250 riders per day, on the average.
27. Sources: DKS Associates (1987); *Transportation Facts* 4, 2, Chicago Area Transportation Study, March, 1987.
28. Level of service is a qualitative measure used to describe the degree of traffic congestion, general speeds, and levels of driver maneuverability on a particular section of roadway. The letter values are related to the following expressions of traffic volumes as a percentage of capacity: A = < 60 per cent (free flow); B = 60–9 per cent (mainly free flow); C = 70–9 per cent (stable flow); D = 80–9 per cent (approaching unstable flow); E = 90–9 per cent of capacity (unstable flow); and F = 100 per cent or > (jammed, forced flow).
29. Exclusive of the Central Corridor and Camelback Corridor in Phoenix, since no freeways exist in either area.
30. See Institute of Transportation Engineers (1985) for a detailed discussion of these network types.
31. Sources: Rodriquez *et al*. 1985, West Houston Association 1984. *Limited-access divided highways in America's twenty largest metropolitan complexes*.

4

Classifying suburban employment centers

4.1 Forms of suburban growth

Urban geographers, regional scientists, and city planners have long classified forms of metropolitan growth in an attempt both to understand the forces shaping it and the consequences of the evolving patterns. Classification, whether used for studying cities, diseases, or insects, is an indispensable tool for distilling sometimes unwieldy volumes of information into more assimilable subgroups. Additionally, it illuminates important relationships among variables by sifting out patterns and differences among classified groups. Following a brief review of theories and writings on suburban growth patterns and spatial forms of office growth, this chapter classifies SECs and assigns case sites to one of six groups based on a number of discriminating variables. The low-to-high ranges of some of the variables discussed in the previous chapter are presented for each of the six SEC groups as well. Case synopses for three of the SECs within each group are also presented. The intention of this chapter is not to create another schema for defining forms of suburban growth, but rather to provide a foundation for sorting out transportation–land use relationships among the case sites studied.

The three classic models of metropolitan structure are concentric zone (Burgess 1925), sector (Hoyt 1939), and multiple nuclei (Harris & Ullman 1945). Burgess saw regions forming as a series of concentric rings of distinct land uses focused on a dominant center, while Hoyt described cities in terms of lineal sectors emanating from the core along major transportation routes, such as railways. Both models dealt primarily with the patterns of residential growth and only considered a single commercial center, though Burgess did acknowledge that some regions seemed to be evolving as "centralized decentralized systems." Harris & Ullman (1945) formalized this notion in their characterization of a metropolis as a hierarchy of individual centers, each featuring a unique pattern of land uses and a separate laborshed. The interdependence of these uses and the scales, forms, and functions of centers were generally overlooked in these early writings.

The migration of factories and retail outlets to the suburbs, ushered in, in part, by the dawning of superfreeways, gave rise to still other visions of metropolitan growth. Some authors characterized the evolving form of urban change as counterurbanization – the erosion of a single-centered metropolis. Others described growth as a dispersion of activities – the seemingly random sprawl of tract housing, shopping malls, and industrial parks, each locating without any specific relation to particular focal points (Blumenfeld 1964). Many saw this emerging form as a mixed blessing, on the one hand increasing the consumption of land and other finite resources, yet on the other easing traffic congestion in the inner-city (Clark 1954). Others cautioned that although downtown congestion would be relieved, the growth in cross-hauling could eventually overwhelm suburbs with traffic (Schnore 1959).

Dissatisfied by this notion of random, unstructured growth, a number of urban economists have developed theories over the past forty years aimed at explicating the spatial relationship among land uses in some systematic way (Carroll 1952, Wingo 1961, Alonso 1964, Mills 1972, Solow 1973). Industrial location theorists viewed the locational decisions of firms with regard to proximity to raw materials, consumer markets, and labor. Other writers focused on patterns of residential location, generally expressed as involving a trade-off of housing and transportation expenses, with the rate of substitution depending on household preferences for low-density living. Over the years, a unified theory of either business or residential location has failed to emerge, in part because empirical work has demonstrated that a multitude of factors influence locational choices (Quigley & Weinberg 1977, Clark & Burt 1980). In particular, with the shift in the nation's economy from a manufacturing to a service base, businesses are becoming increasingly footloose, less encumbered by the need to be near raw materials or transportation lines.

In studying metropolitan growth and change, some authors have sought to define the forms and styles of office and commercial development in the suburbs specifically. In his analysis of the first wave of commercial development outside of America's central cities, Berry (1959) described four types of business locations: (a) urban arterial; (b) highway-oriented; (c) nucleated; and (d) localized. Establishments were said to be drawn to one of these locations according to their degree of specialization in addition to their labor and consumer access requirements. In a later study of office development in Great Britain, Daniels (1974) defined office growth in terms of both scale and form. His four classifications of growth were: (a) small centers; (b) large centers; (c) sprawl; and (d) widely scattered. Baerwald (1982) chose a more basic dichotomy of clustered versus corridor growth in examining office development in the Minneapolis–St. Paul region. A number of more recent studies have similarly differentiated between office growth that is clustered versus more auto-oriented patterns laid out along axial arterials and freeways (Hughes & Sternlieb 1986, Leinburger & Lockwood 1986).

Lastly, several researchers have concentrated on the evolution of suburban economic activities during the post-war era, tracing the transformation of suburbs from predominantly bedroom communities to more mature, urban-like places. Erickson (1983) has described suburban growth in the US through 1960 as a process of "dispersal/differentiation," followed by a subsequent phase (1960–present) of "infilling/multinucleation." More recently, Hartshorn & Muller (1986) have chronicled suburban growth in terms of changing land uses and built environments as well. They maintain that American suburbs have evolved in four distinct stages: (a) "bedroom communities" (pre-1960); (b) "independence" (1960–70, underscored by the arrival of shopping malls and industrial parks that made suburbs more self-sufficient); (c) "catalytic growth" (1970–80, whereby the addition of offices and other diverse uses ushered in an era of maturity); and (d) "high rise/high technology" (post-1980, reflecting dramatic shifts in the nation's economy and the emergence of downtown-type densities).

In summary, suburban growth in general, and suburban office growth in particular, has been described in a number of ways, each with a slightly different connotation in terms of size, density, location, and land use make-up. The wealth of terms used to describe suburban concentrations in the late 1980s – urban villages, satellite centers, outer cities, megacenters, and suburban downtowns – suggests that these places are widely diverse and perhaps resist classification. Based on the findings of the previous chapter, however, it appears that the SECs examined in this study have a number of distinctive characteristics that bear on transportation–land use relationships and thus deserve more systematic analysis. The remainder of this chapter classifies these SEC cases in an effort to sort out these patterns and relationships. Section 4.2, it should be noted, describes the methods used to classify SECs; those less interested in such details can proceed to the third paragraph of section 4.3 for a discussion of the six SEC groups that emerged and the cases which fall into each of the six groups.

4.2   Factors for classifying SECs

As discussed in Chapter 3, SECs can be described along a number of dimensions – size, density, land use composition, site design, ownership patterns, transportation facilities, and so on. Each of these dimensions can be expressed by several different variables, no one of which, alone, fully portrays that dimension, but which together provide a fairly good perspective into the site characteristics of SECs. Some dimensions, such as site design, are fairly qualitative concepts that almost defy measurement and certainly require more than a single variable to capture their full complexity.

In light of this need to use sets of variables to capture the many-sided dimensions of SECs, the multivariate technique of factor analysis was employed. Factor analysis is a statistical method used to identify a relatively small number of underlying factors that can be used to represent relationships among sets of many interrelated variables (Norusis 1986, Dunteman 1984). By merging variables, it enables large numbers of variables to be distilled down to a handful of underlying factors. In our case, it allows variables such as FAR, floorspace per worker, and land coverage ratios to be linearly combined to represent the concept of "density." Qualitative dimensions, such as site design, can also be expressed in terms of more than a single variable to capture their full complexity. Thus, factor analysis can help elucidate some of the underlying, though not always observable, land use dimensions of SECs.

Several features about the factor analysis methodology used in this study should be pointed out. First, since this study focuses on how land use factors influence SEC-related travel behavior, the objective was to classify cases with respect to land use, rather than transportation, variables. Thus, only land use variables entered into the factor analysis. Second, one of the main reasons for carrying out the factor analysis was to obtain factor scores for each of the cases that could then be used for classification in the subsequent cluster analysis. (This point is expanded upon in section 4.3.) Lastly, the seven large corridor cases, each of which exceeded 20 square miles in area, were not included either in the factor or cluster analysis since, by virtue of their sheer magnitude, they would not only have dominated all the other cases, but would also have had disproportionate influence over such underlying dimensions as "size" and "scale."[1] Thus, "large office corridors" were combined as one of the eventual six SEC groups at the outset of this classification effort. Accordingly, 50 rather than 57 cases were used in the following factor and cluster analyses.

The intent of this factor analysis was to combine sets of variables that could collectively capture at least the following four dimensions of the SECs: (a) density; (b) size; (c) design; and (d) land use. Not all of the candidates representing these dimensions entered into the analysis because some variables had a number of missing cases. Their inclusion would have whittled the data set down to those SEC observations for which complete information was available, a fairly small subset.[2]

An exploratory study of the correlation matrix of remaining variables resulted in a further expulsion of some variables in order to prevent certain pairs with high multicollinearity from dominating the analysis.[3] As a result, thirteen land use variables for which complete information was available entered into the analysis.

The final interpretable factor matrix that was obtained for defining underlying factors is shown in Table 4.1.[4] In all, four factors were extracted, meaning that it was possible to distill the thirteen variables down to four basic factors and retain much of the original information.[5] As shown in the bottom row of Table 4.1, these four factors together

Table 4.1   Factor loadings and summary statistics for SECs.

	Factor 1	Factor 2	Factor 3	Factor 4
Variables:				
AVGSTORY	.982			
EMP/ACRE	.880			
FAR	.872			
PARK/EMP	−.745			
COVERAGE	.733		−.443	
EMPLOYMT		.952		
FLOORSPC		.898		
RESTAURT		.820		
ACREAGE			.924	
SQFT/EMP			.871	
OFFICE			.730	−.477
USEENT				.641
RETAIL				.554
AVGLOT				−.527
Summary statistics:				
Eigenvalue	4.490	3.292	2.171	1.467
Percent of variation explained	34.5	25.3	16.7	11.3
Cumulative per cent of variation explained	34.5	59.9	76.6	87.9

Variable definitions:

AVGSTORY	= Number of stories of "average" building, in terms of most frequent height.
EMP/ACRE	= Employees per acre.
FAR	= Floor area ratio.
PARK/EMP	= Number of parking spaces per employee, on average.
COVERAGE	= Proportion of land covered by buildings, on average.
EMPLOYMT	= Size of workforce (thousands).
FLOORSPC	= Square feet of floorspace in office–commercial–industrial uses (millions).
RESTAURT	= Number of on-site restaurants and eateries.
ACREAGE	= Total land acreage.
SQFT/EMP	= Square feet of floorspace per employee.
OFFICE	= Proportion of floorspace in office use.
USEENT	= Land use mix entropy index (see section 4.2 for further definition).
RETAIL	= Proportion of floorspace in retail use.
AVGLOT	= Acreage of "average" lot, in terms of most frequent parcel size.

accounted for about 88 per cent of the variation in the original variables
– that is, only around a 12 per cent loss in information was incurred by
the 70 per cent reduction in the number of "variables" from 13 to 4.

To improve the interpretability of Table 4.1, variables are listed in
order of the size of their factor loadings (i.e., coefficients), first on factor
1, then on factor 2, etc. Also, only those loadings higher than 0.40 (in
absolute terms) are shown. Looking at the loadings, it is apparent that
the factor 1, which accounts for over one-third of the variation in the
data, represents *density*. Based on both the size and signs of loadings,
moreover, one sees that density-related variables have been grouped to
represent cases with high average number of stories, high FARs, high
counts of employees per acre, high land coverage ratios, and relatively
low numbers of parking spaces per employee.

Factor 2, explaining one-quarter of the variation, clearly captures
the *size* dimension of SECs. It reflects some of the commonality
shared by SECs which have large numbers of employees, vast amounts
of floorspace, and numerous eateries. The inclusion of the restaurant
variable suggests that it picks up some of the mixed-use characteristics
of cases as well.

Factor 3, explaining 16.7 per cent of the variation, seems to be more or
less a *design* measure emphasizing the scale and degree of spaciousness
of projects. It appears to be tapping the dimensions of some cases
related to their amount of open space (COVERAGE), working area
(SQFT/EMP), and scale (ACREAGE). In this sense, it captures some
of the amenity and site design features of SECs, along with some
information on size and coverage. Based on the signs of the loadings, it
reflects cases which have large acreages, generous amounts of floor area
per worker, low levels of lot coverage, and high shares of office usage,
i.e., roomy, high-amenity environments. These characteristics seem to
fit the definition of many master-planned, campus-style high-technology
parks, such as the Research Triangle outside of Raleigh and Technology
Park northeast of Atlanta.

Finally, Factor 4 accounts for 11.3 of the variation and is primarily
a *land use* indicator, capturing information on tenant composition as
well as general lotting practices. In addition to office and retail, it loads
high on a variable that was created to reflect the degree of land use
mixture within each SEC – USEENT. USEENT is an index of "land
use entropy", measured as:

$$\text{USEENT} = - \{[\text{OFFICE} * \log_{10}(\text{OFFICE})] + [\text{RETAIL} * \log_{10}(\text{RETAIL})] + [\text{HOUSING} * \log_{10}(\text{HOUSING})] + [\text{OTHER} * \log_{10}(\text{OTHER})]\}, \text{ where:}$$

$$0 \leqslant \text{USEENT} \leqslant \log_{10}(K),$$

OFFICE   = proportion of floorspace in office use;
RETAIL   = proportion of floorspace in retail use;
HOUSING = proportion of floorspace in residential use;
OTHER   = proportion of floorspace in industrial, warehousing, restaurants, hotels, and other uses; and
K   = number of categories, which, in this case, is 4, with categories removed from calculations if the proportion of floorspace is zero.[6]

USEENT provides a logarithmic index for gauging the degree of land use mixture. As used here, it ranges in values from zero (total homogeneity, with all floorspace in one category) to 0.6021 (maximum heterogeneity, with an even mixture of land uses).[7] Thus, single use developments (like office parks) will score low on USEENT while projects with an equal amount of floorspace in office, retail, housing, and other uses will score high values.

Factor 4, *land use*, loads high on cases with high shares of retail and a high level of mixed uses (i.e., a high USEENT value), and low on cases with high shares of office and large average lot sizes. Thus, it appears to be picking up situations with varied mixed-use, retail oriented environments that are on relatively small lots and where office space is not the pre-eminent use. SECs such as Post Oak and South Coast Metro appear to be represented by the fourth factor.

In summary, factor analysis was successful in providing a multi-variable description of the underlying land use and development dimensions of SECs. The extracted factors and their relationships to the original variables are logical and interpretable. The number of extracted factors suggests there are four key underlying site features of SECs – *density*, *size*, *design*, and *land use*. Among these dimensions, density is dominant, followed by size. Intuitively, there is a certain degree of intercorrelation among the factors themselves, i.e., cases with high land use (i.e., mixed-use) scores could also be expected to have high density scores. How such scores can be used to classify cases into distinct groups is discussed next.

4.3   Classification of case sites into SEC groups

The grouping of the 50 SEC cases into homogeneous groups was carried out using cluster analysis.[8] Factor scores for each of the 50 observations served as the primary inputs to the analysis.[9] The process involved combining cases into clusters on the basis of their "nearness" to each other when expressed as squared Euclidean distances.[10] Using the technique of agglomerative hierarchical clustering, clusters were sequentially formed by grouping cases into even larger clusters until all cases were members of a single cluster.[11]

The results of the cluster analysis are summarized in the hierarchical graph, called a dendrogram, presented in Appendix II. This shows the clusters being sequentially combined and the normalized values of the coefficients (i.e., squared Euclidean distances) at each step. The judgemental part of cluster analysis is deciding at what stage to stop joining clusters. This is normally done when the distance coefficients dramatically increase from one agglomeration step to another. For this analysis, this was between the 44th and 45th stage of merging clusters, which meant that five distinct clusters of cases were derived.[12] Because "large office corridors" were set aside as a separate group at the outset, this means that a total of six clusters of SECs were derived for this study.

While in several instances cases which did not fit neatly into any single cluster were subjectively assigned to a group,[13] overall the cluster analysis did provide an intuitive and decipherable grouping of cases. The following descriptions seem to fit the six groups, including the "large office corridor" grouping, that emerged from the cluster analysis:

(a)   office parks;
(b)   office and concentrations centers;
(c)   large-scale mixed-use developments (MXDs);
(d)   moderate scale mixed-use developments (MXDs);
(e)   sub-cities;
(f)   large-scale office growth corridors.

The SECs that clustered together within each group are listed in Table 4.2. The largest single group is "large-scale MXDs," comprising of 14 SECs. Both the "office parks" and "sub cities" groups each have ten cases, while "office concentrations" and "moderate-scale MXDs" have eight. The smallest group consists of the seven "large-scale office growth corridors."

Table 4.3 suggests why these particular titles were chosen for describing the six SEC groups; it presents the low-to-high ranges of several key density, size, land use, and design variables (shown as the next-to-lowest to next-to-highest values).[14] Accordingly, it provides both minimum and maximum thresholds which could be used in assigning other SECs around the country to one of the six categories. Some of the noteworthy traits of each of the six SEC groups are discussed below.

Office parks

The distinguishing characteristics of office parks are their low densities and building profiles, their heavily landscaped, park-like environment, their prodigious supply of parking, and their highly controlled, master-planned appearances. Many attract large corporate tenants who value

Table 4.2 Listing of Cases Within the Six SEC Groups

Office Parks	Office Concentrations	Large Mixed-Use Developments	Moderate Mixed-Use Developments	Sub-Cities	Office Growth Corridors
APOC	Central Ave. Corridor	BWI Area	Bel-Red Corridor	Central Bellevue	Golden Triangle
Bishop Ranch	Central Ft. Lauderdale	Camelback Corridor	Chagrin Blvd. Corridor	Central Stamford	I-5 Portland Corridor
Corporate Woods	Central Walnut Creek	Cyprus Creek	Chesterbrook Village	Central Towson	N. Houston North Belt
Hacienda Bus. Park	Greenway Plaza	East Farmingdale	College Blvd. Corridor	Denver Tech Center	Route 1/ Princeton
Inverness Bus. Park	Greenwood Plaza	East Garden City	Fairlane Town Center	North Dallas Parkway	Route 9/ Boston
Maitland Center	Lake-Cook Corridor	Edina/I-494 Corridor	Hunt Valley	Perimeter Center	Route 128/ Boston
New England Exec. Park	Research Triangle	Gwinnett Place	North Lake	Post Oak-Galleria	Route 495/ Boston
Technology Park	Rocksprings Park	The Meadowlands	Rockside/I-77 Corridor	South Coast Metro	
3M Park-Minnesota		Naperville/ I-88 Corridor		Tysons Corner	
3M Park-Texas		Oak Brook/ I-88 Corridor		Warner Center	
		Plantation/ Broward County			
		Schaumburg Village			
		West Houston Energy Corridor			
		The Woodlands			

high-quality, spacious surroundings. Others emphasize R&D, high-technology, and light-manufacturing activities. Often, speculative space is found in buildings that are grouped together in a campus-like cluster while larger, single-tenant structures and company headquarters are typically set off to themselves (McKeever 1970, Urban Land Institute 1984, Cervero 1986b).

From Table 4.3, it is evident that office parks have the lowest ranges of density, coverage, and building heights and among the highest levels of single-use activities and parking provisions. They frequently have

Table 4.3 Low-to-high thresholds for six SEC groups.[1]

	Office parks	Office centers	Large MXDs	Medium MXDs	Sub-cities	Large corridors
Size:						
Acreage (thousands)	0.25–1.0	0.25–2.8	2.6–19.7	0.35–0.86	0.33–2.24	30.0–300.0
Employment (thousands)	4.1–11.9	6.0–20.3	5.0–53.0	2.2–15.3	16.0–59.5	39.0–480.0
Sq.ft. office, commercial, industrial & floorspace (millions)	1.7–4.3	2.0–10.8	3.6–29.0	1.3–7.1	6.5–25.3	11.0–31.5
Density:						
FAR	0.24–0.42	0.30–2.7	0.50–1.30	0.33–0.92	0.85–3.10	0.20–0.60
No. stories of highest bldg.	5–10	8–30	6–27	3–13	20–28	14–23
Design:						
Parking spaces/ 1,000 sq.ft.	4.0–5.0	3.3–4.0	3.3–5.0	4.0–4.6	3.0–4.0	3.5–4.5
Coverage ratio	0.20–0.40	0.20–0.75	0.25–0.55	0.25–0.48	0.33–0.75	–
Land use mix:						
% floor space:						
office	65–99	85–99	16–66	30–60	50–70	52–74
commercial	01–10	02–10	08–26	10–30	12–34	08–20
No. retail centers	0–1	0–2	1–20	1–4	2–8	–
No. on-site dwelling units	0–100	0–380	0–9,000	0–500	200–5,600	–
Land use mix entropy index[2]	0.25–0.35	0.22–0.35	0.45–0.58	0.47–0.56	0.41–0.51	0.37–0.50

[1] Based on the range of the next-to-lowest to the next-to-highest values for each variable.
[2] Ranges from 0 (least mix) to 0.60 (most mix). See sec 4.2.

little, if any, on-site housing and at most one small retail center. None has a regional shopping facility on site. Compared to the other SECs, they are also fairly small in acreage, employment size, and square footage. As master-planned developments, their territorial boundaries are almost always well defined.

Based on these ranges, SECs that are classified as office parks should have: (a) under 1,000 acres; (b) over 65 per cent of space in office uses and less than 10 per cent in retail; (c) FARs below .45 and coverage rates under .40; and (d) 4 or more parking spaces per 1,000 gross square feet. They also should be master-planned, high-quality work environments with closely coordinated building designs.

Office centers and concentrations

These SECs share some of the characteristics of office parks, however they tend to be much larger and denser. Notably, they generally have about the same proportion of office and retail space as the office parks and comparably few retail centers and on-site housing units. While office parks are centrally controlled and master-planned, these SECs are more agglomerative, i.e., they tend to be concentrations of a number of freestanding office buildings that have sprouted, sometimes independently, in a reasonably well-defined geographic space. Some, such as Greenway Plaza near Houston and Greenwood Plaza outside Denver, have been master-planned and have an architecturally unified character. Thus, they are more like centers than concentrations. Others, such as Phoenix's Central Avenue corridor, have evolved in an *ad hoc* manner and thus represent concentrations of growth. While many of these agglomerations focus on freeways, they tend to be more nodal and far less elongated in shape than some of the SECs defined as "large-scale office corridors."

To some extent, this cluster is a hybrid of the "office park" and "large-scale office corridor" groupings. Some of the large-scale corridors are essentially a collection of office concentrations; in these instances, then, "office centers and concentrations" could be viewed as a subset of large-scale corridors. Other cases, such as the Research Triangle, are low-density, park-like settings, but are far greater in size than the office parks listed in Table 4.2. Thus, this group consists of SECs that do not fit neatly into either the "park" or "corridor" clusters, but which share the common trait of consisting predominantly of office space.

To fit into this cluster, then, SECs should: (a) be larger, have generally higher densities, and offer less parking per worker than most office parks; (b) have at least 2 million square feet of floorspace, with at least 85 per cent in office use; and (c) have more the character of an agglomeration than of a highly controlled, master-planned office development and is focused on a single cluster of buildings.

Large-scale mixed-use developments (MXDs)

The two distinguishing features of these SECs are that they feature a mix of land use activities and encompass a fairly large territory, at least three square miles and usually much more. Additionally, most of these MXDs are widely recognized as being primary growth magnets within their respective regions.

Some of these large-scale MXDs are oriented along freeways and major arterials, and thus have a corridor form (e.g., Edina/Interstate 494 south of Minneapolis and Oak Brook/Interstate 88 west of Chicago). Others are more nodal (e.g., the Meadowlands near Newark and Schaumburg Village northwest of Chicago). Many resemble some of the "sub-cities" listed in Table 4.2, but have far more acreage and generally less of a high-rise profile. Many are also similar to "office concentrations" in density and workforce size, although MXDs generally enjoy a far greater balance of office, commercial, and light-industrial activities. All have at least one major retail center, and most feature a regional shopping center mall of at least 500,000 square feet. Moreover, most have at least several thousand housing units within their perimeters.

The boundaries of many large MXDs are not always clear. In many instances, they are defined in terms of a "study area" that has been designated by the local planning agency (e.g., Camelback corridor north of Phoenix and Cyprus Creek west of Fort Lauderdale). In some cases, a business association or transportation management association (TMA) has been formed to deal with emerging growth problems and has accordingly designated informal boundaries for the MXD.

While in no instance do offices comprise more than two-thirds of floorspace for the cases in this group, non-office functions are not always dominated by banks, restaurants, and retail outlets. Some of the large MXDs (e.g., BWI between Baltimore and Washington, D.C.; Oak Brook/I–88; and East Farmingdale on Long Island, New York) have well over 30 per cent of their floorspace supporting light-industrial and warehousing functions. In all instances, the land use entropy index for large MXDs was at least 0.45 (compared to an average index for all cases of 0.42). The hallmarks of this SEC group, then, are: (a) a large territory of at least 2,000 acres in size; and (b) a mixture of activities, with offices comprising no more than two-thirds of total floorspace.

Moderate-scale mixed-use developments (MXDs)

In almost every respect, these SECs resemble the large MXDs discussed above, with the notable exception that they have far less acreage. Most have only one-third the acreage of the smallest member of the "large-scale MXD" category. In addition, these more moderate-size MXDs tend to be less dense, featuring a varied low-rise and mid-rise skyline. Many, moreover, have a more well-defined core, with clusters of buildings that are architecturally integrated. In general, the growth problems associated with these SECs are not considered to be as serious as those of their larger-scale counterparts.

The mixture of land uses among these SECs spans office, commercial, industrial, residential, and institutional activities. Offices remain the prominent activity in all cases, comprising between 30 per cent and 60 per cent of floorspace. The land use entropy indices for all of the moderate-size MXDs exceed 0.47.

SECs that are candidates for membership of this group, then, should: (a) be less than 1,000 acres in size and have relatively well-defined boundaries; and (b) have a variety of land uses, with office space comprising no more than two-thirds of total floor area.

Sub-cities

These are the places that have been called "urban villages," "mega-centers," "suburban downtowns," and "satellite cities," among other catchnames. They are noted for being downtown-like in their densities and land use mixtures, yet retaining suburban-like characters (e.g., strict zoning controls; wide separation between buildings; plentiful parking; a "white-collar" character; newness of buildings; etc.). Located on the fringes of America's largest cities, however, all remain secondary office and retail centers within their respective metropolitan markets. In this sense, they are second-tier markets, or sub-centers, even though they rival the downtowns of many medium-size cities in size and density. Thus, the term "sub-city" – which suggests the idea of both a sub-market and a suburban city – has been chosen here.

The activities found in these sub-cities read like an inventory of traditional downtown activities – offices, corporate headquarters, hotels, boutiques, conventional halls, performing arts centers, health clubs, doctors' offices, nightclubs, and more. Offices, however, are always a prominent land use. Tysons Corner has more office space than downtown Baltimore or Miami (Urban Land Institute 1987). Nationwide, Houston's Post Oak–Galleria area ranks ninth in office inventory, exceeding that of downtown Atlanta. In many cases, new office towers have gone up at a dizzying pace, with as much as 5 million square feet being added to previously vacant parcels in as few as three years. The North Dallas Parkway, for instance, witnessed a quadrupling of floorspace between 1980 and 1986. Because of this rapid-fire pace of growth, grassroots opposition to new office and commercial projects has generally been more vocal around sub-cities than around any other SEC group.

The sub-cities defined in this study vary along several dimensions, despite the fact that they combined in the cluster analysis. While most are fairly new (e.g., Perimeter Center north of Atlanta and Tysons Corner), others have existed for decades (e.g., central Stamford, Connecticut; central Towson north of Baltimore). Densities also vary somewhat. Some are punctuated by a series of high-rise towers, with only limited amounts of open space (e.g., Post Oak; central Bellevue,

Photo 4.1 Denver Technological Center. Sub-city ten miles southeast of downtown Denver, Colorado. Large patches of open space, architectually coordinated designs, and newness distinguish the Tech Center from the downtown office market. (Photo by the author.)

Washington). Others are more like high-density, multi-use versions of campus-style office parks, featuring attractively landscaped open spaces and prominent signature buildings. Some sub-cities have been centrally planned and are architecturally coordinated (e.g., Denver Tech Center and Warner Center north of Los Angeles), whereas others have evolved incrementally, without the benefit of any unifying plan (e.g., Tysons Corner and Post Oak).

Because of their relatively high densities and land values, all sub-cities have decked parking structures, with commercial rates charged for public parking spaces. All also feature a premium-quality regional shopping mall, generally well over 1 million square feet in total retail space. At least one hotel with convention facilities can be found in each. In addition, all sub-cities have a significant housing component, usually consisting of condominiums and townhouses that are priced for the professional worker.

To qualify as a sub-city, then, an SEC must have: (a) over 10,000 office workers and over 5 million square feet of office and commercial floorspace; (b) fairly high average densities, with the tallest office tower being at least 15 stories high and with some buildings falling within the 20–30 story range; (c) a mixed-use character, with retail and commercial activities comprising at least 10 per cent of floorspace; (d) a regional indoor shopping mall and major convention hotel; (e) on-site housing; and (f) a "feel" for being a downtown-like setting as well as a reputation for being the "other" central place within the region, second only to downtown.

Large-scale office growth corridors

What distinguishes these SECs from others is their tremendous expanses; some extend well over 20 miles in length covering a land area exceeding 100 square miles. In a sense, these cases are a breed apart from the other SECs, representing less of an agglomeration and more of a large swath of office and mixed development within an urbanized region or state. Accordingly, in much of the analysis which follows, this group is treated separately.[15]

All of these large office corridors focus on one or more freeways or major arterials and have a distinct linear form. All are dotted by numerous unrelated office parks, industrial parks, retail centers, commercial strips, and tract housing, much of which evolved in a piecemeal fashion. Most of these developments tend to be much smaller than any of the office parks and other SECs examined in this study; the cumulative effect of numerous small freestanding projects, however, has generally exerted tremendous strains on public infrastructure, including streets, sewers, and water lines. Accordingly, unbridled growth is a politically sensitive issue along all of these corridors. In some cases, the existence of multiple political jurisdictions along the corridor has hampered efforts to coordinate and manage growth.

In general, densities along these mammoth-size corridors are low. Many of the density and site design features of "office parks" and "office concentrations" characterize much of development profiles of individual projects along these corridors. Mid-rise hotels and large regional shopping malls also tend to be common. Though housing tracts can be found in isolated pockets of these corridors, residential development is generally subsidiary to their office functions. Most suffer a significant jobs–housing imbalance.

The noteworthy characteristics of cases which belong to this final class of SECs, then, are: (a) expansive land areas, generally encompassing over 20,000 acres; (b) a dominant freeway or arterial spine which serves to channel growth; (c) a mixture of land uses, with office functions predominating; (d) low average densities; and (e) an employee population that generally far exceeds the residential population.

4.4   Brief case summaries of each SEC group

As a prelude to the tests of hypotheses in Chapters 5 and 6, this final section briefly describes several of the cases within each of the SEC groups. The intent is not necessarily to present the most representative SECs of the six categories, but rather to provide a finer grained perspective into the general make-up of individual centers and corridors within each group. Chapter 7 offers a further discussion of SEC cases in three metropolitan areas: Seattle, Houston, and Chicago.

Office park cases

(a) *BISHOP RANCH*

This a 585-acre, master-planned office and light industrial development which fronts on Interstate 680 in the city of San Ramon, a fast-growing suburb about 35 miles east of downtown San Francisco. The present workforce of 13,000 employees is expected to reach 25,000 employees at build-out, sometime around the year 1995. Around 85 per cent of floorspace is in office use, roughly a quarter of which is speculative space. Five companies own all of the parcels within Bishop Ranch. Three have major company headquarters staffed primarily by back-office workers, one has a light industrial plant which manufactures precision instruments, and the other has a warehouse employing under 100 workers. Numerous covenants control the architectural features of the park and maximum coverage and floor- area ratio limits of 0.35 preserve open space. Plexi-glass, enclosed bus shelters lace the park. A fare-free luxury shuttle for tenant employees connects the Bay Area Rapid Transit (BART) station in Walnut Creek and provides noon-hour service to a nearby shopping center. An on-site Transportation Center has also been created to promote ridesharing and other commute alternatives.

(b) *MAITLAND CENTER*

This is a 250-acre planned business park located in central Florida just north of Orlando along Interstate 4. Over 12,000 employees are spread among 2.89 million square feet of primarily class A office space. The project includes a 400-room hotel, 3,500 square feet of retail space, and 105 condominium units. Strict development controls and considerable attention to landscaping have created a premium work environment. Covenants require that 40 per cent of parcels be left as open space and set minimum front yard setbacks of generally 35 feet or more. Over 20 one-to-six story buildings, most with glass-dominated façades, are spread throughout the compound. Most structures are encircled by surface parking built at 5 spaces per 1,000 square feet. A large interior commons area features exercise trails. A walkpath also meanders through the park. One complex, Maitland Colonnales, is built around a 15-acre lake, with over half a mile of windows overlooking the lake. The four-story building features floor plans designed for flexibility and a ground-level deli.

(c) *NEW ENGLAND EXECUTIVE PARK*
This is a mature 82-acre park with 1.27 million square feet of first-class office space, located off Route 128, 16 miles north of downtown Boston in the community of Burlington. Figure 4.1 shows the project's site plan. The typical building is a two-to-four story structure with a 26,000 square feet footprint and a mix of brick and glass construction. Maximum coverage ratios of 0.36 and 50 feet front lot setback requirements maintain a certain spaciousness throughout the park. Most of the land is covered by asphalt, however. Next to the park is Burlington Mall, New England's largest, featuring more than 100 stores, including 22 restaurants. Also nearby is the Market Place, which offers a variety of restaurants, shops, and business specialty stores. New England Executive Park also boasts a fitness center, a professionally-staffed childcare center, and a helipad where a connection can be made to Logan Airport in eight minutes.

Office centers and concentrations

(a) *CENTRAL AVENUE CORRIDOR*
This roughly two-mile long stretch uptown of downtown Phoenix has several million square feet of office space, including four post-1980 towers totaling 1.3 million square feet. Each of these towers has an anchor tenant and several entry-level retail outlets. The remaining speculative space is leased primarily to financial, legal, and other professional service firms. A number of smaller, freestanding garden office complexes are aligned along the north–south corridor as well. Interspersed among these offices is an assortment of specialty stores, medical buildings, and several condominium complexes. Two major regional shopping centers are also within the corridor. Most low-rise commercial establishments are situated on lots comprised of an assemblage of former 6,000 square feet residential parcels. Although the Central Avenue corridor is not presently served by freeway, it will eventually be at the heart of a 231-mile freeway system, currently under construction, that will be superimposed on Phoenix's one-mile grid arterial system.

(b) *CENTRAL WALNUT CREEK*
A clustering of some 1.3 million square feet of modern mid-rise office space in an area of around one square mile, huddled near an interchange off of Interstate 680 as well as an aerial BART station. Bordered by the freeway and two major thoroughfares, the area is known locally as the Golden Triangle. Most office towers within this triangle have been constructed since 1980 and feature a mixture of granite, marble,

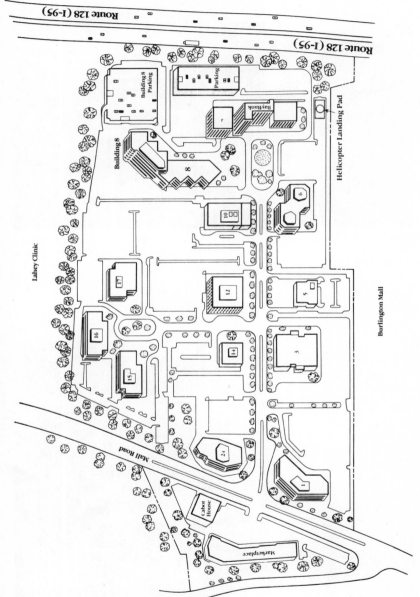

Figure 4.1 New England Executive Park site plan.

Photo 4.2 Office concentration in Walnut Creek, California. Mid-rise towers front a surface parking lot used by patrons of the nearby BART rapid transit system. (Photo by the author.)

Photo 4.3 Peak-period traffic jam at Walnut Creek. Such congestion has given rise to an ordinance which regulates new office and commercial construction according to how well future traffic flows. (Photo by the author.)

and reflective glass, providing a premium, high-tech look. Footprints generally envelop 90 per cent of a site, so open space is limited. Property is divided among some 15 different landholders. A free shuttle connects the triangle area with downtown Walnut Creek, located about a mile to the south. The shortage of nearby restaurants and shops has attracted over 600 passengers shuttling to downtown every day. The prevalence of free parking for employees of several large tenants has encouraged many Golden Triangle workers to drive to work, despite the existence of a BART station within short walking distance. The mixture of these workers' automobiles with the cars of BART patrons who are using the Walnut Creek station to park-and-ride to San Francisco has created a serious congestion problem during peak periods. In response, the citizens of Walnut Creek passed a referendum in late 1985 which halts all future office–commercial development over 10,000 square feet until peak-hour traffic falls below 85 per cent of capacity (level of service D) at 75 key intersections. Although this growth-control ordinance has been challenged in court and remains in legal limbo, a spirited debate continues over how much more office growth can be supported.

(c) *RESEARCH TRIANGLE PARK*
This is a massive 6,600-acre park with over 11 million square feet of floorspace and some 30,000 employees, many of whom are employed in R&D, engineering, and technical–professional positions. Situated between the educational centers of Raleigh, Durham, and Chapel Hill, the Research Triangle is the consummate research and high-technology center, replete with contemporary smart buildings, flexible floorplate designs, and an overall spacious, architecturally coordinated built environment. Although the Research Triangle resembles a traditional campus-style development in many ways, its gargantuan size and regional dominance give it more of an agglomerative character. The compound has several multi-building light-industrial complexes of up to 440,000 square feet. Several low-profile research campuses have 1 million square feet of space each. Interspersed amongst these complexes are a number of individual six-story towers. Four banks, a restaurant, and a retail center are also within the park. In all, some 40 private parties hold title to the Research Triangle property. While a comprehensive set of covenants governs building designs and lotting practices, the park sets no limits on parking other than requiring that all facilities be off-street. A ridesharing office within the park actively promotes employee carpooling and vanpooling. Since the Research Triangle lies in between three urban centers, a variety of through and local trips are inter-mixed along the five major highway corridors serving the park, giving rise to steadily worsening rush-hour congestion.

Large mixed-use developments (MXDs)

(a) CYPRESS CREEK
This is a 5 square mile mixed-use district approximately six miles
northwest of downtown Fort Lauderdale, containing over 6 million
square feet of office, retail, and light-industrial floorspace and over
10,000 workers. Much of the growth centers on Executive Airport and
the Interstate 95 axis north of the airport. Office complexes are generally
of moderate densities, with many buildings ranging from five to ten
stories in height and floor area ratios averaging around 1. The typical
building has 120,000 square feet of class A floorspace, reflective glass
exteriors, and first-floor retail services. Several moderate sized business
parks are also in the area. One, Radice Corporate Center, is situated on
a 33-acre site that includes a 5.5-acre natural preserve with fitness trails
and a four-acre lake. Three office towers with a total of 368,000 square
feet and a 15-story hotel grace the site. Because of shrinking land tracts
and high land prices, most recent projects in the Cypress Creek area have
a distinct mixed-use character. Corporate Park, for instance, features
three restaurants, several banks, and a 250-room hotel, in addition to
premium leasing space. The Zaremba Southeast development, when
completed, will feature three office buildings, a convention hotel, a
retail center, and a centrally located eight-acre aquatic preserve. Traffic
problems along the Interstate 95 corridor have escalated in tandem
with Cypress Creek's expansion. Because of a shortage of lower-priced
multi-family housing nearby, many of the area's workers solo-commute,
resulting in rush-hour tie-ups.

(b) EAST GARDEN CITY
Located about 27 miles east of Manhattan in Nassau County, this is
Long Island's fastest growing office area, with over three-quarters of
space having been erected since 1980. In all, approximately 9.5 million
square feet of mixed office, commercial, and industrial floorspace is
concentrated in an area of four square miles focused on Mitchell
Field, a former military base that has been converted to civilian use.
Most of the estimated 21,700 employees in the area are white-collar
workers, split among professional–technical, clerical, administrative,
and sales occupations. The typical office building in the East Garden
City area is a four-to-eight story glass-façade luxury tower with around
200,000 square feet of space. Many feature on-site amenities, such as
health clubs, banks, and retail shops. Major office complexes include
European American Bank Plaza (1.1 million square feet), Corporate
Center I and II (425,000 square feet), and Mitchell Field Corporate
Center (220,000 square feet). Also in the area are several colleges, a
sports stadium, a racetrack, and two regional shopping centers. Since

only around 300 housing units are sited in the area, the vast majority of workers commute to work – about 75 per cent coming from the eastern two-thirds of Hempstead Township, 13 per cent from Suffolk County, and most of the remainder traveling from New York City. Expansion plans continue for the East Garden City area. Ultimately, 1,170 acres in and around Mitchell Field will be developed, including a proposed college expansion, hotels, office and light industrial space, and assorted R&D projects.

(c) *THE MEADOWLANDS*

A massive 19,730-acre mixed-use district located mainly in Secaucus, New Jersey, the Meadowlands is situated around six miles east of midtown Manhattan, with portions of the district also lying in the cities of North Bergen, East Rutherford, Jersey City, Carlstadt, and Kearny. The Hackensack Meadowlands Development Commission (HMDC) has been charged with the responsibility for planning the Meadowland's growth since it was formed by the state legislature in 1968. Seven major developers and more than 1,800 companies of all sizes, employing over 50,000 workers, are involved in the Meadowland's development. About one-quarter of the district is zoned primarily for low-density residential use, about half is split among office, light industrial, warehousing, and commercial activities, and most of the remainder is in the form of open space and estuary preserves. Among the Meadowland's major office complexes is Berry's Creek East, featuring a 430,000 square foot, 15-story office tower, a luxury hotel, and several restaurants. Two of the district's largest mixed-use centers are Harmon Cove (over 2 million square feet of office space, 500 residential units, and a flagship hotel) and Harmon Meadow (1.2 million square feet of office, two retail plazas, two luxury hotels, several theaters, and numerous stores and restaurants). Other major land uses within the district are the Meadowlands Sports Complex and Teterboro Airport.

Moderate-scale mixed-use developments (MXDs)

(a) *CHESTERBROOK VILLAGE*

This is an 865-acre corporate-retail village that is the centerpiece of the larger master-planned residential community of Chesterbrook, located off Route 202 some 17 miles west of downtown Philadelphia and just to the south of the booming King of Prussia area. Around three-quarters of the corporate center is complete, which is slated eventually to contain around 1.5 million square feet of office space, sometime in the 1990s. Corporate tenants, including law firms and brokerage companies, dominate most of the class A speculative office space. Typical office buildings are three-story brick structures with floorplates of 30,000 square feet

Photo 4.4 Chesterbrook, Pennsylvannia. Bird's eye view of the Chesterfield Corporate Center, surrounded by residences and retail complexes. (Photo provided courtesy of The Fox Company.)

covering around 30 per cent of a lot. Most have coordinated designs and are clustered around commons areas. Six restaurants, two banks, a hotel, and a retail center also populate the core. The most substantial use in Chesterbrook, however, is residential, with over 3,000 housing units priced for varying incomes located within easy walking distance of the corporate center. Over 90 per cent of these are attached, multi-family units. A free shuttle connects surrounding residents with the corporate center as well as a local train station during peak periods.

(b) *COLLEGE BOULEVARD*

A three-mile long office–retail corridor, encompassing 867 acres, College Boulevard is aligned in an east–west direction just south of Interstate 435 in Overland Park, Kansas, across the stateline from Kansas City, Missouri. Over 6 million square feet of office–commercial floorspace are spread along the corridor, with much of the office area found in Corporate Woods, Executive Hills, and Renaissance Office Park. These parks house mainly regional and branch office facilities that are populated largely by middle management and support staff. The workforce exceeds 22,000 and is expected to more than double by the mid-1990s. Most office buildings are low-lying, occupying less than a quarter of land tracts. Four hotels also line the corridor, providing over 1,000 rooms in total. The Shannon Valley Shopping Center occupies a central parcel along the corridor. Total retail square footage, spread among three large centers and several freestanding establishments, exceeds 1 million. Near the corridor, residential construction is booming, with approximately 9,600 dwelling units, half of which are single-family, lying within a one mile radius.

(c) *HUNT VALLEY*

This is a 1,000-acre development that has become Baltimore County's most prestigious corporate address. Located approximately 15 miles north of downtown Baltimore next to Interstate 83, Hunt Valley has been the recipient of over half the county's office space additions since 1980. Mid-rise office buildings, hotels, and a large retail–restaurant complex occupy Hunt Valley's core, surrounded by surface parking and low-rise industrial, warehousing, and office space. Most buildings offer speculative space with flexible floor plans. Typical lots are one acre in size, with front and side lot setbacks of 25–35 feet. Hunt Valley's 850,000 square foot mall features a variety of specialty retail, entertainment, and business service functions. In all, retail uses comprise nearly 20 per cent of total floorspace. The absence of any residential units within the development has resulted in heavy in-commuting and spot congestion at the project's connecting cloverleaf interchange.

Sub-cities

(a) *NORTH DALLAS PARKWAY*

Situated along a T-shaped corridor bounded by the LBJ Freeway (I–635) and Dallas North Tollway, the North Dallas Parkway is located 12–15 miles north of downtown Dallas. The Parkway area contains over 17 million square feet of office space distributed among more than 150 buildings, 7.4 million square feet of commercial inventory, and 5.4 million square feet of light manufacturing uses, all spread over a 5.6 square mile area. Future office development totaling over 24 million square feet has been announced and additional space awaits zoning approval. The area currently has 60,000 workers and could eventually reach 125,000 if all proposed development proceeds. The Parkway area has become a choice location for corporate tenants, rivaling downtown Dallas and the new town of Las Colinas as the region's most prestigious office address. Most office structures are in the 2–4 FAR range, with all-glass façades and well-groomed surroundings. Lots are generally of varying shapes and sizes. The Parkway is noted for having three regional malls, ranging in size from 870,000 to 1.6 million square feet. Eight hotels, providing 3,160 rooms, are also prominently sited near several major freeway interchanges. Among "suburban downtowns" nationwide, North Dallas Parkway has the largest residential population – approximately 14,800

Photo 4.5   North Dallas Parkway, Texas. The more lightly traveled tollway in the center of the photo is bordered by the more heavily traveled non-toll frontage road. (Photo by the author.)

dwelling units are within its boundaries, the overwhelming majority of which are multi-family units. As with most other sub-cities, growth management is a widely discussed issue in the area.

(b) *PERIMETER CENTER*

This is located approximately 12 miles due north of downtown Atlanta near the connection of Interstate 285 and Georgia 400 and within unincorporated portions of DeKalb and Fulton Counties. The Perimeter Center began developing around a large regional mall comprised of three anchors and 1.4 million total square feet. Numerous one-to-two story office buildings built near the mall in the early 1970s were eventually replaced by new 6–18 story executive office towers. Today, over 17 million square feet of office space dots the 2 square mile area, with each structure generally covering 25 per cent of a site.[16] So far, Perimeter Center has been unrivaled in the Atlanta market at attracting corporate tenants. Two-thirds of employees work in service, financial, insurance, real estate, or wholesaling jobs. No other location in Atlanta, including the CBD, houses as many national and regional headquarters of Fortune 500 firms as the Perimeter Center. In addition to several retail centers, four hotels with over 1,400 rooms in total can be found in the development. Rapid land conversion has been a particularly noteworthy feature of the Perimeter Center area. Five residential subdivisions in

Photo 4.6 Tyson's Corner, Virginia. Offices, shops, apartments, and hotels cluster around the Westwood Center south of the Dulles Airport Access and Toll Road. (Photo provided courtesy of JHK & Associates, Alexandria, Virginia.)

the immediate environs have been bought out entirely since the early 1980s to make way for advancing office growth. Landmarks Concourse, for instance, a 65-acre complex with 432,000 square feet in three office buildings and a large hotel, was built on land assembled by the Aruba Circle neighborhood. The clash between office–commercial and traditional residential uses remains a hotly contested, politically charged issue along the Georgia 400 corridor.

(c) *TYSONS CORNER*

Tysons Corner is located approximately 12 miles west of downtown Washington, D.C. near the confluence of Interstate 495 and the Dulles Airport Access and Toll Road in fast-growing Fairfax County, Virginia (Fig. 4.2). Only a country crossroads with a general store several decades ago, Tysons is today easily the largest office–commercial center in Virginia or Maryland. Tysons boasts over 60,000 predominantly white-collar workers within its roughly 1,700 acre boundaries. Its 15 million square feet of office space is complemented by a regional shopping mall, numerous specialty shopping plazas, several hotels, and a high-rise residential building. Currently under way is Tysons II, which will add another 500,000 square feet of office, an 800,000 square foot fashion mall, and two convention-size luxury hotels, all

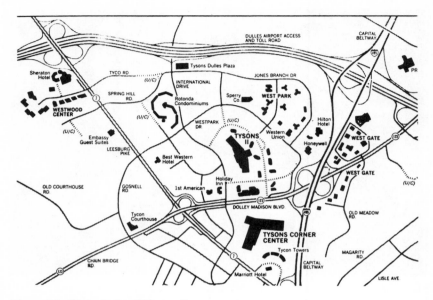

Figure 4.2   The sub-city of Tysons Corner.

interconnected by pedestrian plazas. In some ways, Tysons Corner is a
nodal version of strip development. Despite the best efforts of Fairfax
County planners to orchestrate growth, Tysons remains largely an
assemblage of independent buildings, with very little of an architectural
theme and limited offerings of sidewalks and trails between adjoining
parcels. Besides routine mile-long traffic tie-ups, Tysons Corner is also
experiencing a labor shortage problem, particularly in low-salaried,
unskilled positions. As a result, a number of hotels and retail outlets
in the area have found it necessary to sponsor bus services that connect
many inner-city residents of Washington, D.C. with Tysons. Shortages
of nearby affordable housing have also led to increased long distance
commuting from all corners of Fairfax County as well as from neighboring counties.

Large-scale office growth corridors

(a)   *INTERSTATE 5 PORTLAND CORRIDOR*
This is an 8-mile long mixed-development corridor nestled along Interstate 5 and Route 217 whose northern edge is approximately 6 miles
south of downtown Portland, Oregon. The corridor lies in both Washington and Clackamas Counties within the communities of Tigard, Lake
Oswego, Tualatin, Rivergrove, King City, Sherwood, and Wilsonville.

The I–5 Corridor Association, a coalition of local business representatives and landowners, has defined the boundaries of this corridor as an area encompassing over 30 square miles, rivaling many of Oregon's larger cities in population size and employment. Along with the Sunset Corridor and Columbia Corridor in the Portland area, I–5 has been a primary recipient of offices which have relocated out of downtown Portland. Many new, start-up businesses have also taken up residence there. In all, the corridor boasts over 10.5 million square feet of commercial–office space, around 32,000 employees, and an even larger number of housing units; accordingly, it has a fairly even jobs–housing balance. A mixed bag of business campuses, industrial parks, warehousing districts, retail complexes, and tract housing populate the corridor's landscape. Many business parks feature mid-rise, class A office space in nicely landscaped surroundings. Among the larger office parks in the corridor are Park 217 Business Center (450,000 square feet), Koll Business Center (277,000 square feet), 4000 Kruse Way Place (145,000 square feet), and the Centerpointe (100,000 square feet). The corridor also contains several large shopping facilities, including the Washington Square mall with 1 million square feet of retail space.

(b) *ROUTE 1 PRINCETON "ZIP STRIP"*

This is an 8-mile long stretch, near Princeton, of the larger 19-mile long Route 1 "high-technology" corridor, lying roughly midway between New York City and Philadelphia in the center of the nation's northeast megalopolis. Most of the development is focused on the "Zip Strip," which gets its name because businesses in this area enjoy the prestigious Princeton address and its accompanying zip code of 08540. An estimated 10 million square feet of office–commercial floorspace spans the corridor, an amount which is projected to reach 13.7 million square feet in 1992 and 29.1 million square feet in 2005. Historically, a number of large scientific and corporate research facilities have located near Princeton to take advantage of the area's exceptional educational offerings. What triggered much of the ensuing growth, observers agree, was the opening in the early 1970s of the Princeton Forrestal Center, a 1,604–acre, university–owned, multi-use research and office park. A handsomely landscaped, spaciously designed work environment, the center contains over 50 businesses, foundations, and research institutions, more than 5,000 workers, a 300-room conference center, and residential clusters of townhouses, duplexes, and garden apartments. Many of the office buildings are technologically and architecturally sophisticated, laced with fiber optic cables and state-of-the-art telecommunications equipment. Soon to follow the Forrestal Center's footsteps were the 520-acre Carnegie Center, Nassau Park, Greenlands, Princeton Park, and numerous smaller, independent office projects of

Photo 4.7   Route 1 development, central New Jersey. Low-density office construction under way at the Carnegie Center along Princeton's "Zip Strip." (Photo by the author.)

Princeton Park, and numerous smaller, independent office projects of one to three buildings. The 1 million square foot Quaker Bridge Mall is the largest retail facility in the area. Most research parks have comparatively little retail space; less than 4 per cent of the Forrestal Center's 4 million square feet of floorspace, for example, is devoted to retail use. Because major freeways in central New Jersey do not serve the Zip Strip directly, the largely four-lane Highway 1 has been flooded with traffic in recent years, leading to wrenching traffic jams. Pressures for regional management of growth continue to mount despite New Jersey's strong home-rule form of governance. Tremendous disparities in jobs and housing growth among townships led to the Mount Laurel II decision requiring municipalities to zone for a fair share of the regional need for low and moderate income housing. Proposed legislation providing county planning boards with jurisdiction over major development seems to be gathering bipartisan support.

(c)   *ROUTE 495*

A fast-growing corridor of predominantly computer related industries and communications, electronics, and engineering firms, Route 495 is located around the confluence of the Interstate 495, US Route 20, and State Route 9, some 25 miles due west of downtown Boston. Much of the recent growth has concentrated around Marlborough, a community that has begun charging impact assessments on new commercial projects to cover the cost of expanding infrastructure. An estimated 11 million square feet of predominantly office and light-industrial floorspace and nearly 40,000 workers can be found in the area. Floor area ratios for office and industrial properties range from 0.15 to 0.60. Although high-tech, light manufacturing, and R&D facilities dominate the Route 495 corridor, interest in speculative office buildings and corporate headquarters has intensified around several major interchanges. Most research parks consist of low to mid-rise buildings set in campus-like surroundings and feature sophisticated telecommunications and utilities. Restrictive zoning bylaws introduced by several communities along the Route 495 corridor have limited new commercial construction, increased land prices, and contained residential growth. Traffic and growth management have become highly controversial issues in Marlborough, Westborough, Northborough, Southborough, and several other communities in the Route 495 area.

4.5   Summary

In this chapter, the techniques of factor analysis and cluster analysis were used to combine the 57 case SECs into six fairly homogeneous groups: (a) office parks; (b) office centers and concentrations; (c) large-scale MXDs; (d) moderate-size MXDs; (e) sub-cities; and (f) large office growth corridors. Office parks are generally master-planned developments under 1,000 acres with low FARs and over 65 per cent of total floorspace in office use. Office centers tend to be larger in acreage and floorspace, denser, and architecturally less unified than office parks. Large MXDs are over 2,000 acres in size and support a wealth of activities, with offices accounting for no more than two-thirds of all space. Moderate-size MXDs are fairly similar in make-up, however they tend to be more nodal in form than large MXDs, encompassing no more than 1,000 acres of land. Sub-cities are downtowns in virtually every respect, except they are relatively new and, of course, on the fringes of large metropolitan areas. Finally, large office growth corridors are expansive stretches of office, light industrial, and spot commercial development along major highway axes, with generally low densities and little coordination of design among projects. Overall, the 57 surveyed SECs were found to be split fairly evenly among the six classes, with large MXDs accounting for the largest number of cases with 14, or nearly one-quarter of the sample.

This chapter also presented a brief case summary of three SECs for each of the six groupings. Geographically, these projects are spread around the country, with no one region showing a particular dominance in any one type of SEC. For a discussion of how significantly land use and transportation characteristics vary among these six groups, we now turn to Chapter 5.

Notes

1. As noted in Chapter 3, section 3.2, these seven large corridors are: Routes 9, 128, and 495 in the greater Boston area; Portland's Interstate 5; the Golden Triangle area in Santa Clara County; and the North Houston beltloop area.
2. Factor analysis requires a listwise deletion of missing values, which means that the entire case is purged if any one of its variables used in the analysis has missing information.
3. As might be expected, factor analysis results are strongly influenced by the variables that are chosen for the analysis. Extremely high multicollinearity can distort the analysis by making certain factors dominate disproportionately. See Thurstone (1947) or Dunteman (1984) for further discussion.
4. This is the final rotated factor pattern matrix. Initially, communalities of one were placed in the lead diagonals of the correlation matrix, a concession to no prior knowledge of what share of variation for each variable is common versus unique. This initial phase, then, involved the investigation of Principal Components. Using estimated R-squared values as the communalities in subsequent iterations during the extraction process, four factors were obtained. In order to improve the interpretability of these factors, the Varimax method of rotation was employed. Orthogonal rotation was chosen over oblique rotation because it provided the clearest interpretations and because there was no compelling *a priori* reason to believe that the underlying factors were highly intercorrelated. This was confirmed by the fact that the highest correlation among factors (from the factor correlation matrix) was only 0.203. For further discussion of these points, see Dunteman (1984).
5. Only factors with eigenvalues above one were extracted. This means that only factors which explained *at least* as much of the covariation in the data as any single variable were extracted. The fifth factor, which did not enter the analysis, had an eigenvalue of only 0.64.
6. This is because the $\log_{10}$ of zero is meaningless. See Willemain (1981) for a more detailed discussion of the entropy index.
7. The maximum value of 0.6021 derives from $\log_{10}(K)$, where K is the number of categories, in our case four (land use groups).
8. For a detailed discussion of cluster analysis, see Everitt (1980).
9. Factor scores for each case are derived by multiplying the factor loadings for each variable by that variable's standardized value and summing across variables. In this analysis, factor scores have been used as standardized weights for input into the cluster analysis. The same results could have been obtained by inputting the sum of standardized values (Z scores) across all 13 variables for each case.
10. The measure used for joining clusters was the average linkage between groups, often called UPGMA (unweighted pair-group method using weighted average) (Norusis 1986). Here, the distance measured between two

clusters is the average of distances between all pairs of cases in which one member of the pair is from each of the clusters.

11.   Under this approach, all cases are initially considered as separate clusters, i.e., there are as many clusters as cases. At the second step, the two cases with the most comparable squared Euclidean distances (i.e., the ones whose sum of squared factor scores are the most alike) are combined into a single cluster. At the third step, either a third case is added to the cluster already containing two cases, or two additional cases are merged into a new cluster. The process continues until all cases are grouped together. See Norusis (1986) for further discussion of this approach.

12.   49 (total hierarchical steps) – 45 (cut off steps) = 5 clusters.

13.   Several SECs did not fall into a cluster until after the 45th stage of agglomeration, so they had to be subjectively assigned. This was done by seeing which groups the cases matched most closely based on some of the key factor analysis variables, such as FAR and employment size. To ensure clusters were of somewhat comparable size, moreover, certain clusters were identified based on agglomerations that occurred prior to the 45th stage (see Appendix II for further discussion).

14.   These low to high ranges are "windsorized," meaning the lowest and highest values are purged, i.e., the next-to-lowest and the next-to-highest values are actually shown. Windsorizing clips the far tails of the distribution off so as to provide a better sense of the range of more representative cases and to remove possible outlier cases. Because of sizeable variation in the data, even when groups are clustered, windsorized ranges were felt to be more appropriate for setting thresholds.

15.   In the tests of hypotheses in Chapter 6, these large corridor cases are not used.

16.   For this study, data were only available for the DeKalb County portion of the Perimeter Center which is smaller in size, comprising around 11.2 million square feet in a 950-acre area.

5

Comparison of land use and transportation characteristics among SEC groups

5.1   Introduction

This chapter analyzes the six SEC groups more closely in terms of how they differ in size, density, land uses, employment bases, design features, and various measures of workforce mobility. A combination of statistical tests and summary graphs are presented. Most of the tests compare differences in mean values of variables across the six SEC groups, using the method of Analysis of Variance (ANOVA). The degree to which these differences are statistically significant is highlighted. Bar graphs and diagrams are also used to sift out patterns in the relationships among variables. To the extent that land uses and employee travel behavior vary among SEC groups, inferences can be drawn regarding how physical design practices might influence commuting choices. The specific tests of the affects of project size, density, site design, and land use mixture on travel choices, however, are presented in Chapter 6. This chapter, then, uses SEC groups as the lense for exploring transportation–land use relationships while its successor concentrates on how specific land use variables influence workers' commuting choices and local traffic conditions.

Several caveats about the statistical tests and the materials presented in this chapter should be mentioned at the outset. First, only those variables for which reasonably significant statistical results were obtained are shown in the chapter's tables and discussed in some depth. Second, for some of the variables studied, particularly those where the size of SECs was an intervening factor, the "large corridor" group was not included in the analysis, reducing the number of SEC groups to five. In some instances, furthermore, the "office park" and "office concentration" groups were combined, as were the "large-scale MXD" and "moderate-size MXD" groups, further reducing the number of SEC groups to three. In these cases, size was considered to be an incidental factor, allowing the analysis to be simplified. Finally, it should be noted that because many of the SECs were selected for this study based on data availability, the sites do not necessarily provide a completely random, unbiased sample in the purest of senses. Nonetheless, since the cases capture a fairly large share of the universe of America's largest SECs, the approximate order of magnitude of differences among SEC groups should be reasonably on target. In general, the precise statistical differences in variables are felt to be less important than the general pattern of relationships among land use and transportation factors that emerge from the analysis.

5.2 Differences in size, location, and employment among SEC groups

Since size and employment were two factors used to assign cases to groups, differences across the six SEC categories could be expected. Just how significant are these differences? Table 5.1 shows the ANOVA results for several of the size, location, and employment variables.

Size

The SEC group with the largest acreage is large-scale corridors, followed by large MXDs and then office centers/concentrations. The amount of office, commercial, and industrial floorspace also differs significantly among groups, with all other groups paling in comparison to large corridors. Large-scale MXDs and sub-cities average comparable amounts of floorspace, while office parks average the least footage. Ignoring the large corridor cases, sub-cities have the largest amount of expected future space at buildout – an average of just over 20 million square feet. They also have the longest expected time horizon until buildout – an average expected year of completion of 2008. By comparison, the average office park and center can be expected to reach buildout around 1996 while MXDs are slated for completion, on average, right at the turn of the century. In terms of the percentage of project completion, no discernible pattern was found, with all groups averaging between 50–60 per cent of each SEC in the group being built out.

Regional locations

Table 5.1 also reveals general differences in the regional locations of SEC groups. Large corridors tend to be the farthest removed from the CBDs of regions, although this is partly due to their expansive size. The next farthest group is large-scale MXDs, averaging a distance of 20

Table 5.1 Comparison of Size, Location, and Employment Among SEC Groups

	Means of SEC Groups						
Variables	Office Park	Office Center	Large MXDs	Moderate MXDs	Sub-City	Large Corridor	F Stat. (prob)[1]
Size:							
ACREAGE	549.1	2593.0	7813.0	697.4	1223.3	120530.0	11.73 (.000)
FLOORSPC	2.97	5.69	12.29	3.77	12.72	26.48	4.65 (.001)
Location:							
CBDMILES	18.0	15.4	20.4	13.0	15.7	25.0	1.56 (.188)
Employment:							
EMPLOYMT	8.14	12.91	27.47	7.49	33.56	236.91	13.11 (.000)
MANAGEMT	10.0	17.1	11.1	20.7	18.7	8.8	2.84 (.028)
ADMINIST	20.3	15.9	12.3	15.3	13.9	8.9	2.31 (.061)
TECHNICL	39.1	22.5	15.2	15.5	18.6	19.4	3.05 (.020)

Variable Definitions:

ACREAGE = Total land acreage.
FLOORSPC = Square feet of floor space in office-commercial-industrial uses (millions).
CBDMILES = Approximate radial miles to regional CBD.
EMPLOYMT = Size of full-time workforce (thousands).
MANAGEMT = Estimated percent of workforce in management positions.
ADMINIST = Estimated percent of workforce in administrative positions.
TECHNICL = Estimated percent of workforce in technical positions.

Notes:
1. F statistic and probability.

miles from downtown. Moderate-size MXDs, on the other hand, tend to be closest to CBDs, around 13 miles away.

Employment characteristics

Table 5.1 also compares employment characteristics among groups. Ignoring the massive corridors, sub-cities average the largest employment base with over 33,000 full-time workers. Moreover, Table 5.1 also shows differences in the percentage of employees in several occupational categories. Moderate-size MXDs and sub-cities, for instance, average the largest percentage of management employees. Office parks, on the other hand, tend to have relatively higher shares of administrative staff, quite often consisting of accountants, billing agents, personnel staff, and financial clerks. Office parks average the largest proportion of technical staff (e.g., engineers, scientists, and professional consultants), owing largely to the fact that many parks are aggressively marketed as research and development projects. There is far less variation among groups in the percentage of clerical employees, although office parks and office concentrations average the most with around 25 per cent for both groups. Sub-cities and MXDs, on the other hand, have the largest shares of sales personnel, while large-scale corridors have by far the largest contingent of manufacturing and warehousing workers.

If one considers management, administrative, and technical staffs to represent the "professional" component of suburban laborforces, Figure 5.1 reveals that office parks and centers average the largest shares of these groups with over 50 per cent in both cases. Large-MXDs tend to have the smallest representation of professionals – only around one-third of their workforce. Overall, the predominantly office-use workplaces average the highest shares of technical, administrative, and clerical staffs, reflecting the branch office character of many of these places. MXDs tend to have high shares of managers (e.g., stockbrokers, real estate brokers, and corporate executives) and sales forces. Large corridors generally average the highest shares of light-industrial workers.

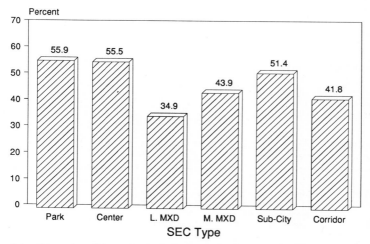

Figure 5.1 Share of workforce in professional job categories, by SEC type.

5.3   Comparison of densities, lotting, and ownership patterns among SEC groups

Density

Group differences in a number of density indices are shown in Table 5.2. Floor area ratios vary significantly among the six SEC groups. Sub-cities average the highest FARs, followed by office centers, settings where freestanding mid-rise and high-rise office towers are common. MXDs average FARs in the 0.76 to 0.89 range, whereas office parks and large-scale office corridors generally have FARs under 0.36. Table 5.2 also shows that the zoning ordinances of sub-cities and large-scale

Table 5.2   Comparison of density, lotting, and ownership patterns among SEC groups.

	Office parks	Office centers	Large MXDs	Moderate MXDs	Sub-city	Large corridor	F stat. (prob.)
Density:							
FAR	0.33	1.55	0.89	0.76	1.80	0.36	3.19 (.014)
MAXFAR	0.61	2.40	3.14	1.59	4.03	1.05	1.53 (.225)
AVGSTORY	2.9	7.3	3.5	3.3	9.2	2.9	5.39 (.001)
EMP/ACRE	18.7	20.4	5.4	11.7	44.7	–	5.47 (.001)
COVERAGE	0.26	0.46	0.31	0.24	0.30	–	1.59 (.193)
Lotting:							
SMALLLOT	2.11	2.54	0.79	1.08	0.36	0.20	1.77 (.141)
LOTVARY	0.096	0.086	0.022	0.062	0.023	0.005	1.72 (.154)
Ownership:							
PROPOWN	13.0	33.5	249.3	248.6	82.4	–	3.01 (.031)
DEVOWN	44.7	67.5	70.0	70.7	75.9	–	2.29 (.081)

FAR	=	Floor area ratio, building square feet/lot size.
MAXFAR	=	Maximum allowable FAR under current zoning.
AVGSTORY	=	Most frequently occurring number of stories for office buildings.
EMP/ACRE	=	Employees/acre.
COVERAGE	=	Proportion of land covered by buildings.
SMALLLOT	=	Acreage of smallest lot.
LOTVARY	=	Smallest lot as a proportion of largest lot.
PROPOWN	=	Number of property-owners, non-residential land only.
DEVOWN	=	Percentage of non-residential property owned by developers.

MXDs generally allow, on average, the highest maximum FARs. In a number of cases, these high density SECs have been designated major growth centers in regional plans, targeted to receive most new office and commercial growth which occurs outside of downtown.

One relationship of interest is the correlation between the size of SECs and densities. Are there any differences among SEC groups in how size and density are related? Figure 5.2 offers some perspective on this. Overall, the random appearance of the pattern in the scatterplot suggests that the relationship between the size of laborforce and FARs is fairly weak among the non-corridor cases. Within SEC groups (whereby office parks and centers are combined, as are MXDs), a more decipherable pattern is apparent. Among office centers (i.e., parks and concentrations), a modest negative correlation appears – as they get bigger, FARs tend to drop. Among MXDs, there is a slight positive correlation; as their employment base increases, so generally do their densities. Among sub-cities, however, there appears to be a fairly strong inverse relationship with the larger ones averaging the lowest FARs. Thus, even though many sub-cities and MXDs share similar land use mixtures, the relationship between size and density seems to be qualitatively different between the two groups.

Table 5.2 also gives mean differences in the most frequently occurring office building height, expressed in stories, among groups. As with the FAR variable, sub-cities and large-scale MXDs likewise appear to average the tallest skylines. When the lowest and highest building stories

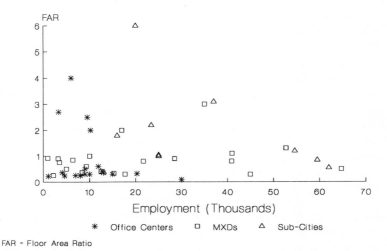

FAR = Floor Area Ratio

Figure 5.2 Plot of FAR versus employment size, by three SEC groups.

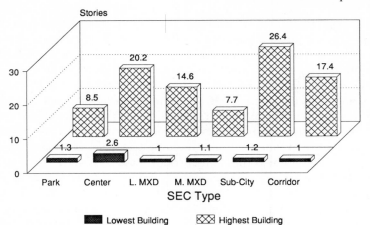

Figure 5.3   Average stories of lowest and highest buildings, by SEC groups.

are compared, several other patterns emerge (see Fig. 5.3). Sub-cities tend to have the tallest average skyline (26-story buildings), followed by office centers. Thus, although the typical building within large MXDs are taller, office concentrations usually have the tallest building among the two groups. All of the SECs tend to have comparably low heights for the lowest building, except office concentrations/centers, wherein the lowest building is generally over two stories. This average is inflated somewhat, however, by the inclusion of several high-rise centers with no buildings under five stories, such as Greenway Plaza in Houston. Figure 5.3 also reveals that sub-cities tend to have the greatest variation in skyline, with some 25 stories separating the lowest and highest edifices, on average.

When density is expressed on an employees per acre basis, Table 5.2 shows that sub-cities again rank the highest – in general, there are over twice as many workers per acre as in any of the other SEC groups. Additionally, Table 5.2 compares average coverage ratios among the groups. All SECs tend to have low building coverage rates, with parking lots, streets, and open space representing well over one-half of total land area and, in the case of office parks, generally around three-quarters. Office centers, on the other hand, average the least amount of open space.

A final indicator of relative employment density is the amount of square feet per employee – an "elbow-room" index. Figure 5.4 reveals that differences are fairly insignificant, with the exception of moderate-size MXDs. Their working environments tend to be more spacious, though part of the explanation is due to the fact that some of these SECs average relatively high shares of retail, light-industrial, and warehouse workers, thus inflating the average. Compared to traditional

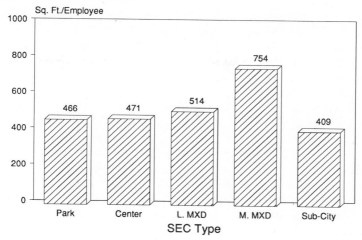

Figure 5.4 Average building square footage per employee in five SEC groups.

downtowns, however, the workers of all of these SEC groups enjoy roomier working environments – in general, over twice as much space per employee (Cervero 1986b).

Lotting

Differences in average front lot and side lot setbacks among SEC groups are summarized in Figure 5.5. Among non-corridor SECs, sub-cities

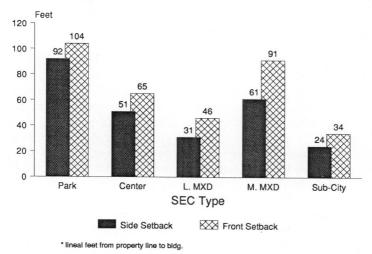

Figure 5.5 Average setbacks for front and sides of buildings, by SEC groups.

average the shortest setbacks while office parks feature the longest ones. Particularly in the case of company headquarters and signature buildings, setbacks exceeding 100 feet in length are not uncommon in many office and executive parks. Another pattern illustrated by Figure 5.5 is that the relative differences among SEC groups in side versus front setbacks are quite similar. Additionally, it is evident that in all SEC environments, front setbacks tend to be 10–20 per cent longer than side ones. In most cases this is because buildings lie closer to the narrower sides of rectangular lots, often with proportionally more front and rear lot space devoted to surface parking.

Average lot sizes were not found to vary significantly among SEC groups. Smallest lots do, however. In general, single-use SECs, i.e., office parks and office concentrations, have much bigger small size lots than any of the other groups. Typically, lotting patterns of suburban office parks consist of 5-acre tracts that can be assembled into 25-acre parcels. If one looks at the smallest lot as a proportion of the largest one, office parks and office centers show the least amount of difference. The greatest variability in lot sizes can be found in large MXDs, sub-cities, and large-scale corridors, where 6,000 square foot residential parcels are sometimes less than $\frac{1}{100}$th the size of the largest property.

Property Ownership

Table 5.2 also compares differences in the number of landholders of non-residential properties among SEC groups. Because of their widely varying uses, MXDs tend to have far greater numbers of property owners than any of the other groups. This probably accounts for the fact that MXDs usually have less of an integrated architectural theme than many sub-cities and most office parks.

Differences in the percentage of land owned by developers versus private companies are shown in the final entry in Table 5.2. All of the SEC groups average between two-thirds and three-quarters of all land in private developer ownership, the lone exception being office parks. In parks, less than half of the land is generally owned by a development company. In many parks, large tracts are sold to major firms which in turn build company headquarters or branch offices, with developers normally retaining control over design features through land covenants and during plan reviews. Typically, covenants govern lotting practices and building lines, not only to ensure access, privacy, light, and air, but also to achieve visual continuity and certain aesthetic ends. Normally, this means control over street design, entrance identities, signage, and the exterior appearance of individual buildings.

5.4 Comparison of land use compositions among SEC groups

Since land use was another variable used to discriminate between groups when clustering SEC cases together, differences in land use mixtures can certainly be expected among groups. This section discusses the magnitude of these differences, concentrating on the relationship between office, retail, and housing components among SEC classes.

Land use mixtures

As discussed in Chapter 1, it is believed that the emergence of numerous suburban job centers with a single dominant use is inducing many employees to drive their own cars to work. Table 5.3 shows that office activities are clearly the predominant function within all of the SECs examined in this study. Among SEC groups, however, the level of office domination varies considerably. Almost by definition, office parks and office centers/concentrations have the highest average share of office floorspace – over 80 per cent in both cases. Excluding sub-cities, all the remaining SECs average less than half of their non-residential floorspace in office uses. The SECs least oriented to office functions are large-scale MXDs.

The dual relationship between office space and retail space is shown in Figure 5.6. Where office uses are most dominant, retail space tends to be minimal, and vice versa. On average, sub-cities have the largest share of commercial–retail space among the SEC groups, owing in large part to the existence of a 1 million square feet or larger indoor shopping mall at most of these megacenters. Figure 5.7 offers a slightly different

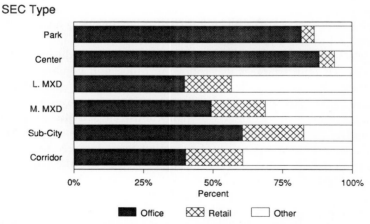

Figure 5.6 Percentage of floorspace in retail and office uses, by SEC groups.

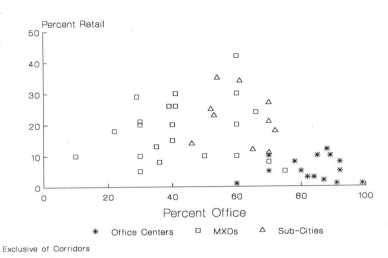

Figure 5.7 Percentage of floorspace in retail versus office use, by three SEC groups.

perspective on this relationship. The scatterplot shows that for MXDs and sub-cities, as more floorspace goes for office functions, relatively more goes for retail space as well, obstensibly as support services for office tenants (e.g., printing and copying services and restaurants). This suggests that other uses (e.g., housing, warehousing, hotels) tend to get squeezed out as MXDs and sub-cities acquire more of a premium office space character. For office centers and parks, however, the share of retail space remains fairly low, whether the development has 75 per cent or nearly 100 per cent office activities. This suggests, then, as office parks and centers begin to diversify, they do so by adding warehousing, manufacturing, hotel, and other business ancilliary uses as opposed to retail functions.

Table 5.3 also shows variation among SECs in light-industrial activity, normally the third largest use following office and commercial–retail activities. MXDs generally have the highest percentages of manufacturing activities while sub-cities and office concentrations average the least. Thus, the existence of light-industrial activities appears to be another factor, besides size and density, which distinquishes MXDs from sub-cities. Among some of the other uses, large MXDs tend to have the greatest share of warehousing as well as of other commercial activities (notably hotels and entertainment offerings).

The degree of variation among different land uses for non-corridor SEC groups is illustrated in Figure 5.8. Ordered from the group with the smallest to the one with the largest entropy index, Figure 5.8 reveals

Table 5.3   Comparison of Land Use Compositions and Housing Provisions Among SEC Groups

| | | | Means of SEC Groups | | | | |
Variable	Office Park	Office Center	Large MXDs	Moderate MXDs	Sub-City	Large Corridor	F Stat. (prob.)
Land Uses:							
OFFICE	81.9	88.3	39.8	49.5	60.7	40.2	19.8 (.000)
INDUSTRY	5.2	1.5	16.2	11.0	1.6	4.7	4.65 (.002)
Services:							
RESTAURT	2.4	14.3	23.0	10.5	54.7	--	8.22 (.004)
SHOPCENT	1.8	2.4	6.9	2.0	2.8	--	2.03 (.098)
RESTINT	3875	10490	914	546	675	--	1.08 (.368)
Housing:							
HOUSUNIT	84	275	2988	583	2496	--	3.61 (.014)
MULTIFAM	40.0	37.7	21.2	36.3	87.0	--	4.70 (.004)
AVGRENT	625	477	549	550	664	--	1.90 (.117)

Variable Definitions:

OFFICE	= Percent of floorspace in office use.
INDUSTRY	= Percent of floorspace in light-industrial and manufacturing use.
RESTAURT	= No. of eateries and restaurants on-site.
SHOPCENT	= No. of shopping centers over 100,000 sq. ft. of floorspace within 3 miles.
RESTINT	= Restaurant intensity index -- Employees per on-site restaurant.
HOUSUNIT	= No. of on-site housing units.
MULTIFAM	= Percentage of dwelling units within 3 mile radius that are multi-family.
AVGRENT	= Estimated monthly rent of multi-family units within a 3 mile radius.

that office centers are the least varied while large MXDs are the most diversified. (As discussed in chapter 4, this index ranges from 0 to 0.60, with the low range representing little land use variety and the high range signifying much.) In general, office parks tend to be a little more diversified than centers, whereas MXDs are slightly more diversified than sub-cities. All things equal, then, one would expect office centers to average the highest share of workers who commute to work alone,

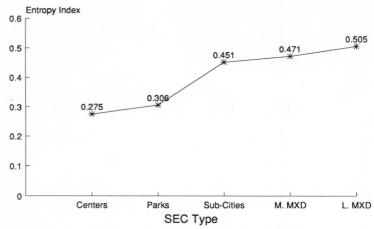

Figure 5.8 Comparison of land use entropy index among five SEC groups.

while MXDs should average the largest proportion of carpoolers and transit patrons.

Consumer services

Comparisons of different levels of consumer and tenant support services for SEC groups are also shown in Table 5.3. By far, sub-cities average the largest number of on-site eateries – over 50 per SEC. Office parks, on the other hand, generally have fewer than three on-site eateries, often in the form of first-floor delis and snack shops. Significant differences in the number of on-site banks were also found. While sub-cities average around 12 banks and savings institutions each, the other SEC groups (excluding corridors) generally have no more than four, and in the case of office parks, normally only around one.

As shown in Figure 5.9, the SEC group averaging the largest number of retail centers exceeding 50,000 square feet in floor area, equivalent to at least a retail plaza of around five shops and a large grocery store, is large-scale MXDs, which have about nine per site. Only around half of the office parks, by comparison, have shopping plazas or centers of at least this size. The degree to which the number of retail plazas and centers vary as a function of density is shown in Figure 5.10. The scatterplot reveals that as SECs become denser, the number of on-site retail centers generally falls. The relationship is the strongest for MXDs and the weakest for office centers and parks. This finding likely reflects two factors: first, other uses, such as offices and hotels, outbid retail establishments for prime real estate in high density MXDs, resulting in high rates of land conversion; second, in denser MXDs, smaller, more local-oriented retail plazas are often consolidated or sometimes

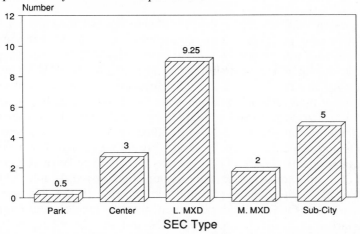

Figure 5.9 Average number of retail centers with floorspace over 50,000 square feet.

replaced by large regional shopping centers and malls. This is somewhat confirmed by Table 5.3, wherein large MXDs average, by far, the largest number of shopping centers exceeding 100,000 square feet within a three-mile radius of the site – on average, around seven. None of the other SEC groups averages more than three large-size shopping centers either on-site or nearby.

As discussed in Chapter 4, the availability of on-site and nearby retail facilities is best expressed when these variables are indexed to

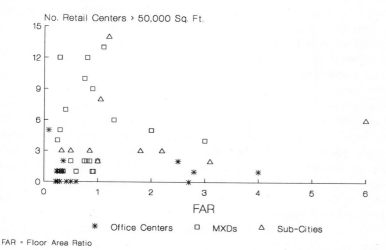

FAR = Floor Area Ratio

Figure 5.10 Plot of number of retail centers versus FAR, by three SEC groups.

the number of SEC employees, producing a retail intensity measure. The fifth row of Table 5.3 shows differences in the average number of employees per on-site restaurant/eatery (RESTINT). Although the relationship in not statistically significant, in part because of missing values for a number of cases, it is apparent that office centers and parks offer their tenants' employees the fewest lunchtime opportunities. Moderate-size MXDs and sub-cities, by comparison, have roughly 15 times the restaurant intensities of office centers/concentrations. For MXDs and sub-cities, there generally are no more than 1,000 workers for every on-site eatery. These groups also tend to have the greatest level of retail intensity when the number of employees is indexed to the number of on-site banks and retail centers, though the relationship is not as strong. One would expect, then, that the incidence of employee ridesharing is relatively high in MXDs and sub-cities because of the availability of nearby consumer services. The extent to which this is borne out is presented in section 5.6 and Chapter 6.

Housing Provisions

Differences in the number of on-site dwelling units are summarized in the bottom section of Table 5.3. In part because of their sheer size, large-scale MXDs and sub-cities average the largest number of on-site units – well over 2,000 each. Office parks, by comparison, average fewer than 100 units. The percentage of these units that is multi-family is also shown. Sub-cities tend to be made up predominantly of multi-family condominiums and townhouses, whereas the housing component of large MXDs consists primarily of single-family dwellings. This housing orientation seems to be another qualitative difference that distinguishes sub-cities from MXDs. All other SEC groups have, on average, fewer than half of their housing stock in the form of multi-family units.

Most relevant from a transportation standpoint, however, is the general balance of jobs and housing. Figure 5.11 compares differences across five SEC groups. While the mean ratio of jobs to housing is around 30 for all cases combined, the two groups which vary most dramatically from this average are office parks and large-scale MXDs. Parks tend to have the least housing offerings while large MXDs have the most, with the two groups differing in jobs/housing by a factor of about four. This is further illustrated by Figure 5.12, where dwelling units and employment are plotted against one another. In general, regardless of how large the employment base might be, office centers and parks average the fewest number of on-site housing units. For MXDs, dwelling units generally increase with employment size, however the correlation is fairly modest. In the case of sub-cities, the relationship between these two variables is the strongest – the sub-cities

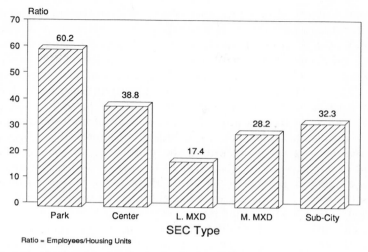

Figure 5.11 Average jobs–housing ratios for five SEC groups.

with the largest employment bases (e.g., North Dallas Parkway and Tysons Corner) also tend to have the largest number of on-site housing units. One might expect, then, that because of the availability of nearby multi-family housing, larger shares of the workforces in MXDs would be walking and cycling to work. We shall explore this hypothesis in section 5.6.

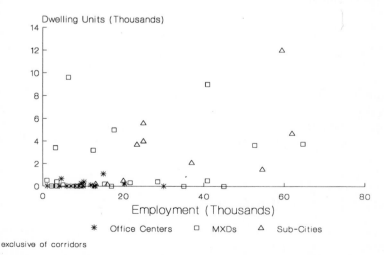

Figure 5.12 Plot of dwelling units versus employment, by three SEC groups.

From a mobility standpoint, more important than the number of on-site units is the availability of housing within a reasonable commutershed of an SEC. Office parks and moderate-size MXDs were generally found to have the largest number of nearby housing units relative to their workforce size, whereas large-scale MXDs tended to have the fewest, although the relationship was not statistically strong. In general, these nearby housing units tend to be single-family dwellings for all SEC groups, with sub-cities featuring the largest share of multi-family units within a three-mile radius. As was discussed in Chapter 3, just because there is some degree of equality in the number of jobs and housing units does not necessarily mean that SEC workers will reside nearby and enjoy easy commutes. The cost of these units, and in particular the match between employee earnings and housing prices, is probably the single strongest determinant of how close employees reside to work. The last entry in Table 5.3 shows that average monthly rents for multi-family units are generally the highest in the vicinity of sub-cities and office parks, while they tend to be the lowest near office centers. Generally, the same pattern held in terms of differences in the average purchase price of nearby housing, although this variable was statistically insignificant. Office parks, it should be recalled, average the highest share of clerical workers, while sub-cities tend to have the largest share of sales personnel – two occupational groups with traditionally low earnings levels. While differences in housing rents are not glaring across SEC groups, there does appear to be some degree of mismatch between workforce earnings and nearby housing costs that could account for some of the mobility problems around America's office parks and sub-cities.

5.5   Transportation facilities and services

In addition to land use and design characteristics of SECs, of course, the amount and quality of transportation facilities and services also influence commuting choices and local traffic conditions. This section compares differences in the supply-side characteristics of the six SEC groups.

On- and off-site roadway facilities

The directional miles of roads within SECs vary to a large extent according to the acreage of each SEC. Among the non-corridor SECs, large MXDs and sub-cities tend to have the most miles of collectors

Table 5.4 Comparison of Transportation Facilities and Services Among SEC Groups

Variable	Office Park	Office Center	Large MXDs	Moderate MXDs	Sub-City	Large Corridor	F Stat. (prob.)
			Means of SEC Groups				
Roadways:							
EMP/RWM	1357.3	1250.6	2197.5	1498.3	2796.1	--	2.21 (.045)
EMP/FWM	2099.4	1797.6	3488.8	2339.6	8067.2	--	3.87 (.005)
EMP/INC	2789.5	5804.7	7317.1	3521.3	11685.6	8077.5	3.27 (.013)
SPACING	2.56	4.09	2.33	2.33	2.20	2.03	2.05 (.089)
Parking:							
PARK/EMP	1.04	0.95	1.10	1.09	0.96	1.13	1.49 (.212)
PARK/SQF	3.90	3.58	4.02	4.13	3.55	3.90	1.29 (.284)
PARKING$	0.00	1.17	0.73	0.00	1.08	--	3.93 (.009)
Buses/Vans:							
COMUTBUS	1.5	3.8	8.8	0.3	2.6	--	1.68 (.164)
EMP/VAN	1068.9	3394.6	3920.8	1284.3	3196.5	--	1.26 (.314)

EMP/RWM	= Employees/directional mile of roadways within site.
EMP/FWM	= Employees/directional mile of freeways within 5 miles of SEC.
EMP/INC	= Employees/freeway interchange within five miles of SEC.
SPACING	= Freeway directional miles/interchange.
PARK/EMP	= Parking spaces/employee.
PARK/SQF	= Parking spaces/1,000 gross square feet.
PARKING$	= Most frequently occurring daily price for parking, in dollars.
COMUTBUS	= Number of daily private commuter buses serving SEC.
EMP/VAN	= Employees/company-sponsored van operation.

and major arteries since they encompass the largest geographic areas. A better indicator of the relative supply of roadways is the ratio of employment size to directional miles for an SEC. Table 5.4 compares this ratio among SEC groups for on-site surface roads (EMP/RWM) and freeway facilities (EMP/FWM) within five radial miles of an SEC. A similar pattern is evident for both variables. Office concentrations and office parks average the largest supply of road space and freeway capacity per employee whereas sub-cities average the least. Moderate-size MXDs are closer to office centers in their levels of roadway supply while large MXDs more closely resemble sub-cities.

Table 5.4 also compares the relative number of access points, expressed as nearby freeway interchanges, among the SEC groups. Based on the ratio of employment to the number of freeway interchanges within a 5 mile radius of SECs, Table 5.4 shows that office parks enjoy the highest level of site accessibility to freeways. Sub-cities, on the other hand, tend to have the fewest number of freeway interchanges relative to their workforce size. Among the six groups, all average spacings of around 2 to 2.5 freeway miles between interchanges, with the exception of office centers, wherein interchanges are normally spaced 4 miles apart. This longer spacing reflects the fact that most office centers and concentrations abut a single interchange whereas other SEC developments tend to be spread out over several interchanges.

In all, it is evident that office parks enjoy the highest relative level of roadway supply among the SEC groups, while sub-cities have the least in relation to their employment base. Accordingly, all other things being equal, one would expect office parks to be most oriented to auto-commuting and sub-cities to be the least among the groups. The extent to which this is the case is discussed in section 5.6.

On-site parking provisions

The supply and cost of parking probably influence employee travel behavior as much as on-site and nearby roadway supply, and perhaps even more. Table 5.4 compares the average number of parking spaces per employee (PARK/EMP) and per 1,000 square feet (PARK/SQT) among the six SEC groups. In general, there is not very much variation – all groups average relatively high levels of parking supply, roughly one space per worker. Because of their higher densities and land values, sub-cities tend to have the lowest level of parking provision, however parking is still plentiful even in these settings. Evidently, developers of virtually all SECs appear to be heeding the advice of their financiers and brethren to "overbuild parking when in doubt."[1] This predisposition toward parking probably reflects a skepticism over the possible success of alternative travel modes in suburban work settings as much as it does a belief in parking's salesmanship value.

While the supply of parking is fairly constant across SEC groups, general pricing practices do not appear to be. Table 5.4 shows that while all office parks and moderate-size MXDs studied provided free parking for everyone, the most frequent all-day rate for office centers and sub-cities averaged over one dollar.[2] Large-scale MXDs averaged around 75 cents as the most common daily rate. Commercial parking rates, of course, do not reflect what employees actually pay. As discussed in Chapter 4, an overwhelming majority of workers in many office settings receive vouchers to pay for most, if not all, of monthly parking expenses. On the whole, office workers in most SECs pay nothing to park, an in-kind subsidy that acts as a strong inducement for many to drive to work alone.

Transit and ridesharing services

Few significant statistical patterns emerged when various measures of public transit provisions were compared across SEC groups. In general, sub-cities average far more bus runs both on-site and nearby than the other SEC groups. When indexed to the size of workforce, MXDs were found to have the highest relative level of transit services; however, again, the relationship was statistically weak.

A somewhat stronger pattern emerged when the level of private commuter bus operations was compared among groups. Table 5.4 shows that large MXDs average, by far, the largest number of private subscription bus services, with approximately nine buses serving each center daily. Most of these are premium services offering office workers guaranteed padded seats, a pleasant temperature-controlled climate, and front-door drop-off and pick-up.

Differences were also evident in the level of company support of vanpool services among SEC groups. Figure 5.13 shows that large-scale MXDs and sub-cities tend to have the most companies underwriting van

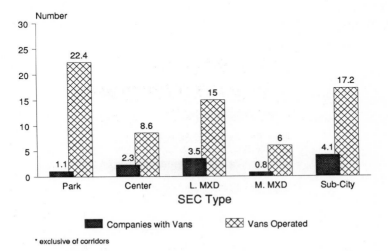

Figure 5.13 Average number of companies sponsoring vanpools and vans operating in SECs.

services for their employees, in the neighborhood of three to four firms in both cases. These firms sponsor, on average, around four vans each, for a total operation of 15 or more vans within each SEC. While office parks generally only have one company running employee van services, compared with the other groups, these were large operations, averaging around 22 vans per company. Thus, whereas the other SEC groups tend to have multiple companies sponsoring fairly moderate-size van services, office parks tend to have one large company that operates nearly two dozen vans. As shown in the final entry of Table 5.4, moreover, office parks also tend to enjoy the highest intensity of van services – around 1,000 or so employees per van in service.

Finally, Figure 5.14 compares differences in levels of rideshare support among the six SEC categories. The group with the highest proportion of full-time or part-time rideshare coordinators is office centers – nearly two-thirds of its SEC cases have coordinators. Sub-cities, on the other hand, have the largest proportion of designated ridesharing offices – seven of the ten cases have a specific on-site office devoted to ridematching, marketing, and other support services. Moderate-size MXDs tend to be least involved in rideshare promotion and coordination.

5.6   Comparison of commuting choices and local traffic conditions among SEC groups

So far, differences in the general land use and transportation supply characteristics of SEC groups have been examined. Most significant from a policy standpoint, however, is the degree to which commuting

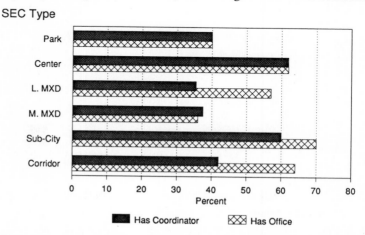

Figure 5.14   Average per cent of SECs with rideshare coordinators and offices.

behavior and local traffic conditions vary among the six groups. To the extent that certain patterns are evident, inferences may be drawn regarding how variations in land use patterns are related to variations in transportation conditions. This section attempts to illuminate any such patterns that exist.

Time, speed, and distance of journey to work

Mean travel times and distances for journeys to work among SEC groups were found to be fairly comparable.[3] Oneway commutes ranged from a low average travel time of 21.6 minutes for office center workers to a high of 25.9 minutes for sub-city workers. Oneway distances were also fairly similar, ranging from an average of 9.5 miles for sub-city employees to a high of 11.9 miles for office park workers. Because of the relative high variation in travel times and distances within SEC groups, these differences were insignificant from a statistical standpoint, however.

A slightly stronger pattern emerged when average commuting speeds were compared among SEC groups. As shown in the first row of Table 5.5, average commuting speeds were in the range of 29 to 32 m.p.h. for all of the groups except large MXDs (27.4 m.p.h.) and sub-cities (22.9 m.p.h.). Thus, even though sub-city employees reside, on average, closest to work, they tend to commute at comparatively slow speeds.

The most plausible explanation for why sub-city and, to a lesser extent, large-scale MXD employees commute at slower average speeds is that these centers tend to be relatively dense and consequently more crowded, both inside buildings and out on the street, all things equal. This chapter has already shown that sub-cities average FARs and employees per acre levels that are over 15 per cent higher than for any other SEC group. Additionally, as discussed previously, both sub-cities and large-scale MXDs tend to have the least amount of road capacity per employee among the SEC groups. Thus, higher densities and comparatively limited amounts of road space likely account for, at least in part, these slower average commuting speeds.

Modal choices for work trips

The built environment probably has as much influence on the travel modes workers choose as any single aspect of commuting (Pushkarev & Zupan 1977). Figure 5.15 compares the average per cent of work trips made by the two dominant modes of commuting – drive-alone auto and ridesharing (carpooling and vanpooling combined).[4] Two things stand out in Figure 5.15. First, driving alone is by far the dominant means of commuting among all SEC groups, constituting at least four out of

**Table 5.5 Comparison of Workforce Travel
Characteristics and Areawide Traffic Volumes Among SEC Groups**

Variable	Office Park	Office Center	Large MXDs	Moderate MXDs	Sub-City	Large Corridor	F Stat. (prob.)
			Means of SEC Groups				
Work Trip:							
SPEED	29.1	30.6	27.4	32.2	22.9	30.6	1.21 (.317)
VANSHAR	3.4	2.1	3.6	2.0	2.6	1.2	1.16 (.340)
WALKSHAR	0.3	0.5	1.2	0.5	1.4	--	2.01 (.053)
DRIVDIFF	9.1	13.0	6.4	10.9	6.8	--	1.43 (.229)
BUSRIDE	139.4	525.6	1614.3	248.3	3041.1	--	2.89 (.036)
ARIVTIME	8:10	8:10	8:25	8:26	8:05	8:17	1.51 (.205)
DEPRTIME	4:49	4:57	4:58	5:00	5:01	4:55	1.10 (.371)
STAGGER	38.0	26.1	21.3	17.9	21.8	--	1.03 (.411)
Traffic:							
ADT	45.3	70.3	61.5	45.6	113.0	78.2	3.29 (.012)

Variable Definitions:

SPEED	= Estimated average travel speed for work trip in m.p.h.
VANSHAR	= Percentage of work trips in vanpools.
WALKSHAR	= Percentage of work trips by walking.
DRIVDIFF	= Drive alone work trip percentage minus regional drive alone percentage.
BUSRIDE	= Average weekday ridership of all bus runs serving SEC.
ARIVTIME	= Most frequently occurring time of arrival, a.m. peak.
DEPRTIME	= Most frequently occurring time of departure, p.m. peak.
STAGGER	= Estimated percentage of workforce with staggered work hour privileges.
ADT	= Average daily directional traffic volume on main freeway or roadway serving SEC.

five work trips made to SECs within each group, on average. Second, the SEC groups which average the lowest levels of solo-commuting are large-scale MXDs and sub-cities; these groups, by no coincidence, also average the highest shares of vehicle-pooling. In the case of large-scale MXDs, on average, slightly over 15 per cent of all journeys to work take place in carpools or vanpools.

The comparatively high incidence of ridesharing among large MXDs and sub-cities seems to confirm several hypotheses set out in this

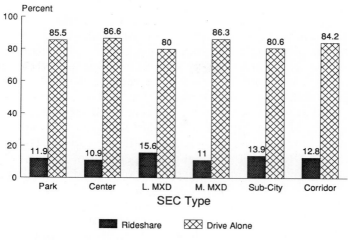

Figure 5.15 Average per cent of work trips made to SECs, by drive-alone versus ridesharing.

research. First, the SEC groups with the highest densities average the highest share of vehicle pooling. And second, these two groups also tend to have the greatest variety of land uses, and in particular the largest retail components. The inference is clear: SECs that are denser and have restaurants, shops, banks, and other consumer services on-site (e.g., sub-cities and MXDs) are better able to lure workers out of their private automobiles and into carpools and vanpools, all things equal.

For specific non auto modes (e.g., carpools, vanpools, transit, walking, and cycling), variations in mode splits among SEC classes were generally found to be modest, in part because these individual modes represent such a small share of total trips.[5] The largest group differences were for vanpooling and walking. Table 5.5 shows the share of commutes via vanpools to be highest in large-scale MXDs, followed closely by office parks. As noted above, vanpooling's relative popularity in large-scale MXDs can be attributed partly to density and retail services. Company support of vanpools in large MXDs has probably also been conducive to vanpooling. For office parks, supply appears to explain much of vanpooling's relatively high market shares. As discussed earlier, office parks average more company vans per worker than any other SEC group. For the variable WALKSHAR, the SEC groups with the highest densities and land use mixtures – large MXDs and sub-cities – again average the highest shares. The relatively high proportion of walk commutes made to large MXDs and sub-cities is also consistent with the earlier finding that both groups tend to have the highest shares of multi-family housing nearby. A reasonable inference, then, is that the close proximity of apartments and townhouses has enabled larger shares of MXD and sub-city workers to reside close by and walk to work.

Of course, mode splits are influenced by far more than the site characteristics of individual SECs. For instance, the quality of regional bus services, along with a host of other contextual factors, could be expected to influence transit modal shares. So far, such factors have been treated as constants. One way to account for regional differences in the quality of transit services and other commute alternatives is to include a control variable. This is done with the variable DRIVDIFF in Table 5.5. DRIVDIFF is equal to the per cent of work trips to an SEC that are drive-alone minus the per cent of drive-alone work trips for the entire region in which the SEC lies.[6] Thus, a positive value indicates that a larger share of employees solo-commute to the SEC than do the region's "typical" employees. The magnitude of this percentage point difference reflects roughly just how much more SEC workers appear to be auto-dependent than all other workers within the region. Since mode shares for both worker groups are influenced by the quality of regional transit services, the cost of automobile usage, and other factors, these factors are controlled for when differences are taken between the two percentages.

From Table 5.5, office center employees appear to be the most dependent on their automobiles for commuting relative to all other workers in the region. On average, workers in office centers solo-commute 13 percentage points more than employees in other work settings in the region. Employees in large-scale MXDs and sub-cities, on the other hand, seem to be less heavily dependent on their cars than workers in the other SEC groups. Thus, even when factors such as quality of regional transportation are controlled for, large-scale MXDs and sub-cities prevail as the SEC environments which are least oriented to solo-driving and, accordingly, most favorable to other commuting options.

Other worker commuting characteristics

Table 5.5 compares group differences for several other indicators of employee travel behavior. Consistent with findings so far, the SEC groups with significantly higher ridership levels for bus routes serving their employees (BUSRIDE) are sub-cities and large MXDs. Thus, these two groups average comparatively high levels of transit usage in both absolute and percentage terms.

Table 5.5 also shows differences in average employee arrival and departure times among groups. Although differences are not statistically significant, several time values are noteworthy. One, the later average arrival times for MXDs reflect their higher shares of retail workers.

Many sales personnel do not arrive at work until 9:00 a.m., or later, thus inflating the average figure. Also of note is the fact that the workforces of sub-cities average the earliest arrival times and the latest departure times – that is, they seem to be putting in more hours per day than their counterparts in other SECs. What these figures most likely reflect, however, is the variety of occupational roles found in sub-cities, giving rise to atypical average arrival and departure times.[7] The presence of stockbrokers who punch in early time clocks, for instance, may deflate the average arrival time figure for some sub-cities. The relatively high share of theater workers during the evening, on the other hand, might inflate the average evening departure time for others. Most importantly, it may be the case that the mixed-use character of sub-cities has served to spread out worker arrival and departure times, thereby reducing the intensity of peaking.

The level of work-hour staggering is revealed by the penultimate entry in Table 5.5. Office parks appear to have the highest estimated percentage of employees working under staggered arrangements – around 38 per cent. This percentage reflects the high share of clerical and back office employees found in office parks, the majority of whom work in staggered shifts. MXD firms, by comparison, appear to offer their employees fewer staggered work opportunities.

Areawide traffic conditions

The final set of comparisons made among SEC groups looked at differences in areawide traffic volumes and conditions. The last entry in Table 5.5 reveals a significant difference in average daily traffic (ADT) volumes in the vicinity of sub-cities relative to average ADTs for other SEC groups. Sub-cities average well over 100,000 daily vehicle trips per direction on the main freeway or arterial serving them. Major roadways serving office parks and moderate-size MXDs, by comparison, average less than half this volume. Large growth corridors average the second highest directional traffic volumes along their primary road axis. However, these volumes are still only around two-thirds of the daily counts found on freeways serving sub-cities.

Traffic conditions are best reflected, of course, when vehicle volumes are indexed to road capacity. Average peak-period volume-to-capacity ratios for major surface arterials and major freeways serving SECs are compared among the five non-corridor groups in Figure 5.16.[8] Along both surface streets and freeways, peak traffic conditions are generally the worst around sub-cities. On average, peak traffic volumes on the primary freeway serving sub-cities are 89 per cent of capacity, whereas the major connecting arterial operates at around 83 per cent of capacity. The next most congested SEC setting appears to be office

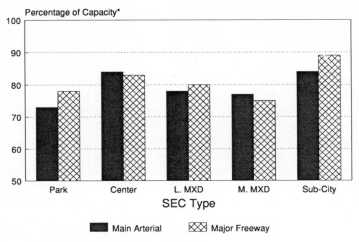

Figure 5.16 Average traffic volumes as per cent of capacity on main roadways serving SECs.

centers, wherein nearby freeways and arterials operate, on average, at around 82 per cent of capacity. Thoroughfares serving large-scale MXDs are generally the third most congested. Office parks, on the other hand, average the least congestion on adjoining surface streets, while moderate-size MXDs tend to have the least congested adjoining freeways. For both groups, the primary connecting roadways tend to operate at level of service C during the peak – that is, volumes remain under 80 per cent of capacity, with relatively stable flow conditions.

The common feature of the SEC groups with the most congested traffic conditions is their relatively high employment densities. In SEC settings, then, density appears to be a double-edge sword: while it works in favor of ridesharing and other commute alternatives, it at the same time generates traffic volumes that frequently saturate local thoroughfares. Thus, the SECs with the highest shares of transit usage and ridesharing are also the most congested.

The decision of local policy-makers to restrict densities in some SECs reflects the preference given to accommodating the automobile over the encouragement of ridesharing or transit commuting. Within the two- to four-year time frame that many local officials are elected, this is a rational choice since the marginal gains in vehicle-pooling induced by higher densities are usually insufficient to make up for the higher levels of nodal congestion. Density, however, must be viewed within a time context. Although denser suburban work environments may increase congestion in the near term, in the long run, they concentrate activities so as to make ridesharing and mass transit viable alternatives to solo-commuting. When it comes to density in suburban work settings, a general tenet might be: short-term pain is necessary for long-term gain.

5.7 Summary policy inferences

This chapter's comparison of differences in commuting behavior and conditions among SEC groups yielded several insights which appear to support some of the propositions set out in Chapter 1. Invoking the *ceteris paribus* assumption, the following can be said:

(a) The share of commute trips made in some manner other than by driving alone increases as an SEC becomes denser and features a wide variety of land uses. Large-scale MXDs and sub-cities average the highest share of non-solo commuting. This is so even when controlling for the quality of transportation services and other contextual variables.

(b) The incidence of ridesharing is the highest in settings with substantial commercial components, most notably sub-cities and MXDs. The availability of retail activities appears to induce a number of employees to carpool and vanpool to work because in these settings they can access banks, shops, restaurants, and the like without a motor vehicle.

(c) The share of work trips made by foot is the greatest at sub-cities, the SEC group with the highest proportion of multi-family housing units within a three mile radius. This suggests that the availability of moderate-priced housing could be inducing some employees to reside nearby and walk to work.

(d) Sub-cities appear to have the least degree of peaking of commute trips. This is most likely due to the ability of highly varied land uses to shift trips to the shoulders of the peak and thus achieve a more even temporal distribution of travel.

(e) SECs with the slowest average speeds for employee commutes and the most congested local streets and freeways are sub-cities and large-scale MXDs, the two groups with the highest employment densities.

Based on these findings, the three major site variables which appear to have the greatest influence on employee travel behavior and local traffic conditions around SECs are density, size, and land use mixtures. The SEC groups with the highest densities have the highest incidence of ridesharing and transit usage, but also the most congested local streets. The paradox of density in suburban work settings appears to be that in the near term, as long as most employees drive to work alone, local streets invariably become more congested as activities intensify; however, over the long haul, density is necessary to build up a ridership base to sustain transit and ridesharing services. Additionally, ridesharing tends to be most prevalent in large SECs, suggesting that a critical mass of employees is necessary for mounting successful vanpool and carpool programs in suburbia. Lastly, land use mixing also emerged as an important determinant of travel choice – those SECs with the greatest variety of activities were found to average the highest shares of non-solo commutes, including walks trips. In tandem, then, high densities, a large concentration of workers, and mixed-use development appear to be necessary, though probably not in themselves sufficient, prerequisites if reasonably significant levels of ridesharing, transit usage, cycling, and foot travel are to be achieved in suburbia.

It bears repeating that these inferences are based on comparing differences among SEC groups and fleshing out patterns that emerge. How variables such as density, size, and land use mixes directly influence travel choices and traffic conditions directly are tested in Chapter 6.

Notes

1. For a discussion of this general industry rule to overbuild parking, see Lenny (1984) and O'Mara & Casazza (1982).
2. Recall that this is the average of the most frequent rate. For some centers, parking was entirely free while for others the most frequent rate was, say, over $3 per day. The average of these most frequent rates tended to result in a figure somewhere in between these extremes. In general, the average of the most frequent rate is not representative of the specific rates charged, but does provide an accurate gauge of the relative differences among groups.
3. The figures in this subsection, it should be recalled, are "averages of averages" – that is, they are averaged across cases within each SEC group based on the average statistics for employees within each SEC.
4. The summary statistics for variation across groups were: drive alone (F statistic = 1.78; probability == 0.163) and ridesharing (F statistic = 0.708; probability = .620). Thus neither mode registered statistically significant variation across groups, although drive alone percentages do seem to be moderately influenced by SEC type.
5. Differences in transit modal shares were quite small across groups (F statistic = 0.682; probability .649). The same applied for carpooling. Consistent with expectations, the two SEC groups with the highest transit and carpool shares are sub-cities and large-scale MXDs. Large corridors average the highest shares of "other" modes (e.g., drop-off).
6. Regional drive-alone percentages are for 1980 and were obtained from Rodriquez *et al.* (1985).
7. The relatively large extremes in arrival and departure times for sub-cities could reflect a more negatively skewed distribution of arrivals in the

morning and a more positively skewed distribution of departures in the evening than for other SEC groups. Median times of arrival and departure would probably be more similar among SEC groups.

8.   These were estimated by computing the "average" level of service within each group, wherein a level of service A was assigned a value of 1, B was assigned a value of 2, C was assigned a value of 3, and so forth. The average level of service of 3.30 for main arterials serving office parks, for instance, was translated as 73 per cent of capacity since it was 3 percentage points above the floor for level of service C (70 per cent of capacity) and 7 percentage points below the floor for level of service D (80 per cent of capacity).

6

Land use and work site factors influencing commuting choices in SECs

6.1 Introduction

How the land use and site characteristics of SECs directly influence the commute choices of SEC employees and local traffic conditions is studied in this chapter. While Chapter 5 focused on variations in different work site and travel variables among SEC groups, here we shall directly model land use–transportation relationships within SECs.

The primary purpose of this chapter is to test empirically the hypotheses posited in the first chapter of the study. The basic hypothesis, again, is that the *low-density*, *single-use*, and *non-integrated* character of SECs have compelled many workers to rely upon their automobiles for accessing work and circulating within projects. Thus, the primary dependent variable used in the analysis is the per cent of work trips made by solo-commuters. Various density, land use mixture, and site design variables are entered into the analyses to evaluate the hypothesis. In addition to modeling mode choice decisions, this chapter tests how land use and site characteristics appear to influence local traffic conditions, measured in terms of average commute speeds and levels of service on connecting facilities.

While the thrust of the analysis is on land use–transportation interactions, several other relationships are studied as well. For one, site factors most related to high parking standards are probed. Additionally, variables which seem to be associated with high jobs–housing imbalances, both on-site and nearby, are identified. Land ownership patterns are also modeled to investigate which site environments seem to be most related to multiple property holdings.

In studying all of these relationships, the technique of stepwise regression analysis was employed. Here, the emphasis is placed on uncovering those combinations of variables which best account for variation in the dependent variable. In stepwise analysis, each variable which enters the equation adds something new, providing some information about the dependent variable that none of the other variables offers. Because of the high inter-correlation among various land use and site variables gathered for this study, the stepwise approach was considered to be most appropriate. If a number of closely correlated land use and site design variables were forced into the equations, the models would have broken down due to multicollinearity problems. Thus, although stepwise results do not provide insight into the influences of all variables of interest, they do offer a foundation for understanding the unique influences of those few variables that do enter into the analysis.[1]

One of the shortcomings of modeling land use and transportation relationships for areas (like SECs) rather than for people is that aggregation biases invariably occur. It is individuals, not SECs, who make choices on how, when, and where to travel. Just because the "average" parking fee is not related to the "average" rate of solo-commuting among SECs does not necessarily mean that parking costs have no influence on whether individuals will drive alone to work. By aggregating data, some of the richness in choice decisions is unavoidably lost. With this in mind, this chapter also presents a sub-analysis of how various work site characteristics are related to modal choices and time periods of travel of employees from the suburban community of Pleasanton, California. The intent here is to enrich the more aggregate level study by providing a finer grain perspective on the influence of work site characteristics on commute choices in a particular suburb.

Following these analyses, the chapter concludes with a summary overview of the results of the empirical tests. Our general state of knowledge on land use-transportation in suburban employment settings is also discussed.

6.2   Factors influencing mode choices in SECs

Land uses and design practices are thought to influence the modal choices of suburban workers as much as any one aspect of commuting. This section presents the stepwise regression findings of those variables

Table 6.1 Stepwise regression results on factors influencing percentage of work trips, by drive-alone mode.

Variable	Dependent variable: DRIVALON Beta coefficient	Standard error	t statistic	Probability
OFFICE	0.12073	0.04973	2.428	.0200
VANSRUN	− 0.09058	0.02762	− 3.279	.0022
EMP/INTC	− 0.00053	0.00019	− 2.713	.0100
RIDECOOR	− 3.36511	2.32610	− 1.446	.1562
Intercept	82.24903	3.70500	22.200	.0000

Summary statistics:
  Number of observations = 46
  R-squared = .436
  F statistic = 7.345
  Probability = .0002

Variable definitions:
  DRIVALON = Percentage of work trips by drive-alone mode.
  OFFICE   = Percentage of total floorspace in office use.
  VANSRUN   = Number of company vans in daily operation.
  EMP/INTC = Employees per freeway interchange within a five mile radius.
  RIDECOOR = Rideshare coordinator in SEC: 1 = yes, 0 = no.

that do the best job at explaining drive-alone, ridesharing, and walking–cycling choices.

Drive-alone models

Table 6.1 summarizes the stepwise results for the dependent variable DRIVALON – percentage of work trips by individuals who drive alone to their suburban jobs. For the 46 SEC cases with complete data,[2] a model with reasonably good predictive powers was obtained, explaining over 43 per cent of the variation in DRIVALON. Three "supply-side" variables and one "land use" explanatory variable entered the stepwise equation. On the supply-side, the model indicates that the share of work trips to SECs by solo-commuters declines as the number of vans in operation (VANSRUN) increases and the relative number of site access points decreases (i.e., EMP/INTC rises),[3] all else equal. The equation also suggests that, *ceteris paribus*, drive-alone shares fall around 3.4 per cent if there is a designated rideshare coordinator at the SEC (RIDECOOR).[4] Promotion and support of vanpools and carpools, then, seems to be paying off in SECs. According to the model, an SEC with 20 vans in operation and a rideshare coordinator could be expected to reduce the share of work trips made by solo-commuters by about 5 per cent over an SEC with no vanpools or coordinator position.

The sole land use variable that entered the stepwise equation was OFFICE – the percentage of floorspace in office use. Based on the sign on the variable OFFICE, as SECs become more office-oriented, the share of solo-commute trips can be expected to rise. All else being equal, an SEC with a share of total floorspace in office use that is 20 per cent higher than an otherwise comparable SEC can be expected to have a 2.4 per cent higher share of work trips made by solo-commuters. This finding, then, clearly supports the supposition that single-use office environments induce vehicle commuting. Hence, by inference, mixed-use work environments will reduce auto-dependency and encourage workers to seek out other commute options.

As was discussed in Chapter 5, the analysis of site factors that influence solo-commuting generally ignores the effects of larger regional influences (e.g., the quality of the regional bus system) on mode splits. These regional factors can be controlled for by taking the difference in drive-alone shares for an SEC and drive-alone shares for the entire region in which the SEC lies. The variable which measures these differences, DRIVDIFF, was modeled, and the stepwise results are shown in Table 6.2. The results are fairly similar to those of the previous model, except that two land use variables and only one supply-side variable entered this model. A reasonably good fit of the data was obtained and all of the variables that entered the model have coefficients which match *a priori* expectations.

Table 6.2 shows, as before, that the introduction of a modal competitor, namely vanpools, decreases the dominance of the private

Table 6.2   Stepwise regression results on factors influencing SEC drive-alone commuting relative to regional average.

	Dependent variable: DRIVDIFF			
Variable	Beta coefficient	Standard error	t statistic	Probability
OFFICE	0.13623	0.05803	2.347	.0255
RSFT/EMP	−0.00969	0.00427	−2.269	.0304
VANSRUN	−0.09665	0.03141	−3.077	.0043
Intercept	0.09738	0.03897	0.028	.9402

Summary statistics:
  Number of observations = 37
  R-squared = .373
  F statistic = 6.145
  Probability = .0021

Variable definitions:
  DRIVDIFF = Drive alone work trip percentage minus regional drive alone percentage.
  OFFICE   = Percentage of total floorspace in office use.
  RSFT/EMP = Retail square footage within 3 mile radius of SEC per on-site employee.
  VANSRUN   = Number of company vans in daily operation.

automobile in SECs.[5] Every 20 vans reduce the share of trips made
to an SEC by solo-commuters by about 2 per cent over the share for
a typical workplace in the region. And as before, office environments
seem to increase the relative dependency of SEC workers on their
automobiles (i.e., relative to the "typical" worker in the region). The
additional land use variable that has entered this second model gauges
the relative amount of retail space nearby (RSFT/EMP). The negative
sign on this variable suggests that the relative automobile dependency
of SEC workers declines as the amount of retail space per employee
in reasonable proximity to the SEC increases. As an indicator of
land use diversity, it is clear that nearby retail and other mixed-use
offerings encourage workers to choose other commuting options to
driving alone.

In sum, the primary site factor which seems to influence how dominant solo-commuting will be in an SEC setting is land use composition.
Specifically, the share of space in office use and the relative availability
of nearby retail activities appear to have a significant affect on the share
of work trips that are driven alone. Other work site variables, such
as density, size, and lotting practices, did not enter either equation.
This does not necessarily mean that these factors are irrelevant,
but rather that land use composition appears to be a particularly
influential factor. Despite the relatively high explanatory powers of
these models, however, land use, in and of itself, did not emerge as a
tremendously strong predictor of mode choice. For instance, an SEC
with 20 per cent of floorspace devoted to office use could be expected
to average only around a 6 per cent smaller share of work trips made
by solo-commuting than an SEC with 70 per cent office space that
was otherwise identical. Thus, land use mixing only seems to yield
marginal dividends in reducing solo-commuting. Combined with other
initiatives, however, this could mean the difference between gridlock
and circulation in some settings. Overall, more varied land uses appear
to offer a reasonably good potential for reducing auto dependency in
suburban employment settings.

Rideshare model

Solo-commuting constitutes over 80 per cent of all work trips made
to the overwhelming majority of SECs studied. The only serious
competitor in most instances is vehicle-pooling, whether by private
automobile or van. Table 6.3 presents the best model obtained for
predicting RIDESHAR – the percentage of work trips by vanpool or
carpool. The model, which explained one-half of the total variation
in RIDESHAR, offers a slightly different perspective on the mode
choices of SEC workers from the two prior ones.

Table 6.3 **Stepwise regression results on factors influencing percentage of work trips, by rideshare modes.**

	Dependent variable: RIDESHAR			
Variable	Beta coefficient	Standard error	t statistic	Probability
VANSRUN	0.15264	0.03618	4.218	.0002
EMP/INTC	0.00044	0.00017	2.582	.0151
J/HAREA	0.08632	0.04566	1.850	.0804
OFFICE	− 0.05686	0.03477	1.635	.1089
Intercept	11.10422	2.96415	3.746	.0008

Summary statistics:
  Number of observations = 35
  R-squared = .499
  F statistic = 7.226
  Probability = .0004

Variable definitions:
  RIDESHAR = Percentage of works trips by vanpool or carpool.
  VANSRUN = Number of company vans in daily operation.
  EMP/INTC = Employees per freeway interchange within a five mile radius.
  J/HAREA = Ratio of on-site employees to estimated housing units within a three mile radius of SEC.
  OFFICE = Percentage of total floorspace in office use.

The two supply-side variables that entered the equation reinforce what was learned from the prior models. The share of work trips by vanpools or carpools rises as more vans are sponsored by companies and the relative number of access points to the site falls (i.e., the variables EMP/INTC rises). Both variables are statistically significant at the 0.05 probability level.

The variable OFFICE further confirms the importance of land use mixing on commute choices. The equation suggests that as office uses become more dominant, ridesharing can be expected to slip in its share of the commuting market. It follows that unless other facilities are situated at a site – most importantly, consumer services such as restaurants and banks – then SEC employees will be less inclined to participate in a vanpool or carpool program.

The inclusion of the other land use variable in Table 6.3 poses an interesting paradox, of sorts. The variable J/HAREA, which reflects the degree to which jobs and housing units are in balance, suggests that when there is a relative shortage of nearby housing, employees are more likely to live farther away and vehicle-pool. By extension, when housing is more plentiful nearby, relatively fewer commutes will be made in carpools or vanpools. Thus, jobs–housing balances tend to work against carpooling and vanpooling. For short distances, ridesharing is unattractive because the time spent picking up other passengers en route is generally viewed as excessive. Thus, balancing jobs and housing can not be expected necessarily to reduce solo-commuting. It might even encourage some to drive to work. In a balanced environment, however, more commuters would be driving short distances on mainly local streets rather than mixing with through traffic on freeways. The other primary benefit of jobs–housing balances, of course, is that some employees would be more inclined to walk or cycle to work. The next subsection explores whether this has been the case.

Walking–cycling models

The difficulty in studying the influence of jobs–housing levels on the incidence of walking and cycling trips is that the majority of SEC cases have no on-site units. Thus, the inclusion of the variable measuring on-site jobs indexed to on-site housing units would eliminate many cases from the analysis. Accordingly, two separate models were produced for estimating the shares of trips by walking and cycling modes, one without the jobs–housing variable and the other with it.

The first model is shown in Table 6.4. It fits the data fairly closely, explaining about two-thirds of the variation in the dependent variable WALKBIKE. The supply-side variable that entered the first equation reflected the level of vanpool service (EMP/VAN). The sign on EMP/VAN's coefficient suggests that where there are few vans relative

Table 6.4 Stepwise regression results on factors influencing percentage of work trips by walking and cycling modes.

Variable	Beta coefficient	Standard error	t statistic	Probability
		Model One		
	Dependent variable: WALKBIKE			
EMP/VAN	0.00009	0.00002	5.323	.0000
RETAIL	0.05861	0.02363	2.480	.0190
EMPLOYMT	0.00529	0.00303	1.746	.0910
Intercept	−0.01309	0.04455	−0.029	.9768

Summary statistics:
  Number of observations = 36
  R-squared = .663
  F statistic = 19.727
  Probability = .0000

Variable definitions:
  WALKBIKE = Percentage of work trips by walking or cycling.
  EMP/VAN   = Employees per on-site company sponsored van in operation.
  RETAIL   = Percentage of total floorspace in retail use.
  EMPLOYMT = Size of full-time workforce, in thousands.

to the number of employees, the share of commutes made by foot or via bicycle increases, all things equal. This probably reflects less the fact that walking can serve as a substitute for vanpooling, but rather that more balanced, mixed-use settings tend to have high shares of walking and relatively low shares of vanpooling. One can surmise, then, that factors like jobs–housing balance and land use mixtures are intervening influences on the relationship between walking and vanpooling.

The two land use variables that entered the model shown in Table 6.4 are RETAIL and EMPLOYMT, tapping the "compositional" and "size" dimensions of SEC sites. Importantly, the equation suggests that walking and cycling trips are more likely to occur as the share of floorspace devoted to retail activities increases. The availability of on-site retail activities, one can infer, allows workers to take care of personal business and other chores by foot, freeing them of the need to have an automobile available. The equation further suggests that as the employment base of an SEC increases, so does the share of walking and cycling trips.

The second model sought to explore the direct influence of jobs–housing balances on the variable WALKBIKE. The resulting equation, which is summarized in Table 6.5, was based on 18 fewer cases since a number of SECs had missing values for JOB/HOUS. As in the first model, both EMP/VAN and RETAIL entered this model of reduced cases, suggesting that these variables are fairly

Table 6.5 Stepwise regression results of factors influencing percentage of work trips, by walking and cycling modes.

	Model Two			
	Dependent variable; WALKBIKE			
Variable	Beta coefficient	Standard error	t statistic	Probability
EMP/VAN	0.00011	0.00003	4.507	0.0009
JOB/HOUS	−0.01757	0.00963	−1.825	0.0885
RETAIL	0.05486	0.02739	2.007	0.0622
Intercept	0.70761	0.78366	0.903	0.3859

Summary statistics:
  Number of observations = 18
  R-squared = .693
  F statistic = 8.271
  Probability = .0037

Variable definitions:
  WALKBIKE = Percentage of work trips by walking or cycling.
  EMP/VAN = Employees per on-site company sponsored van in operation.
  JOB/HOUS = Employees per on-site housing unit.
  RETAIL = Percentage of total floorspace in retail use.

robust.[6] The sign on JOB/HOUS is consistent with expectations. In general, where there are many more jobs than on-site housing units, the share of commutes made by foot or bicycle falls. Although the relationship is not very strong, the equation does suggest that one of the marginal benefits of jobs–housing balancing is to invite more foot travel and cycling.

Summary of mode choice models

Overall, the models presented in this section seem to confirm the hypotheses posited regarding the affects of mixed-use environments on commuting.[7] Single-use office settings seem to induce solo-commuting, whereas work environments that are more varied, both on-site and nearby, generally encourage more ridesharing, walking, and cycling. Particularly important to ridesharing is the availability of consumer retail services. While the synchronization of job and housing growth in an SEC setting could be expected to encourage more foot and bicycle travel, at the same time, ridesharing and vehicle occupancy levels could be expected to fall off somewhat. The benefits of jobs–housing balancing, therefore, relate more to the shortening of vehicular trips and the easing of local through traffic conflicts than to inducing people to walk or cycle to work.

6.3   Factors influencing traffic conditions around SECs

This section examines the affects of site variables on average commuting speeds, travel times, and levels of service on principal thoroughfares serving SECs. Since so many other off-site factors affect local traffic conditions, the estimated models rest heavily on *ceteris paribus* assumptions. Thus, the analyses presented below examine the joint affects of density, project size, scale, and workforce composition on traffic conditions, with all other influences held constant.

Commuting speed model

Table 6.6 summarizes the best fitting model for explaining average commuting speeds to SECs based on available data. All of the variables that entered the stepwise model seem logical and the overall model has reasonably good predictive abilities, as suggested by the R-squared statistic of 0.53.

The variable which reflects the relative level of highway capacity is EMP/FWYM. All else equal, the more employees per mile of freeway within a 5-mile radius of the SEC, the slower workers generally travel

Table 6.6 **Stepwise regression results of factors influencing average commuting speeds.**

| | Dependent variable: SPEED | | | |
Variable	Beta coefficient	Standard error	t statistic	Probability
EMP/FWYM	− 0.00059	0.00032	− 1.852	.0789
JOB/HOUS	− 0.09093	0.04079	− 2.229	.0374
EMP/ACRE	− 0.10190	0.05178	− 1.968	.0631
Intercept	37.22287	2.31963	16.047	.0000

Summary statistics:
  Number of observations = 26
  R-squared = .532
  F statistic = 7.555
  Probability = .0014

Variable definitions:
  SPEED   =   Average travel speed for journey-to-work trip (m.p.h.). See Table
               3.6, n. 2 for further definition.
  EMP/FWYM =   Employees per directional mile of freeways within 5 miles of SEC.
  JOB/HOUS =   Employees per on-site housing unit.
  EMP/ACRE =   Employees per acre.

to work. Thus, employees working at large office complexes served by a single freeway can generally expect to commute at slower average speeds than a contemporary who works in a small development served by two freeways.

The two work site variables that entered this equation are JOB/HOUS and EMP/ACRE. Those who work in settings with far more jobs than on-site housing units and large numbers of workers per acre can generally expect to commute at relatively slow average speeds. For the typical SEC with a jobs–housing ratio of 30, workers generally could be expected to commute at speeds 2.6 m.p.h. below workers in new towns with roughly comparable numbers of jobs and housing units. The relationship between jobs–housing levels and commuting speeds, of course, is an indirect one. Most likely, SECs with high ratios of jobs–housing have other characteristics which influence commuting speeds, such as higher densities and single-use characters that increase the relative auto-dependency of workers. The inverse relationship between SPEED and EMP/ACRE does suggest that high employment densities are associated with slower average travel speeds.

Travel time model

The best-fitting model developed for explaining average commute times of SEC employees demonstrates fairly modest predictive abilities. From Table 6.7, only two variables entered the model. EMP/FWYM again

Table 6.7 **Stepwise regression results of factors related to average journey-to-work travel time.**

| | Dependent variable: TIME | | | |
Variable	Beta coefficient	Standard error	t statistic	Probability
EMPENT	−74.97186	22.08247	−3.395	0.0016
EMP/FWYM	0.00047	0.00021	2.188	0.0349
Intercept	63.22291	12.13402	5.210	0.0000

Summary statistics:
　Number of observations = 44
　R-squared = .305
　F statistic = 8.337
　Probability = .0010

Variable definitions:
TIME 　　　= 　Average one-way travel time for journey to work, in minutes.
EMPENT 　 = 　Employment entropy index, computed as: $\Sigma p_i*(\log_{10}p_i)$, where p_i is the proportion of employees in job classification i. In this analysis, five job classifications were used: management; administrative; technical; clerical; and others. The minimum value for this index is zero, signifying all jobs are within one category. The maximum value is $\log_{10}(K)$, where K is the number of categories which in this case is 5, which thus equals 0.699. This signifies maximum heterogeneity, which means an equal spread of jobs among all groups. Thus, this index is used to reflect the relative degree of job variation across employment classifications for each SEC. See chapter 4, section 4.2, for a further discussion of the entropy index.
EMP/FWYM = 　Employees per directional mile of freeways within 5 miles of SEC.

reflects the relative supply of nearby freeway capacity. In general, where there are comparatively few directional miles of freeway per SEC employee, travel times increase. The other variable that entered, EMPENT, reflects the degree of job diversification at the work site. Those working in SECs with the greatest variety of jobs among administrative, technical, and clerical positions seem to enjoy shorter average commutes. Of course, the relationship here is an associative one rather than a direct causal one. Since EMPENT was found to be slightly negatively correlated with average commuting distances, one can infer that the shorter commute times for more varied workforce settings is due, in part, to the fact that employees of these places tend to reside closer to their jobs.

Level of service models

Of course, the two factors that directly account for level of service are the volume of traffic and the amount of roadspace. In this analysis, the intent was less to build a predictive model and more to identify which set of site variables was most closely associated with levels of service. Since level of service is measured on an ordinal scale, using

Table 6.8 Stepwise regression results on factors related to level of service on main freeways serving SECs.

| Variable | Dependent variable: FWYLOS | | | |
	Beta coefficient	Standard error	t statistic	Probability
FLOORSPC	0.03638	.01301	2.796	.0072
EMP/ACRE	0.01792	.00694	2.581	.0127
JOB/HOUS	0.01279	.00713	1.794	.0872
Intercept	3.36931	.25909	13.005	.0000

Summary statistics:
  Number of observations = 26
  R-squared = .335
  F statistic = 6.492
  Probability = .0030

Variable definitions:
  FWYLOS   =   Numeric index of peak period level of service on primary freeway serving
                SEC, wherein ordinal values are assigned to level of service as follows: A
                =1; B = 2; C = 3; D = 4; E = 5; F = 6. Thus, a low value represents a
                high, or free flow, level of service. A high value for FWYLOS, on the
                other hand, represents a low, or forced flow, level of service. See chapter
                3, section 3.7 for further discussion on level of service.
  EMP/ACRE =   Employees per acre.
  JOB/HOUS =   Employees per on-site housing unit.
  FLOORSPC =   Total commercial–office–industrial floorspace, in millions of square feet.

a regression framework to account for variations in service quality can be problematic. Specifically, least squares estimation rests on the assumption that the dependent variable is continuous and that the unknown sources of variation (represented by the error term) are normally distributed. Since cases were assigned values of 1 for level of service A, 2 for B, 3 for C, and so forth, the normality assumption of least squares estimation is violated when the dependent variable, level of service, is estimated. Regression analysis, however, can still provide useful insights into factors affecting ordinal variables like level of service, since reasonably reliable estimates can be obtained when there are five or more discrete ordinal values, such as in this case (Blalock 1979). As long as the goodness-of-fit statistics are interpreted with caution, models estimated for ordinal-scale dependent variables can prove informative.

Table 6.8 summarizes the stepwise equation estimated for the variable FWYLOS – peak-hour level of service on the primary freeways serving SECs. Three work site variables entered the model. In interpreting these variables, it should be kept in mind that high values of FWYLOS denote congested service quality (i.e., levels of service D, E, and F). Thus, major connecting freeways tend to be most congested around SECs with large amounts of office–commercial floorspace, high

Table 6.9 Stepwise regression results on factors related to level of service on main surface arterials serving SECs.

| | Dependent variable: RWYLOS | | | |
Variable	Beta coefficient	Standard error	t statistic	Probability
FAR	0.2320	.0938	2.475	.0166
PROFSHAR	−0.02189	.0083	−2.619	.0115
FLOORSPC	0.0291	.0105	2.772	.0077
Intercept	4.3448	.4384	9.911	.0000

Summary statistics:
  Number of observations = 57
  R-squared = .272
  F statistic = 6.377
  Probability = .0009

Variable definitions:

RWYLOS	=	Numeric index of peak period level of service on primary surface roadway serving SEC, wherein ordinal values are assigned to level of service as follows: A = 1; B = 2; C = 3; D = 4; E = 5; F = 6. Thus, a low value represents a high, or free flow, level of service. A high value for RWYLOS, on the other hand, represents a low, or forced flow, level of service. See chapter 3, section 3.7 for further discussion on level of service.
FAR	=	Floor area ratio, equals to total square footage of floorspace divided by total square footage of land in SEC.
PROFSHAR	=	Percentage of workforce in management, administrative, or technical job classifications.
FLOORSPC	=	Total commercial-office-industrial floorspace, in millions of square feet.

employment densities, and large jobs–housing imbalances. Thus, size, density, and land use composition appear to be working in tandem to influence levels of service on nearby freeways. All things equal, suburban centers that are big, dense, and housing-free in character tend to suffer the worst nearby freeway conditions.

Site factors associated with level of service on major arterials serving SECs were found to be only slightly different. From Table 6.9, it is seen that surface arterials tend to be most congested around large, dense suburban work settings as well. Take, for instance, an SEC with 1 million square feet of non-residential floorspace, a FAR of one, and a peak hour level of service of C on its main connecting arterial. Based on the coefficients in Table 6.9, if that same SEC were to double in size and if the FAR was to catapult from one to five, then, all else equal, peak hour level of service could be expected to fall one notch to D. The workforce variable in Table 6.9 that was found to be most associated with roadway level of service was PROFSHAR – the percentage of employees in professional positions. Where this percentage is high, traffic on surface streets tends to flow more smoothly. The most logical explanation for this is that, although professional workers tend to be heavily auto-reliant, they also tend to enjoy more flex-time privileges, giving rise to a more even temporal distribution of trip-making during morning and evening hours. This point is confirmed in the Pleasanton analysis in section 6.7.

Summary of models on traffic conditions

The analysis in this section was able to demonstrate that several site characteristics are closely related to local traffic conditions. Denser and large-scale SEC settings tend to have more congested nearby thoroughfares and relatively slow employee commutes. Where jobs far exceed housing, average commute speeds also tend to be slower and connecting freeways are more likely to be jammed. Where there is a closer match-up between jobs and housing, on the other hand, freeways tend to flow better, possibly because the conflict between through and local traffic is reduced.

While land use composition emerged as the key site factor influencing mode choices of SEC workers, density appears to exert the most influence on local traffic conditions. In many ways, density performs a multiple role: by inducing congestion, it encourages people to find alternatives to driving to work; at the same time, higher densities enable alternative modes, like bus transit, to operate more efficiently and successfully compete with the private automobile. The transfer of trips from automobiles to buses and vans in turn helps to free road space and perhaps induce latent travel. To the extent that viable alternatives to the automobile are available, then, the congestion-producing affects of high density SECs may only be transitional. In the long term, higher density work environs could be expected to lure enough employees to buses and vans so as to keep congestion below the level it would have reached had workers remained highly auto-dependent. Unfortunately, determining exactly what this density threshold is for suburban work settings can only occur over time, as our knowledge base on land use–transportation relationships in the suburbs accumulates.

6.4   Factors related to parking standards at SECs

As already noted, the one prominent feature of nearly all suburban work settings is the abundance of off-street, surface parking. This section investigates those site factors which appear to be most closely associated with high levels of parking at SECs. Table 6.10 presents the best-fitting stepwise model developed for the dependent variable PARK/EMP – average parking spaces per employee in an SEC. Several different dimensions are reflected in this model. One, parking rates

Table 6.10 Stepwise regression results of factors related to parking per employee standards.

| | Dependent variable: PARK/EMP | | | |
Variable	Beta coefficient	Standard error	t statistic	Probability
RETAIL	0.00674	.00251	2.688	.0104
PARKING$	−0.06781	.02634	− 2.574	.0139
EMPLOYMT	−0.00079	.00052	− 1.510	.1390
Intercept	1.01285	.04255	23.804	.0000

Summary statistics:
  Number of observations = 43
  R-squared = .316
  F statistic = 5.537
  Probability = .0031

Variable definitions:
  PARK/EMP   =   Parking spaces per employee.
  RETAIL   =   Percentage of total floorspace in retail use.
  PARKING$ =   Most frequently occurring daily price for parking, in dollars.
  EMPLOYMT   =   Size of full-time work force, in thousands.

are generally the highest in SECs with proportionally high shares of retail use. Many parking spaces for retail establishments, however, are designed for customers rather than employees, so average parking rates become inflated. The equation also indicates that parking per employee generally decreases as daily parking fees rise. Prices, then, appear to ration parking demand, reducing the number of spaces offered. Finally, the size of the laborforce also interacts negatively with rates of parking supply – SECs with the largest employment bases tend to have the fewest number of parking stalls per worker.

When parking standards are examined on a per square foot basis, several other variables enter into the best-fitting equation. Table 6.11 shows that besides retail percentages and employment size, parking rates per 1,000 square feet are also influenced by density and regional location. The model suggests that parking rates tend to be lower in denser, closer-in SECs. This probably reflects influences of higher land values in higher-density, more central suburbs, prompting developers to cut back somewhat on their parking supplies. Higher land costs force decked parking structures to be built; these normally consume around 8 per cent less space than equivalent size surface facilities because tenants accept narrower aisles and smaller stalls in return for closer proximity to their offices (Gauldin 1979). According to the model in Table 6.11, a suburban office building with a floor area ratio of 3.5 could be expected to have one less parking stall per 1,000 square feet of space than an otherwise comparable building with an FAR of 1.0. Where parking seems to be most overbuilt, then, is at low density

Table 6.11 **Stepwise regression results of factors related to parking per square footage standards.**

| Variable | Dependent variable PARK/SQFT | | | |
	Beta coefficient	Standard error	t statistic	Probability
FAR	−0.2926	0.0898	− 3.259	.0025
RETAIL	0.0382	0.0108	3.539	.0012
CBDMILES	0.0257	0.0106	2.431	.0203
EMPLOYMT	−0.0042	0.0023	− 1.819	.0775
Intercept	3.3015	0.2624	12.583	.0000

Summary statistics:
  Number of observations = 43
  R-squared = .375
  F statistic = 5.246
  Probability = .0020

Variable definitions:
PARK/SQF	=	Parking spaces per 1,000 gross square feet of floorspace.
FAR	=	Floor area ratio, equal to total square footage of floorspace divided by total square footage of land in SEC.
RETAIL	=	Percentage of total floorspace in retail use.
CBDMILES	=	Approximate radial miles to regional CBD.
EMPLOYMT	=	Size of full-time workforce, in thousands.

SECs situated some distance from downtown, which seems to describe campus-style business parks in most regions of the US.

The relationship between parking supply and the independent variables FAR and RETAIL is further illustrated in Figures 6.1 and 6.2. Figure 6.1 shows the slight inverse relationship between parking

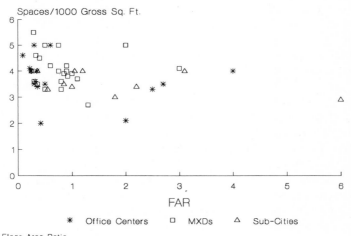

Figure 6.1 Plot of parking supply versus FAR, by SEC groups.

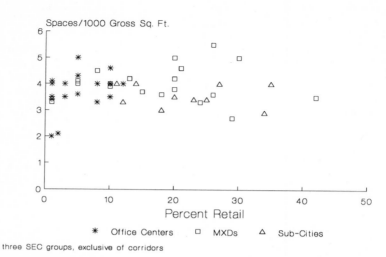

Figure 6.2 Plot of percentage of floorspace in retail use versus supply, by SEC groups.

per 1,000 square feet and FAR among all cases. Within SEC groups, however, slightly different patterns emerge. The strongest inverse relationship between parking supply and density is for MXDs. The lower parking supplies of denser MXDs likely reflect the tendency of businesses and shopkeepers in these areas to share parking facilities, particularly in the face of higher land prices. A far weaker pattern exists for sub-cities. Most sub-cities appear to provide facilities at the level of 3 to 4 spaces per 1,000 square feet, regardless of density levels. Office parks and centers do seem to shave their parking supplies per worker as their density increases, however the relationship is not a particularly strong one.

Figure 6.2 shows the influence of retail space on supply levels. Among all SECs, the relationship appears to be fairly weak, appearing as a cloud of points in the scatterplot. Among groups, however, a stronger pattern emerges. For office parks and centers, parking rates clearly increase as the share of floorspace in retail use rises. For MXDs, however, rates appear to decline slightly as retail becomes more dominant, perhaps reflecting the existence of more shared-use arrangements in these settings. Finally, as was the case for the FAR variable, sub-cities seem to provide consistent parking levels regardless of the prevalence of the retail component.

In sum, high densities and large employment bases seem to lower parking standards of SECs while retail uses generally inflate parking levels. It should be kept in mind, however, that many retail spaces are reserved for customers as opposed to workers. On the one hand, retail settings drive up parking standards to meet peak season demands for parking. On the other hand, retail settings can help lower parking standards because shared-use possibilities increase. In general, the net impact of retail uses in SECs has been to raise parking supplies slightly, but also to allow a more even distribution of usage throughout the day, week, and year.

6.5 Factors related to jobs–housing levels around SECs

This research has demonstrated that jobs–housing mismatches induce SEC workers to use motorized travel modes to get to work and lower the incidence of walking and cycling commutes. While around 4 per cent of suburban workers in the US walked or cycled to work in 1980 (Pisarski 1987), among the SECs studied, the average share was about 2 per cent. Moreover, it has been argued, jobs–housing mismatches force larger shares of SEC commuters on to regional thoroughfares, setting the stage for conflicts between SEC-oriented traffic and regional through trips. Providing nearby housing targeted to the earnings levels and taste preferences of suburban workers, it is felt, could reduce these mismatches.

What site factors seem to be related to jobs–housing levels both within and close to SECs? Table 6.12 shows the stepwise results for predicting JOB/HOUS – the ratio of SEC employment to on-site housing units. A very good fit was obtained for the 21 cases with complete data, evidenced by the high R-squared and F statistics.

Table 6.12 **Stepwise-regression results of factors related to on-site jobs–housing ratios in SECs.**

| Variable | Dependent variable: JOB/HOUS | | | |
	Beta coefficient	Standard error	t statistic	Probability
PROFSHAR	3.1518	0.4842	6.509	.0000
SQFT/EMP	−0.0437	0.0199	−2.191	.0458
CBDMILES	−1.0698	0.4021	−2.661	.0186
AVGHOUS $	0.1612	0.0892	1.807	.0922
Intercept	−7.5153	20.8232	−0.361	.7236

Summary statistics:
  Number of observations = 21
  R-squared = .818
  F statistic = 15.736
  Probability = .0000

Variable Definitions:
  JOB/HOUS = Employees per on-site housing unit.
  PROFSHAR = Percentage of workforce in management, administrative, or technical job classifications.
  SQFT/EMP = Square feet of non-residential floorspace per employee.
  CBDMILES = Approximate radial miles to regional CBD.
  AVGHOUS $ = Estimated average purchase price of single-family housing unit within a 3 mile radius of SEC, in thousands of dollars.

Looking at the signs of the coefficients, there appears to be the highest excess of jobs over housing units within SECs in the settings where: the workforce is made up predominantly of professional employees; densities are low (reflected by the square feet of workspace per employee); average single-family homes nearby are comparatively expensive; and the SEC is relatively close to the regional CBD. Of all the predictors, the composition of the laborforce appears to be most strongly related to jobs–housing levels. The model suggests that every 1 per cent increase in the share of jobs in professional positions is associated with an increase in the ratio of jobs relative to on-site housing units of about three. Overall, it appears that the fewest on-site housing provisions tend to be provided in SECs that are low density, professionally oriented office parks that are located in more inner-tier suburbs.

Again, people do not have to live and work within the same compound for the benefits of jobs–housing balancing to accrue. Striking a balance in job and housing growth within a reasonable radius of an SEC is perhaps more important from a regional mobility standpoint. Table 6.13 presents those site variables that were found to be most closely associated with the ratio of SEC jobs to housing units within a 3 mile radius of the SEC, expressed as the variable J/HAREA. In general, SECs with the least amount of nearby housing relative to their workforce sizes tend to have large shares of retail space and clerical workers, and comparatively few management personnel. Thus, SECs comprised of significant shares of clerical workers, a group that usually earns moderate salaries, tend to have the fewest housing opportunities nearby.

Table 6.13 Stepwise regression results of factors related to ratio of jobs to nearby housing units.

Variable	Dependent variable: J/HAREA			
	Beta coefficient	Standard error	t statistic	Probability
RETAIL	0.5532	0.2138	2.588	.0147
CLERICL	0.4582	0.2498	1.834	.0766
MANAGEM	−0.3558	0.2215	−1.606	.1187
Intercept	−7.2178	8.3901	−0.860	.3965

Summary statistics:
  Number of observations = 35
  R-squared = .245
  F statistic = 3.241
  Probability = .0358

Variable definitions:
  J/HAREA   = Ratio of on-site employees to estimated housing units within a 3 mile
                     radius of SEC.
  RETAIL   = Percentage of total floorspace in retail use.
  CLERICL   = Percentage of workforce in clerical positions.
  MANAGEM = Percentage of workforce in management positions.

An interesting relationship between jobs–housing levels and workforce composition has thus emerged from this analysis. SECs with high shares of non-professional (e.g., clerical, sales) workers tend to have more housing units on-site however comparatively few housing opportunities nearby. Chapter 5 showed that the housing units available near SECs with high shares of non-professional workers also tend to be more expensive. The inference that can be drawn seems well-supported: many SEC employees are unable to live within short commuting distances of their workplaces because nearby housing tends to be in short supply and relatively expensive.

6.6   Factors related to property ownership patterns in SECs

A final set of relationships explored in this chapter involved land ownership patterns. It has been hypothesized that centralized control over SEC projects allows more coordinated designs as well as the sharing of facilities, such as access roads, parking, and tenant support services. As a result, projects developed by relatively few landholders could be expected to have higher average densities and be less spread out.

   Do SECs with fewer "chefs in the kitchen" average higher site densities? The stepwise regression results shown in Table 6.14 shed some light on this. Ignoring the large corridor cases, the model reveals that

Table 6.14   Stepwise regression results on factors related to property ownership patterns.

| Variable | Dependent variable: PROPOWN | | | |
	Beta coefficient	Standard error	t statistic	Probability
OFFICE	−3.8575	0.9752	−3.956	0.0004
LAND/EMP	0.0030	0.0007	4.133	0.0002
RSQT/EMP	0.2241	0.0566	3.958	0.0004
Intercept	287.0762	74.0195	3.878	0.0004

Summary statistics:
   Number of observations = 40
   R-squared = .740
   F statistic = 33.18
   Probability = .0000

Variable definitions:
   PROPOWN   = Number of property owners, non-residential land only.
   OFFICE   = Per cent of total floorspace in office use.
   LAND/EMP = Square feet of land per employee, in thousands.
   RSQT/EMP = Retail square footage of floorspace within a 3 mile radius per on-site employee.

the number of non-residential property owners within an SEC tends to be large in settings with relatively large retail components (RSQT/EMP) and low employment densities (LAND/EMP). Predominantly office environments, on the other hand, are associated with comparatively few property owners. This equation, it should be noted, is not meant to be a causal expression. In fact, the causality between the variables shown in Table 6.14 is probably in the other direction – the number of property owners influences density and land use composition, not vice versa. Still, the hypothesis postulated above appears to be borne out. SECs associated with fewer property owners tend to have higher average employment densities (i.e., less land area per employee).

Table 6.15 provides an additional perspective on SEC land ownership influences. SECs with higher FARs and closer match-ups of employees and on-site housing units tend to have larger shares of land owned by developers than by private firms.[8] While the statistical fit of this model is only of moderate significance, it does appear that in SEC settings where developers retain control over most of the land, densities are higher and on-site jobs and housing units tend to be more closely aligned.

Table 6.15 Stepwise regression results on factors related to developer land ownership shares.

| | | Dependent variable: DEVSHARE | | |
Variable	Beta coefficient	Standard error	t statistic	Probability
JOB/HOUS	−0.2067	0.1145	−1.805	.0899
FAR	5.1850	3.1051	1.670	.1144
Intercept	0.7225	0.0731	9.886	.0000

Summary statistics:
  Number of observations = 22
  R-squared = .291
  F statistic = 3.276
  Probability = .0642

Variable definitions:
  DEVSHAR   =   Percentage of non-residential land owned by developers.
  JOB/HOUS =   Employees per on-site housing unit.
  FAR   =   Floor area ratio, equal to total square footage of floorspace divided by
                total square footage of land in SEC.

Photo 6.1   Pleasanton, California. New low-rise office buildings dot the landscape along Interstate 580 in suburban Pleasanton. (Photo by the author.)

6.7   Case summary of work site factors influencing commuter choices in Pleasanton, California

To augment the national-level analysis, a disaggregate study of commute choices was conducted among individual employees of Pleasanton, California, a fast growing suburb in the San Francisco Bay Area. The following analysis focuses on how work site characteristics were related to the travel choices of Pleasanton workers, with choice expressed in terms of mode and time period of travel.

Case setting and data sources

The city of Pleasanton was selected as a case setting both because it has a substantial suburban office concentration and because survey data on the travel characteristics of Pleasanton's workers have been collected annually since 1984. Figure 6.3 depicts the location of Pleasanton in the San Francisco Bay Area. The community lies approximately 35 miles east of downtown San Francisco in the north-central portion of Alameda County, near the confluence of two major freeways, Interstate 580 and Interstate 680. Pleasanton's population jumped from 18,328 in 1970 to 45,500 in 1986 (California Department of Finance 1986). Employment has similarly grown at a rapid pace, rising from 9,090 in 1980 to an estimated 18,500 in 1985. Consequently, Pleasanton has become more of a mixed community over time, changing from a place with a predominantly bedroom character to one with more of a balance of jobs and residents.

A significant share of Pleasanton's office growth since the early 1980s has occurred in the Hacienda Business Park, one of the case

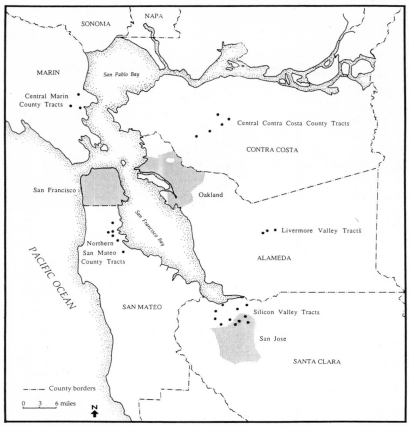

Figure 6.3 Location of Pleasanton in the San Francisco Bay Area.

SECs used in this study. The 860-acre Hacienda project presently has
over 5,000 workers and is expected to grow to over 40,000 at build
out, sometime after the year 2000.[9] It was the announcement of the
Hacienda project, coupled with steadily worsening congestion on local
thoroughfares, that prompted a number of Pleasanton citizens to form
an action committee in the early 1980s to respond to mounting traffic
problems. The overwhelming consensus of local citizens was to hold
employers accountable for the traffic impacts of their workers and to
take action to contain peak hour, single-occupant automobile travel.
In response, a Transportation System Management (TSM) ordinance
was passed by local referendum in late 1984 (Diamond 1985, Cervero
1986b). The ordinance stipulates that no company with 50 or more
employers (or firms in multi-tenant complexes) can have over 55 per
cent of its workforce driving alone to work during peak hours in
1988. Moreover, all participating employers are required to appoint

a "workplace coordinator" to promote ridesharing, post information on vanpooling and other commute alternatives, and conduct annual surveys to monitor progress toward meeting the ordinance's goals. Those failing to comply with the ordinance are subject to fines of $250 per day, or more.

The 1986 Pleasanton Employee Travel Survey formed the basis for the analysis presented in this section. The surveys were mailed to Pleasanton workers in the spring of 1986, eliciting responses on mode, distance, time period, and other characteristics of the commute trip. The 1986 survey secured a response rate of 77 per cent of all Pleasanton workers, representing 14,424 cases among the 1,074 Pleasanton firms subject to the TSM ordinance. In that a large share of these responses was from employees of the Hacienda Business Park and adjoining office parks, this data base offers insights into the travel choices of employees working in a mixed office park/office concentration type of SEC setting.

Summary workforce composition and commuting characteristics

The 1986 survey revealed that Pleasanton's workforce was made up predominantly of management/administrative personnel (26.2 per cent), followed by clerical (21.1 per cent), service (21 per cent), and professional technical workers (17.6 per cent). Pleasanton's workforce was also predominantly female in 1986 – 62 per cent of all survey respondents were women. Indeed, one of the chief reasons why many Bay Area firms have relocated their back office and clerical functions to places like Pleasanton has been to take advantage of suburbia's substantial female labor market.

As in other SECs around the country, the survey showed that the drive-alone automobile was, by far, the most prevalent means of commuting among Pleasanton workers in 1986. Despite Pleasanton's pioneering TSM ordinance, 84.3 per cent of the workforce solo-commuted in 1986, while only 10.2 per cent shared rides. Bus transit carried just 1.7 per cent of Pleasanton employees to work in 1986.

Finally, the survey also showed that around one-third of Pleasanton workers enjoyed flex-time privileges. This far exceeds the share of Bay Area employees who are able to flex their work schedules, which in 1980 was estimated to be around 10 per cent (Jones & Harrison 1983). Commutes made by Pleasanton workers were also generally longer than those made by typical Bay Area workers. The average one-way commute distance was found to be 15.1 miles, markedly higher than the 11.1 mile average home–work distance for Bay Area workers as a whole (US Bureau of Census 1982).

Workplace factors influencing mode choice

To explore factors influencing the modal choices of Pleasanton's workers, binomial logit analysis was performed. Because the Pleasanton survey did not collect information on the cost and service characteristics of different modes, the influences of these variables could not be directly explored. Rather, the survey compiled data primarily on the characteristics of the workplace, allowing the modal influences of factors such as employer size and tenant composition to be studied. Thus, it was only possible to examine the affects of a handful of site variables, notably scale and tenant mixture, on commuting behavior. Accordingly, the collective influences of other factors are assumed to be constant in the analyses which follow.

Table 6.16 summarizes the maximum likelihood estimation results of the stepwise logit model derived from the 1986 survey, where mode choice was expressed in terms of choosing either drive-alone (value=0) or all other travel options (value=1). Because of the dominance of solo-commuting in Pleasanton, mode selection was treated as a simple binary choice – either drive-alone or commute by an alternative means. Moreover, since over two-thirds of the remaining commute trips were by carpool or vanpool, the "other" category largely captured shared-ride forms of commuting. Thus, in the discussion below, the alternative to "drive-alone" is referred to as "shared-ride."

From Table 6.16, all of the explanatory variables were highly significant and had signs consistent with *a priori* expectations.[10] The pseudo R-squared statistic suggests that the model has modest predictive abilities, however, this statistic is only a rough gauge of goodness-of-fit for discrete choice models and is not inviolable (Ben-Akiva & Lerman 1985). All things equal, Table 6.16 suggests that Pleasanton workers are most likely to rideshare if they commute relatively long distances, work for a large company at a single-tenant site, and work in non-professional and non-management positions (i.e., clerical and sales). The tendency to share rides declines, however, when flex-time programs exist and workers arrive to and depart from work at times that vary substantially from the norm.

A number of dimensions of mode choice are being tapped in these findings. Distance works in favor of ridesharing because only over long distances does the time spent picking up carpool and vanpool passengers become a relatively small portion of the total travel time. The propensity to rideshare increases with company size because a critical mass of employees is generally needed if workers are to be successfully matched into carpools. Having workers concentrated in a single-tenant complex also favors ridesharing; multi-tenant complexes, on the other hand, seem to impede the formation of carpools and vanpools because the coordination of ridematching among multiple employers tends to be more complicated than within a single company. Clearly, the odds of attracting suburban workers into carpools and vanpools are much higher for a national headquarters staffed with 5,000 employees than for a building housing 5,000 workers divided among numerous small firms.

From Table 6.16, factors that work against ridesharing are equally revealing. The negative association between professional employment and ridesharing was expected, reflecting both the affect of higher incomes on mode choice as well as the fact that professionals and managers generally place a higher premium on flexible and convenient forms of transportation, notably the drive-alone automobile, than other

Table 6.16   Binomial Logit Results on Likelihood of Selecting Share-Ride Modes

Dependent Variable: SHARIDE

Variable	Beta Coefficient	Standard Error	t Statistic
DIST	0.0237	0.0015	248.21
EMPTYPE	-0.3148	0.0501	-39.37
TENANT	0.3301	0.0559	34.78
NUMEMP	0.0007	0.0002	16.67
FLEXTIME	-0.1452	0.0528	-7.56
ARRIVDIF	-0.0003	0.0001	-4.78
DEPARDIF	-0.0002	0.0001	-2.44
Intercept	-2.0660	0.0541	-1457.93

Summary Statistics:
    Number of observations = 13,483
    Chi-Square = -2(log likelihood ratio) = 447.78, p = 0.000
    Pseudo R-Squared = 1 - (likelihood ratio) = 0.192

Variable Definitions:

SHARIDE = Commute by shared ride or other non-drive alone mode: 1=yes, 0=no.

DIST   = Respondent's reported one-way trip length, in miles.

EMPTYPE = Employment type: 1=professional/management, 0=all other.

TENANT = Tenant composition at worksite: 1=single tenant, 0=multi-tenant.

NUMEMP = Total number of employees at respondent's workplace.

FLEXTIME= Flexibility of respondent's work hours: 1=work hours flexible by 45 minutes, 0=work hours not flexible by 45 minutes.

ARRIVDIF = Difference between respondent's reported arrival time and the modal arrival time at his or her worksite, in minutes.

DEPARDIF= Difference between respondent's reported departure time and the modal departure time at his or her worksite, in minutes.

commuters. The affects of flexible working arrangements and atypical arrival and departure times on ridesharing also seem intuitive since the need to pool rides is less imperative as peak demand is spread over a longer period. Ridematching, moreover, becomes more difficult the more workers' arrival and departure times vary. Cross-tabulating survey results, it was found that only 7.6 per cent of Pleasanton workers with flex-time privileges carpooled or vanpooled, compared to 11.4 per cent of the entire Pleasanton workforce. Clearly, the existence of flex-time opportunities has hampered ridesharing efforts in the case of Pleasanton. This is consistent with the findings of Wegmann & Stokey (1983) that giving employees at the Tennessee Valley Authority near Knoxville greater choice in working hours reduced participation in the Authority's ridesharing program.

While Table 6.16 summarizes statistical associations between mode choice and various workplace factors, it discloses little about the probability of Pleasanton commuters opting for different modes under different circumstances. Figures 6.4 and 6.5 provide a graphic perspective on how sensitive Pleasanton workers are to changes in trip length and firm size as well as several categorical variables when making mode choices. Comparing Figures 6.4 and 6.5, it is

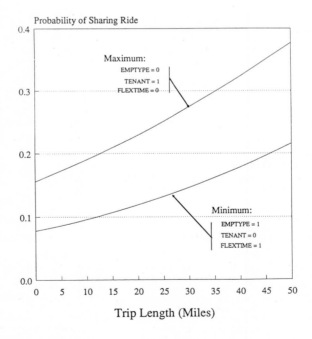

Figure 6.4 Probability of shared-ride commute, by one-way trip length for employees of Pleasanton, California.

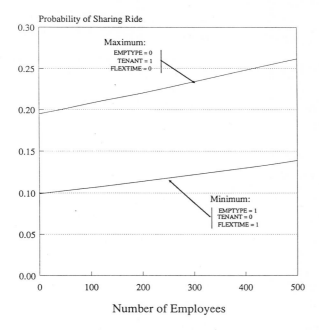

Figure 6.5 Probability of shared-ride commute, by member of employees at worksites in Pleasnaton, California.

evident that ridesharing is more strongly influenced by shifts in trip distance than by changes in employer size. For a clerical employee in a single-tenant project who has no flex-time opportunities, all else equal, the probability of ridesharing is 0.37 if he makes a 50-mile trip and only 0.17 if he commutes 4 miles. However, if this 4-mile commuter is a professional in a multi-tenant project who is able to flex his work schedule, the probability of ridesharing falls even more, to 0.08. From Figure 6.5, the probability of ridesharing also drops noticeably as the firm size variable is perturbed. The clerical worker in a single-tenant project with no flex-time arrangements has a 0.27 probability of ridesharing if his company has 500 workers, compared to a 0.20 probability if the company has just 40 workers.

Overall, the incidence of ridesharing among Pleasanton workers is highly sensitive to changes in commute distance and moderately influenced by changes in company size. The fact that the lines for the minimum and maximum ranges in Figures 6.4 and 6.5 are not parallel, moreover, indicates that significant interaction exists between the variables. Because the top lines are steeper as one moves to the right in both figures, one can infer that the affects of employment type, tenant mix, and flex-time work arrangements on mode choice are proportionally greater for someone traveling 50 miles versus someone traveling 5 miles.

Factors influencing time period of travel

The Pleasanton data also allowed the peaking characteristics of travel to be studied. The logit results summarized in Table 6.17 show factors which are causally related to workers commuting outside of Pleasanton's designated morning peak (7:30–8:30 a.m.) and evening peak (4:30–5:30 p.m.).

The model's coefficients indicate that the likelihood of commuting outside of both peaks increases as an employee's arrival and departure

Table 6.17 Binomial Logit Results on Whether Employee Commutes Outside of Both Peak Hours

Dependent Variable: OUTPEAK

Variable:	Beta Coefficient	Standard Error	t Statistic
ARRIVDIF	0.0071	0.0002	897.03
DEPARDIF	0.0024	0.0001	421.29
SHARIDE	0.4239	0.0586	52.32
NUMEMP	-0.0013	0.0002	-46.89
FLEXTIME	0.2807	0.0465	36.35
TENANT	0.2345	0.0528	19.75
DIST	0.0039	0.0015	6.74
EMPTYPE	-0.1108	0.0451	-6.05
Intercept	-1.6452	0.0497	-1097.41

Summary Statistics:
  Number of observations = 12,332
  Chi-Square = -2(log likelihood ratio) = 2911.91, p = 0.000
  Pseudo R-Squared = 1 - (likelihood ratio) = 0.433

Variable Definitions:

OUTPEAK = Commute outside both the morning (7:30 to 8:30) and evening (4:30 to 5:30) peak hours: 1=yes and 0=no.

ARRIVDIF = Difference between respondent's reported arrival time and the modal arrival time at his or her worksite, in minutes.

DEPARDIF = Difference between respondent's reported departure time and the modal departure time at his or her worksite, in minutes.

SHARIDE = Commute by shared ride or other non-drive alone mode: 1=yes, 0=no.

NUMEMP = Total number of employees at respondent's workplace.

FLEXTIME = Flexibility of respondent's work hours: 1=work hours flexible by 45 minutes or more, 0=work hours not flexible by 45 minutes.

TENANT = Tenant composition at worksite: 1=single tenant, 0=multi-tenant.

DIST = Respondent's reported one-way trip length, in miles.

EMPTYPE = Employment type: 1=professional/management, 0=all other.

times vary significantly from his co-workers', and his commute distance increases, and when he enjoys flex-time privileges. Several variables related to characteristics of the worker and workplace were also significant. The chances of an employee commuting outside of both peaks appear to be the highest when that person is in a non-professional occupation and works for a small, single-tenant company. One can infer that because professionals–managers shoulder major business responsibilities, they tend to arrive at work during peak periods when most other employees arrive.

A sensitivity analysis for the variable OUTPEAK as a function of number of employees (NUMEMP) is shown in Figure 6.6. The figure indicates, for instance, that if John Doe works for a company with 100 employees, the probability that he commutes outside of both peaks is 0.24 if he is a professional–manager who works in a multi-tenant complex, drives alone, and has no flex-time opportunities. If Jane Smith works for a similar size company, but is a clerical worker in a single-tenant complex, shares a ride, and is allowed to flex her work schedule, her probability of commuting outside of both peaks is much higher – 0.47. It is clear from the graph that the likelihood of someone

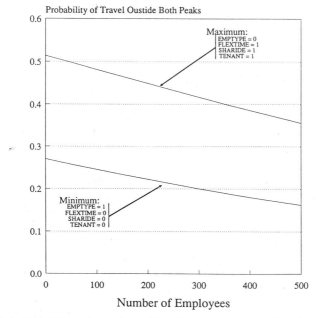

Figure 6.6 Probability of travel outside of a.m and p.m peak hours, by number of employees at work sites in Pleasanton, California.

commuting in non-peak periods is strongly related to their employer's size, their flex-time opportunities, and whether their workplace has a mixture of tenants.

Summary of Pleasanton case analysis

Pleasanton is fairly representative of other suburban areas around the US experiencing rapid growth. It has a largely back-office workforce which predominantly solo-commutes. From this analysis, the following work site characteristics were found to have a strong influence on commute choices in Pleasanton:

(a) *Employment composition*: The incidence of ridesharing increases as the share of the workforce in non-professional occupations increases. Non-professionals are more likely than other workers to commute during the peak period, in part because they tend to enjoy fewer flex-time privileges.

(b) *Firm Size*: The share of commute trips in carpools and vanpools increases with company size. Larger firms also average larger shares of employees commuting at peak hours, also partly because they tend to offer their workers fewer flex-time opportunities.

(c) *Tenant Mixtures*: If a work site is occupied by a single tenant, the odds are greater that employees will share rides.

Collectively, these findings suggest that companies which relocate their predominantly clerical back office staffs in large single-tenant sites and which have rigid work schedules will tend to have relatively high shares of employees who carpool and vanpool to work. On the other hand, they will also tend to have large shares of their employees commuting during peak hours. The implication, then, is that SECs that are designed to accommodate back office workers in large branch facilities are most likely to experience the highest rates of ridesharing as well as the greatest degree of peaking. If ridesharing is deemed important to preserving mobility in an area, then developments catering to large, back office firms might be sought. If, on the other hand, a primary objective is to spread out peak loads, then other kinds of developments might be considered more appropriate for an area.

6.8   Summary of hypothesis tests

The affects of specific site and land use factors on SEC mobility levels are summarized below:

(a) *Density*. Employment densities and FAR appear to influence local traffic conditions more than any single site factor. High density SECs average the slowest employee commutes and the worst levels of service on connecting freeways and arterials. Additionally, high densities appear to work in favor of commute alternatives to the drive-alone automobile. High density SECs also generally have relatively low levels of parking supply, a factor which also likely reduces the share of solo-commutes.

(b) *Land use composition*. Among all of the site variables examined, the degree of land use mixing appears to have the greatest influence on the modal choices of SEC workers. Projects made up almost wholly of offices are associated with solo-commuting. Overall, every 20 per cent increase in the share of total floorspace devoted to office uses was found to result in a 2.4 per cent increase in the share of work trips made by single-occupant drivers, all else equal. The availability of nearby retail services, on the other hand, induces ridesharing. On-site retail facilities are also essential toward attracting more walking and cycling work trips. In general, highly mixed-use centers allow workers to take care of personal chores on foot in a contained area, freeing some of the need to have an automobile at their disposal. Mixed-use environments also allow for more shared parking arrangements, which reduce the total number of spaces in a site and, potentially, the overall scale of a project.

(c) *Size and scale*. The size of SEC activities appears to influence both local traffic conditions and mode choice. SECs with expansive floorareas average the poorest levels of service on connecting freeways and arterials. On average, every additional 1 million square feet of office-commercial floorspace was related to an increase in traffic volume-to-capacity levels of 3–4 per cent, all other factors held constant. Large developments also tend to experience greater peaking of employee arrivals and departures. Large-size employers, on the other hand, are generally more successful in winning their workers over to carpools and vanpools. In Pleasanton, California, for instance, it was found that every 5,000 workers added to office developments increased ridesharing by 3.5 per cent, all else equal. Buildings occupied by a single tenant, moreover, average higher shares of carpoolers and vanpoolers. Overall, suburban work environments with a critical mass of employees appear to be an important prerequisite for mounting and sustaining successful ridesharing programs.

(d) *Jobs–housing balances*. Suburban work settings with a more even balance of jobs and housing tend to have higher shares of employees walking and cycling to work, however they at the same time average lower percentages of ridesharing. These more balanced environments also tend to have less congestion on connecting roadways, possibly because the conflicts between SEC-oriented trips and other through travel are reduced. Jobs–housing mismatches appear to be most common in areas with large shares of employees in clerical, sales, and other moderate-salaried positions. Nearby housing in these settings also tends to be relatively expensive. A logical inference is that appreciable numbers of clerical and service-industry workers in many SEC settings are being priced out of local neighborhoods and forced to live farther from their workplace than they would otherwise choose. The farther away workers live, the greater the likelihood that suburban freeways will become oversubscribed.

Overall, the hypotheses posited in this research appear to be borne out by these empirical findings. While the relationships that were found were not as strong as might be hoped for, in view of the fact that the analysis occurred at a fairly aggregate scale, the findings appear convincing nonetheless. Clearly, changes in site designs, land use mixtures, and densities, in and of themselves, will not bring about dramatic shifts in commuting behavior, at least not in the near term. Other initiatives not directly studied in this research – such as regional TSM ordinances, new freeway construction, or improved areawide transit service – also strongly affect commuting behavior. In tandem with broad-based programs to manage traffic congestion, however, it is felt that the design of higher-density, more mixed-use suburban workplaces with nearby affordable housing could yield substantial mobility dividends in the long term.

Our knowledge of the affects of site and land use variables on suburban commuting behavior is still only partial. Further research is needed, for instance, on the influences of site practices, such as lot configurations and building placements, on travel choices. More work on the affects of parking standards and jobs–housing mismatches on commuting to suburban centers is also required. Determining the density thresholds necessary for mass transit to become a viable alternative to the private automobile in different SEC environments also needs to be studied more fully. Still, the findings of this research provide some insight into these topics and, in general, should provide a useful framework for designing future suburban employment centers with mobility objectives in mind.

As a follow-up to this empirical work, chapter 7 offers some embellishment to these relationships by discussing various transportation–land use issues in SECs in three metropolitan areas: Seattle, Chicago, and Houston. It is followed by the concluding chapter on recommended policy directions for designing workplaces of the future.

Notes

1. For a thorough discussion of the stepwise method, see Blalock (1979).
2. Multiple regression equations delete cases listwise. If data are missing for any single variable under consideration, the case is removed from the analysis. Since some variables had a number of missing cases, their inclusion would have substantially reduced the size of the data base. Accordingly, variables with more than six missing cases were not considered in the stepwise analysis.
3. Keep in mind that high values of EMP/INTC represent low levels of site access. Thus, the negative sign on EMP/INTC suggests that as site access improves (i.e., EMP/INTC rises), then the per cent of trips by solo-commuters drops off.
4. RIDECOOR is a dummy variable. If it takes on values of 1 (i.e., a rideshare coordinator position exists at the SEC), then DRIVALON rises by 3.36 per cent.
5. While vanpool provisions appear to influence solo-commuting, the availability of transit services was found to have little effect. This is consistent with the findings of other researchers that "modal split to suburban offices is not significantly affected by the availability of public transit" (Brown *et al.*, 1984, 20–4).
6. That is, both variables resisted change when the sample size was reduced, demonstrating their strength at predicting WALKBIKE in both small sample and comparatively large sample situations.
7. It should be noted that no model was developed for predicting transit usage because the relationships that were produced during the stepwise process were fairly weak. No site variables were found to have any significant predictive abilities in explaining transit modal shares for this particular data base.
8. Again, the causality likely lies in the direction of property ownership patterns influencing density and land use, rather than vice versa.
9. For a more in-depth discussion of the Hacienda Business Park, see Cervero (1986b).
10. The high significance could have been anticipated because of the large number of cases (13,483) that entered into the analysis.

7

Case studies of land use–transportation issues in SECs in greater Seattle, Chicago, and Houston

7.1 Introduction

Insights into specific land use and transportation issues affecting SECs can also be gained by examining case experiences. This chapter summarizes an assortment of topics regarding site designs, land use planning, parking standards, jobs–housing relationships, and other issues for SECs in three metropolitan areas – Seattle, Chicago, and Houston. Of course, these and other issues vary considerably among metropolitan areas in degree of importance and level of local response. No one case, in and of itself, can represent the full depth of any single topic. Cases, however, help bring issues down to the field level, offering a finer-grained perspective into land use–transportation relationships.

Much of the information for the cases that follow was obtained through field research. Interviews with developers, employers, and local officials were conducted in each instance. They were supplemented by local reports, newspaper accounts, and other information sources gathered during the course of field study. Thus, compared to the prior chapters, the summaries which follow are based on both factual information and the opinions and impressions offered by others.

The three cases presented in this chapter, it should be noted, are not meant to be comprehensive. Emphasis is placed on highlighting assorted land use, site development, and mobility issues surrounding some of the SECs in these metropolitan areas. Success stories as well as problem areas are discussed. In most instances, SECs are still growing and thus it is too early to tell what affects certain design and land use strategies will have on mobility. Still, the assortment of issues covered in the following sections should offer insights into important transportation–land use issues around some SECs and the kinds of policy responses that are being crafted to preserve future mobility.

7.2   Seattle area case study

In the greater Seattle region, two of the primary areas of office growth outside of downtown Seattle since 1980 have been downtown Bellevue and the Bel-Red corridor just east of it (see Ch. 2, Fig. 2.18 for the general location of these two areas). The case summary in this section concentrates mainly on downtown Bellevue, in part because some of the most innovative responses to traffic management through land use initiatives are to be found there.

Overview of growth and development trends

The eastern shore of Lake Washington, known locally as Eastside, has been one of the fastest growing corridors in the greater Seattle area in recent years. From 1980–87, the city of Bellevue grew from 73,900 to 82,000 residents, an 11 per cent rise. Just to the north, Redmond's

Photo 7.1 Sub-city of Bellevue, Washington. Glass-textured office towers provide a striking backdrop for a newly opened public park in central Bellevue. (Photo by the author.)

population rose even faster during this period, from 23,300 to 30,300, nearly a 30 per cent increase. In both places, however, employment has significantly outpaced population growth, increasing at a rate exceeding 5 per cent annually since 1980.

Downtown Bellevue encompasses a 330-acre zone west of Interstate 405, a major north–south facility serving the Seattle area (see Fig. 7.1). This district presently contains around 8 million square feet of office and commercial floorspace and supports a workforce numbering

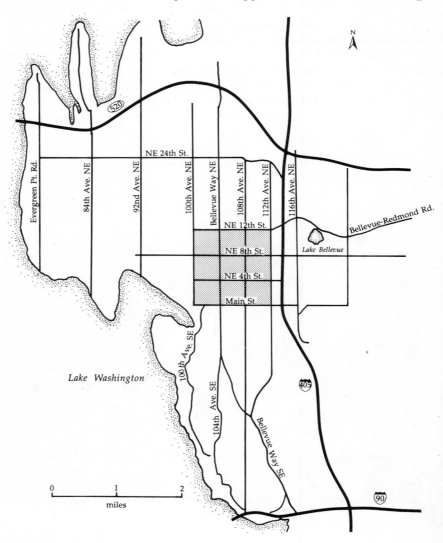

Figure 7.1   Location of Bellevue CBD.

over 20,000. Since 1980, Bellevue has been in a state of transition from Eastside's primary retail center to a major regional employment hub. Prior to 1980, office buildings comprised less than half of downtown Bellevue's floorspace, with retail outlets ranging from neighborhood convenience stores to a regional shopping center dominating the streetscape. This built environment was best suited to motorized travel. Most businesses provided over five parking spaces per 1,000 square feet of floor area. Offices and shops were generally spread throughout downtown, prompting many workers and shoppers to use their cars when circulating between buildings. In general, central Bellevue was not distinguishable from other suburban communities of the 1960s and 1970s.

Since 1980, downtown Bellevue has undergone a dramatic face-lift. One of the major catalysts behind this transformation was the upgrading of Bellevue Square from a suburban community shopping center to a regional super-mall. An overhaul of the downtown master plan in 1981 soon gave way to higher densities and parking reductions. Within a few years, many of Bellevue's one- to two-story office and retail buildings were replaced by high-rise office towers set atop underground parking facilities. Most new office additions have ranged from 10- to 25-stories in height, with floor area ratios between 6.0 to 8.0, comparable to the downtown densities of many medium-size cities. Today, Bellevue is the archetypal suburban city, featuring a high-rise skyline and a lively mix of offices, shops, restaurants, hotels, and theaters.

The Bel-Red corridor is poles apart from downtown Bellevue in both land use and employment composition. Short for the Bellevue Redmond Road axis, Bel-Red is largely a strip of freestanding one- to two-story office buildings, small business and industrial parks, warehousing, and independent retail centers. Over 7 million square feet of non-residential floorspace straddles the 4 mile corridor from Interstate 405 to the southern portion of Redmond. Since over 90 per cent of the corridor is already built out, however, the role of land use and design initiatives in shaping travel behavior along the Bel-Red corridor is somewhat limited. Still, traffic congestion continues to worsen along the corridor. In response, the Eastside Transportation Program was formed in 1987. Comprised of transportation professionals from surrounding communities, the program aims to forge a subregional consensus on managing growth and traffic along the Bel-Red corridor as well as other major concentrations of development on the eastside of Lake Washington.

Redesign of downtown Bellevue

The 1981 Downtown Plan was a watershed in Bellevue's transformation. The central idea was to convert downtown from a place for automobiles to a place for people. The primary instrument for doing this was land use regulations. Bellevue's downtown was rezoned to allow a "wedding cake" pattern of densities, with a high-rise central core surrounded by a tapering of densities toward the edges. Setback requirements were also eliminated so that structures could be built closer together.

One of the obstacles faced in creating a pedestrian environment was the layout of much of downtown Bellevue on a superblock grid. Many parcels in central Bellevue are quite large, spanning 600 feet or more on each side, thus creating long walking distances between properties. The response to this was to create several pedestrian spines with first-floor retail and people-oriented places that would be attractive to pedestrians. N.E. 6th Street, which links Bellevue Square with high-rise office buildings to the east, was designated as the principal spine along which pedestrians would receive priority over cars. An ordinance was subsequently passed that requires all buildings along these spines to have ground-level retail shops, office structures included. A system of "edge conditions" was also set governing the orientation of buildings to sidewalks and the massing of abutting structures. Requirements were introduced to ensure that all new buildings provide distinguishing features at the ground level, such as arcades, artwork, or architectural recesses, so as to make passageways more interesting visually. In sum, the overriding objective of these measures was to create a unified and aesthetically pleasing series of pedestrianways that would make walking through downtown Bellevue's large superblocks enjoyable, thus hopefully drawing people out of their automobiles.

Density bonus system

In addition to ordinance requirements, Bellevue has enticed developers to provide pedestrian amenities and introduce mixed-use activities through a progressive system of density bonuses. Referred to as the "FAR Amenity Incentive System," developers are given bonuses as high as 10 additional square feet of building space for every square foot of amenity provided, with amenities defined as including: enclosed plazas, arcades and marquees, public sculptures, water fountains, and performing arts space. In some zones, moreover, developers can add 2 square feet of office space for every square foot of retail space provided. Throughout the downtown district, developers receive an 8:1 floorspace exchange for providing childcare facilities.

Bellevue's bonus system also encourages jobs–housing balances. For most downtown zones, developers can build an additional 4 square feet of office space for every square foot of housing provided. Housing units can either be built into the work complex or constructed separately within Bellevue's downtown perimeter. This bonus system seem to be paying off. A 15-story residential tower was completed in 1985 and a number of other large-scale residential projects are in various stages of completion. Through this bonus system, Bellevue policy-makers aim to create a lively, mixed-use core which is active around the clock.

While density bonuses have created a more pedestrian-oriented environment, they have also played a vital role in increasing the amount of transit services Bellevue residents and employees receive. This is because of a novel agreement entered into between the city of Bellevue and Seattle Metro, the regional transit authority, in the early 1980s. The agreement outlined a schedule of Metro transit service increases that were indexed to the city increasing its employment densities and lowering its parking ratios over time. By 1984, Bellevue had earned nearly 4,000 annual hours of additional bus service. In Bellevue, higher densities and higher levels of transit service have mutually reinforced one another.

Parking standards

The containment of parking was also considered to be essential in creating a more people-oriented environment in downtown Bellevue. Since 1981, the city has gradually reduced parking by setting both minimum and maximum allowances that fall every two years. In 1987, the code required a minimum of two spaces and a maximum of 2.7 spaces per 1,000 net square feet of office space, far below that found in most suburban work settings. The city also allows up to a 20 per cent reduction in required parking for developments in mixed-use complexes that share parking. The introduction of a parking ceiling is a particularly novel feature of Bellevue's ordinance, preventing developers from following the common practice of overbuilding parking as a marketing ploy.

Other features of Bellevue's parking program are also noteworthy. Because surface parking often pushes buildings apart, thus creating an environment less conducive to walking, Bellevue officials have also introduced zoning incentives to encourage the placement of new facilities underground. Every 2 square feet of parking built below surface allows an additional square foot of office space to be provided. Since a typical parking stall consumes nearly as much area as the typical suburban worker, this amounts to a substantial increase in potential building space. Because of the higher cost of providing underground parking, moreover, most office developers have opted for the minimum parking requirement of two spaces per 1,000 square feet over the 35 per cent higher maximum. Parking fees have also become fairly common in downtown Bellevue. A recent survey found that half of those who

Photo 7.2 Bellevue Transit Center. The bus terminal and transfer point is dwarfed by a 26-story office building. (Photo by the author.)

park in garages underneath new high-rise offices pay for parking, on average around $20 per month.

Transit center ~Public transport~

One of the centerpieces of downtown Bellevue is the new transit center. At the eastern edge of the pedestrian corridor, the center is the largest terminal-transfer point for the Metro system outside of downtown Seattle. Designed with six bus bays, an overhead canopy, benches, information kiosks, and a sheltered waiting area, the center is served by 17 transit routes. During the midday, up to 12 buses are synchronized to arrive and depart every 30 minutes to facilitate transfers. The transit center is viewed as a vital element in creating a people-friendly suburban work environment. In light of the fact that 7 per cent of Bellevue's workforce commute via transit each day, a much higher percentage than that attained by most other suburban workplaces around the country, the transit center seems to have been a worthwhile investment.

Future development

A number of major projects currently under way promise to accelerate Bellevue's transformation to a major suburban center. One is Bellevue Place, a massive mixed-use complex that will add over 1 million square feet of additional floorspace, spread among a 21-story office tower and smaller companion, a 25-story 400-room hotel, a retail arcade, a restaurant, a bank, an athletics club, and a performing arts center. As a condition of the project's approval, city officials required that a Bellevue Place transportation management program be established. The program calls for the creation of a transportation coordinator position and the institution of various educational programs to promote ridesharing. The developer is also being held accountable for introducing programs that restrict single-occupancy vehicle travel to certain permitted limits at various stages of project occupancy. Another set of performance standards restricts the maximum amount of peak employee parking to 1,117 spaces. Where these maximums are exceeded, certain initiatives, such as the sponsorship of subsidized transit passes, will become mandatory.

Case summary

In summary, Bellevue has pioneered some of the most aggressive policies anywhere designed to create a rich environment of density, transit service, and pedestrian activity. A variety of density bonuses and performance standards has been introduced to ensure that future development is consonant with the <u>objective of creating a people-friendly environment, one where the interests of pedestrians take priority over those of the private automobile.</u> No other SEC in the country has sought to <u>restrain parking</u> as much as Bellevue. While some spillover problems are being encountered at retail centers during peak season, overall the parking containment program, along with the density incentives, seems to be paying off. Among SECs nationwide, Bellevue has one of the lowest rates of solo-commuting – only 75 per cent. One out of four currently arrive to work by carpool, vanpool, or bus. Given the city's ambitious program to harness automobile usage, if anything, the market percentages for ridesharing and transit usage should increase in coming years.

[handwritten in margin: Slight Problem with P. space restriction]

7.3   Chicago area case study

While a casual observer walking through Chicago's downtown loop district might be stuck by the number of cranes and skeletal structures stretching skyward, most recent office construction in the Chicago region has been in the suburbs. Downtown Chicago's share of the region's total office inventory has dropped steadily, from 91 per cent in 1970 to 68 per cent in 1986 (Urban Land Institute 1988). Several corridors and townships have received the lion's share of office growth outside the city of Chicago since 1980. These have been: the Interstate 88 East–West Tollway between Oak Brook and Naperville; the village of Schaumburg; the Chicago O'Hare Airport area; and the Lake–Cook corridor straddling the line between these two counties, among others (see Ch. 2, Fig. 2.8 for locations). This section discusses growth trends in these areas, along with issues related to site designs and jobs–housing mismatches.

Development trends

In 1986, 12.7 million square feet of office space was added to the Chicago market; approximately 4 million square feet of this went downtown, while the remaining 8.7 million square feet ended up in the suburbs (Urban Land Institute 1987). This explosive pace of growth has wreaked havoc on many suburban roadways. Worsening traffic congestion has led some Chicago area suburbs to take more restrictive stands on new development. Several suburban communities have begun asking developers to reduce their projects' size as a condition of permit approval. In suburban Schaumburg, developers already make "contributions" for public road improvements related to both residential and commercial projects, while the western suburb of Naperville recently passed an ordinance that exacts developer fees. Development trends in specific subareas of the Chicago region are summarized below.

(a) *INTERSTATE 88 EAST–WEST TOLLWAY*

This is an 18-mile stretch of burgeoning office development from Oak Brook on the east end to the booming community of Naperville on the west. Suburbs along the tollway have coalesced into a massive linear complex of office parks, company headquarters, R&D facilities, retail centers, warehouses, hotels, and upscale restaurants. Total office floorspace exceeds 12 million square feet along the corridor, accommodating an estimated 77,000 workers. Since 1980, office space along the Tollway has doubled (Dunphy, 1987). The eastern and western poles of the Interstate 88 corridor are quite distinct. Around Oak Brook, office buildings are fairly tall, offering an impressive array of interior and exterior amenities. The west end, near Naperville, is dotted with well-manicured office complexes, averaging much lower densities. High-technology and research parks have become particularly prominent in the Naperville area.

A number of fairly large office complexes have been built along the Interstate 88 corridor since the mid-1970s. Among the largest have been: Commerce Plaza (1.5 million square feet); Naperville Office Park (1.29 million square feet); Corporate West (1.25 million square feet); and the Corporetum Office Campus (1.1 million square feet). Most of these complexes offer a mix of multi-story and single-story Class A office space in addition to flexible office/showroom or office/warehouse space. Office functions are dominant along most of the tollway, with relatively few mixed-use complexes existing. Three regional shopping malls, each with 1.4 million square feet of floor area or more, are the other major trip generators along the corridor.

(b) *SCHAUMBURG*

Located 26 miles northwest of Chicago near the intersection of Interstates 90 and 290, Schaumburg has experienced phenomenal population and employment growth in recent years. Between 1970 and 80, its population doubled from 50,500 to 104,000. No longer just a bedroom community, over 45,000 people presently work in Schaumburg. Current office and retail floorspace exceeds 22 million square feet. Many office structures are class A high-rises, featuring glass-textured exteriors and atrium entrances. The largest regional shopping complex in the Chicago area, the Woodfield Mall, is in the heart of Schaumburg. Sales from the mall and ancillary businesses make Schaumburg second only to Chicago in total retail sales for the entire state of Illinois. Schaumburg has thus become a major destination for both workers and shoppers in

Photo 7.3 Woodfield Corporate Center, Schaumburg, Illinois. Office cluster in the fast-growing, mixed-use Village of Schaumburg, 26 miles northwest of Chicago. (Photo by the author.)

recent years. In 1970, for instance, only 2,385 work trips were made to Schaumburg; by 1980, this figure ballooned to 34,799 work trips (Regional Transportation Authority 1987).

(c) *LAKE–COOK CORRIDOR*
This corridor straddles the line between Lake and Cook Counties. Most of the growth here has taken the form of light-industrial parks and free-standing office complexes, concentrated in the communities of Deerfield and Riverswood in Lake County and Northbrook in Cook County. Projects slated for completion by 1995 will increase employment to an estimated 45,000 workers and total floorspace to over 10 million square feet. Compared to some of the Chicago area's other growth corridors, there are relatively few retail activities along the Lake–Cook Corridor, giving rise to a workforce that is becoming increasingly automobile-reliant. With an average of 4.5 parking spaces per 1,000 square feet of office floorspace along this corridor, solo-commuting has become quite prevalent, capturing around 92 per cent of all work trips made.

(d) *O'HARE AIRPORT AREA*
Over 8 million square feet of predominantly mid-rise speculative office space was built around the perimeter of O'Hare International Airport from 1980–5. Major projects in the area have included the 273-acre

Forest Creek Industrial Park and the 224-acre Hamilton Lakes Business Park. While historically the O'Hare area has catered to smaller office tenants, more recently it has attracted several large corporations, giving rise to a more diverse tenant mix. With office growth, congestion not only afflicts O'Hare Airport itself; connecting roadways are also becoming increasingly saturated. In general, the mixing of airport-destined traffic with workers heading to nearby office complexes has overburdened Interstate 294 and other major thoroughfares serving the O'Hare area.

Site design issues

The suburbs of Chicago offer a case context where the issue of site design has received serious attention. This has been especially so along the Interstate 88 corridor from Oak Brook to Naperville. As discussed above, much of this stretch consists of independent office parks and freestanding towers that are unrelated to one another in any design sense. Buildings between parcels are typically thousands of feet apart and have few sidewalk amenities connecting them. Site layouts and circulation paths do little to welcome mass transit vehicles. Many parks along the Interstate 88 corridor offer few transit amenities, such as front-door boarding and drop-off areas. If a worker is motivated enough to patronize mass transit to work, typically he alights the bus off-site, facing long walking distances to his office, compounded by vast parking areas, wide boulevards, disconnected sidewalks, imposing freeway interchanges, and other physical barriers. Such physical settings create transit-hostile environments, dissuading even the staunchest transit advocates from busing to work. As a consequence, only 1 per cent of commuters who work along the Interstate 88 corridor use some form of public transportation (Dunphy 1987).

In recognition of this problem, the DuPage County Development Department recently formed a committee of public and private interests to look at design issues along the Interstate 88 corridor. Guidelines were developed as part of this effort which call for a number of site planning and design treatments that are more conducive to transit access. The overarching theme of these guidelines is to create higher densities that will form the ridership base to support transit. FARs exceeding 0.3, representing densities higher than those typically found at campus style office parks, are recommended for new office developments in areas currently supported by transit services. Besides higher densities, the guidelines also call for the following design reforms along the Interstate 88 corridor:

(a) Future buildings should be clustered, with main entrances oriented as close to the street as possible. This would limit the number of bus stops and minimize walking distances.

(b)   Plans should ensure that site access is coordinated with adjacent office complexes and other nearby land uses. Access between office clusters, whether by frontage road, sidewalks, or side access points, should be designed to minimize travel time.

(c)   Parking layouts should not create long walking distances between buildings and off-site land uses. Close-in, priority parking should be given to vanpools and carpools, to encourage ridesharing.

At present, these are only guidelines. However, the DuPage County Development Commission hopes eventually to use these and other pre-established policies during the development review process of new office and commercial applications with an eye toward creating more transit-sensitive work environments. Whether the Commission will be successful or not hinges on building an *esprit de corps* among the County's 35 municipalities. DuPage County controls land development only in unincorporated areas, which account for one-sixth of the population and a smaller percentage of the jobs. Thus, for the remainder of the County, the Development Commission can attempt to build a consensus on land use policies; however, it remains only an advisory body.

To date, competition for tax revenues have been intense throughout the County. A case in point is the proposal made by a developer in the early 1970s to build a regional shopping mall adjacent to Naperville under the proviso that the city annex the land. When Naperville officials hesitated because of concerns over traffic congestion, water, and sewers, the neighboring city of Aurora promptly annexed the land and the 1.5 million square foot Fox Valley Center was built soon thereafter. Naperville not only lost tax revenues, it also suffered traffic impacts (Dunphy 1987). As long as cities remain so fiercely competitive and and use decisions remain highly fragmented, it is questionable whether voluntary programs to build denser workplaces and more transit-sensitive office projects will work in places like DuPage County. Presently, there are discussions in the Illinois state legislature to tie funding for transportation and other infrastructure to the development of sub-regional plans that all municipalities within a county are willing to buy in to. The chances of site design guidelines being enforced by jurisdictions along the Interstate 88 corridor certainly would increase if such strings were attached to state grants.

Jobs–housing imbalances

The Chicago metropolitan area also represents a case context where the jobs-housing imbalance issue has received considerable attention in recent years. Acute housing shortages near job centers have forced a growing number of workers to reside long distances from their workplaces. Much of the region's imbalance can be attributed to the shortage of housing suited to the earnings of the workforce. In DuPage County, for instance, there are an estimated 6,400 more service jobs than there are service workers who live there (DuPage County Development Department 1986). Local officials estimate that at least several thousand service workers are residing outside of the 332 square mile county because housing is too expensive.

Perhaps the most serious mismatches are at the eastern edge of the county, near the Oak Brook axis of the Interstate 88 East–West Tollway. This area is jobs-rich but housing-poor. Oak Brook's 1985 employment count was around 35,100, compared with a residential population of only 6,600 – roughly five jobs for every resident (Sachs 1986). Consequently, the overwhelming majority of Oak Brook employees in-commute from outside the city every morning and out-commute in the evening. Figure 7.2 shows where Oak Brook workers are coming from. Workers' residences fan out in all directions, with the majority of workers residing three or more municipalities away from Oak Brook. With such an expansive laborshed, freeways serving the Oak Brook area are becoming jammed as workers converging on the area merge with traffic heading elsewhere. For instance, appreciable numbers of workers reverse-commuting from Chicago to the booming area of Schaumburg mix with Oak Brook-destined traffic along major suburban freeways such as Interstate 294; Figure 7.3 shows Schaumburg's laborshed, whose southern portion clearly overlaps Oak Brook's. Thus, while the individual laborsheds of suburban communities might appear reasonably well circumscribed, when one considers there are dozens and dozens of other overlapping laborsheds in the Chicago area, the congestion problems posed by thousands of workers sharing the same limited freeways to commute long distances become evident.

Suburban Chicago's jobs–housing dilemma is further evidenced by recent surveys on the percentage of employees who live and work in the same municipality (Sachs 1986). Only 18.1 per cent of Schaumburg's 1985 workforce of 32,000 resided in the community. In Oak Brook, just 2.5 per cent of the 35,100 workers live there. The survey further showed that two-thirds of Schaumburg employees resided more than 10 miles from their workplaces (a distance corresponding to Chicago's regional average). In Oak Brook, just over 60 per cent of workers commuted farther than 10 miles each direction. The survey further revealed that employees in traditionally lower-paying manufacturing and service jobs in both places averaged longer commutes than those working in finance and administrative positions (Sachs 1986). Clearly, part of the jobs–housing mismatch problem in the Chicago area is rooted in the shortage of nearby affordable housing for moderate-salaried workers.

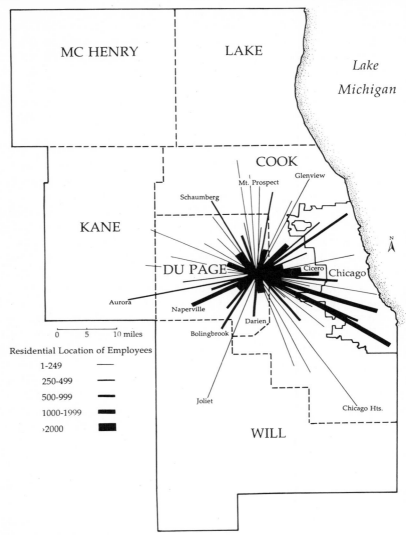

Figure 7.2 Residential locations of Oak Brook, Illinois employees.

Besides creating traffic problems, there is some indication that these mismatches are retarding economic development and restricting the job opportunities of unemployed residents of poor Chicago neighborhoods. From a survey of employers in suburban Chicago, when asked the hardest jobs to fill, clerical-support ranked the highest – 30.6 per cent of respondents felt these positions were the most difficult to fill, compared to 21.8 per cent who felt that management and professional positions were (Sachs 1986). The same survey, moreover, found that the highest

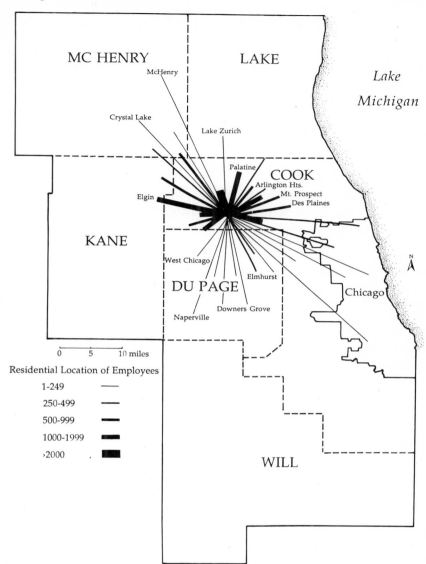

Figure 7.3 Residential locations of Schaumburg, Illinois employees.

number of job vacancies were for clerical-support positions, which comprised 31.7 per cent of total vacancies. Another study demonstrated how inaccessible suburban employment areas have become to Chicago's poor. For the 35 quartersection zones in the city with the highest unemployment rates, the average zone-to-zone travel time to major suburban employment centers was estimated to be around 45 minutes in 1980 (Northeastern Illinois Planning Commission 1984). This travel time was found to be double the regional average for access to suburban job centers. The analysis concluded that: "individuals in high unemployment areas are already spending more than the average amount of time traveling to work; many major job sites are, for all practical purposes, inaccessible to residents of high unemployment areas by reason of excessive travel-times" (Northeastern Illinois Planning Commission 1984, 1).

Case summary

Office growth in suburban Chicago has generally been linear in form, aligned along major thoroughfare corridors like the Interstate 88 East–West tollway and Lake–Cook road. There generally has been little coordination among independent projects, resulting in a settlement pattern of disconnected office complexes with site plans that emphasize circulation within, rather than between, developments. Site plan guidelines have been formulated to encourage closer project coordination and to promote work environments that are more transit-sensitive. Another land use problem in suburban Chicago has been severe jobs–housing imbalances in several major work centers. Surveys suggest that significant numbers of lower-salaried employees in Oak Brook and Schaumburg are priced out of the local housing market, forced to reside considerable distances from their workplaces. Jobs–housing mismatches have been recognized as a critical problem linked to growing suburban congestion; however, little consensus has emerged on what to do about it. In general, the multitude of jurisdictions in DuPage and suburban Cook Counties has hampered efforts to forge any regional program that would work toward providing more affordable housing near major suburban job centers. Some observers believe that citizens will eventually take to the ballot box to restrict new growth unless something is done to relieve worsening traffic congestion. Such "ballot box zoning" would likely exacerbate the jobs–housing imbalance problem since little new affordable housing would be added to regional inventories. To the extent that new growth is forced on to the far ex-urban fringes of the Chicago area, a likely future scenario is one of longer distance commutes and the geographic spread of traffic jams.

7.4   Houston area case study

Houston is a city of centers. While the city's overall density is relatively low, under 3,000 persons per square mile, there are at least 22 identifiable high-density employment centers. The locations of some of the larger ones, including downtown, Post Oak, Greenway Plaza, and the West Houston Energy Corridor, are shown in Figure 7.4. Overall, the Houston area probably has the largest number of widely dispersed activity centers of any major city in the world. Some observers attribute this to the free-wheeling, entrepreneurial policies of local government, perhaps best exemplified by Houston's rejection of zoning as a land use planning tool. Because of few natural restrictions on growth, moreover, there is generally land suitable for development in abundant supply in almost every direction. The possibility that the free market, unencumbered by zoning constraints and left to plow its way along a flat landscape, has given rise to high-density, well-defined employment nodes is an intriguing one that invites spirited policy debates.

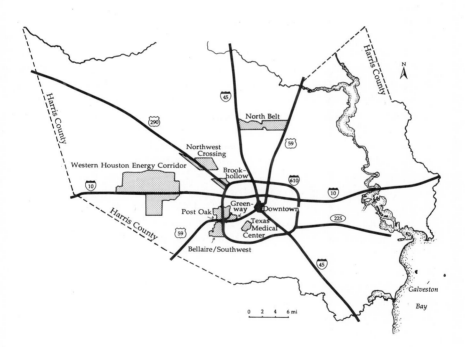

Figure 7.4 Major activity centers in Houston.

This case study examines the scope of office–commercial growth in several of Houston's larger suburban activity centers. Issues related to pedestrian circulation, mixed-use development, and parking standards are emphasized.

Growth and traffic trends

Houston's booming oil economy triggered a surge in office construction during the first half of the 1980s, when over 60 per cent of Houston's 164 million square feet office inventory went up. In 1985, more than three-quarters (124 million square feet) of this office space was located in the suburbs (Urban Land Institute 1987). Post-1980 office additions have been of all shapes and sizes, featuring a pot-pourri of small office centers, campus-like business parks, office–commercial strips, and well-defined high-rise clusters. Many large petroleum companies opened up branch offices throughout suburban Houston during the 1980s. Several international headquarters were also built in the suburbs, notably along the Energy Corridor of west Houston. The downturn in Houston's economy following the recession of 1982–4 has since given rise to a situation of severe oversupply. While office vacancy rates hover around the 50 per cent mark in some areas, several million square feet of new retail space is still being added to Houston's office inventory annually (Urban Land Institute 1987).

The rapid pace of office construction and employment growth in Houston over the past two decades has taken its toll on areawide thoroughfares. Average speeds on Houston's freeways during the afternoon peak fell from 36.6 m.p.h. in 1969 to 24.4 m.p.h. in 1979.[1] The congested period increased from an average of less than three hours in 1970 to nearly eight hours in 1980. In some areas, 12- to 14-hour rush periods are not uncommon. The Houston Chamber of Commerce (1982) has estimated that every Houstonian pays a "traffic congestion tax" of almost $800 apiece each year due to lost time, wasted fuel, and vehicle depreciation. Public opinion polls further suggest how serious the situation is: an overwhelming majority – 53 per cent – of citizens polled in 1985 cited traffic congestion as the biggest problem facing Houston, three times the percentage for the second most frequently cited problem, crime. In response to worsening congestion, the world's most extensive system of vanpools and park-and-ride bus services can be found in Houston. Around 70 miles of restricted busways and traffic lanes have been provided along Houston freeways, part of a planned total of 209 miles when the system is completed. Still, mile-long traffic tie-ups remain common in Houston, prompting calls for growth management – even in zoning-free Houston. Other steps being taken to cope with traffic congestion include the recent opening of the Hardy Toll Road in western Houston and the first round of construction on a second, outer beltloop which will eventually collar the city.

Suburban activity centers

The varying densities and styles of office growth in the Houston area are evidenced by the variety of activity centers that exist. Five major suburban concentrations of employment are described below.

(a) *POST OAK*

The Post Oak/Galleria area 6 miles west of downtown Houston has come to be recognized as the largest suburban downtown in the nation, boasting 25 million square feet of office–commercial floorspace and a day-time workforce of 76,000. In recognition of its pre-eminence as Houston's second downtown, the local business association has chosen to call the area Uptown in recent years. Prominent within the Uptown area are the Galleria shopping complex, one of the nation's most celebrated fashion malls, and the landmark Transco Tower, the tallest building outside of a downtown anywhere. Although Uptown resembles a downtown in terms of density and skyline, most buildings

Photo 7.4 Post Oak, Houston. High-rise skyline on the western edge of Houston that would rival most American downtowns in height and density. (Photo by the author.)

occupy a defined space and feature spacious setbacks. Because of the long distances separating many towers, the area generally has few walking trips.

(b) *GREENWAY PLAZA*

Whereas Post Oak has evolved in a piecemeal fashion over the past several decades, Greenway Plaza, several miles to the southeast, is a master-planned development, featuring a mixture of uses spread over 13 towers of ten stories or more. The 127-acre, 5 million square feet complex boasts a luxury hotel, underground retail, 378 on-site executive condominiums, assorted restaurants, a health club, and the Summit, Houston's 18,000-seat sports and entertainment facility. Unlike other suburban centers in Houston, Greenway Plaza is architecturally unified, giving the appearance of a carefully thought-out development. Although five skywalks connect buildings, only 60 per cent of surface streets have sidewalks (Rice Center 1987). As a consequence, many trips made within the compound and to nearby destinations are by car.

Around one-quarter of Greenway Plaza employees travel to work in a vanpool, one of the highest rates in the nation for a suburban center. The existence of a rideshare coordination office, company-sponsored vanpools, private commuter bus connections to residential areas (including the new town of The Woodlands), and the restriction

Photo 7.5   West Houston Energy Corridor. New glass facade buildings tower over the east-west Richmond Avenue corridor, part of the Energy Corridor. (Photo by the author.)

on parking to just over two spaces per 1,000 square feet of floorspace have all had a part in vanpooling's success.

(c) *WEST HOUSTON ENERGY CORRIDOR*
The entire West Houston area has experienced tremendous population and employment growth since 1980. In all, 27.8 million square feet of office space, two-thirds of which was built from 1981 to 1983, are spread over 41 business parks in an area of around 7,500 acres. Most office growth has concentrated on the 10-mile axis of the Katy Freeway (Interstate 10) shown in Figure 7.5. Since a number of world headquarters of petroleum firms line this stretch, it has become known as the Energy Corridor. Projects along this corridor are generally unrelated, with low and mid-rise buildings spread over large tracts of land. Among the major business parks are Park 10, Oakbrook, and Sundown, each offering nicely landscaped environs and class A rental space. Although most retail space is internal to individual developments

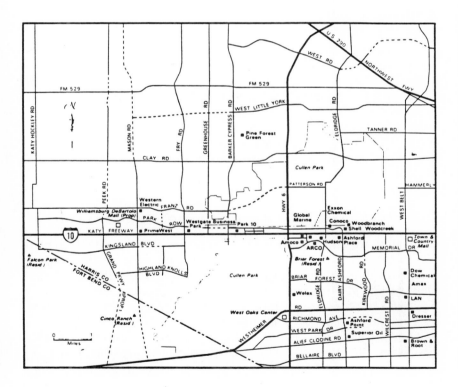

Figure 7.5 West Houston Energy Corridor.

or else absent, two shopping malls, West Oaks Center and Town and Country Mall (each with over 1 million square feet of space), are major trip generators in the area.

(d) *NORTH BELT*

Over 20 office parks are located near the Houston Intercontinental Airport in an area known as North Belt. Office inventories total over 15.5 million square feet spread among 157 buildings, varying from single-story to mid-rise towers. Most office parks in the area are master-planned and have few on-site retail services. Among the largest office complexes in the North Belt area are Greenspoint Plaza, Greenspoint Park, and Northchase. The entire north Houston area does have a substantial retail component, however. In all, over 13 million square feet of retail space is spread among 77 centers, including three large regional malls. The 22-mile Hardy Toll Road, presently under construction, will eventually link many of the office parks and retail centers near the airport to Interstate 610 to the south and residential developments to the north.

(e) *THE WOODLANDS*

A master-planned suburban community 25 miles north of downtown Houston, The Woodlands has matured beyond a residential new town to become a major employment destination in recent years. The heart of the 23,000-acre development is Metro Center, a mixture of offices, light-industrial uses, and retail stores. Presently, over 6,000 employees work in low-rise buildings surrounded by shady trees and open spaces. The Metro Center will eventually feature a technology park, a medical park, and a regional shopping mall.

High densities and mixed uses in Houston's suburban centers

Compared with most other suburban centers around the country, Houston's centers are extraordinarily dense and multi-use in character. The average heights of office buildings in Greenway Plaza and Post Oak are 12 and 24 stories, respectively. Both centers, moreover, enjoy a rich mix of office, commercial, and residential activities. In Houston, it is not uncommon to find an office tower, hotel, and apartment building standing side-by-side. Indeed, many premium quality office complexes on Houston's burgeoning west side are surrounded by apartments, condominiums, and moderate-to-expensive single-family housing tracts. This intermingling of land uses has generally given rise to closer jobs–housing balances in outlying Houston than in many suburbs around the country, which is evidenced by the short average one-way commutes for employees of many centers. Employees of Post Oak, for instance, average one-way distances of 7 miles, while those working in nearby Greenway Plaza commute an average of 9.5 miles in each direction, both under the regional average of 10 miles (Rice Center 1987). The 24–8 per cent modal shares of work trips captured by vanpools and buses in both places, moreover, suggest that higher densities have help curb worker dependency on the private auto.

The common explanation given for Houston's high nodal densities and commingling of uses is the absence of zoning controls. In Houston, planning has occurred in the guise of deed restrictions placed on the land. Deeds normally govern aesthetics, with matters such as density or land use mixture often receiving less attention. By removing land use restrictions and allowing the market to mediate suburban development, it could be argued, Houston's centers have become more heterogeneous and less segregated from residential housing than their counterparts elsewhere around the country.

While the unique affect of non-zoning on Houston's development patterns is difficult to isolate, there can be little doubt that higher densities and greater land use diversity have been net benefits from a mobility standpoint. Vanpooling's success in suburban Houston relative to other parts of the country is a testament to that. As applied in most other suburban areas around the country, zoning has been an obstacle to mixed-use development. The strict segregation of residences, offices, and commercial centers into distinct zones has become one of suburbia's trademarks. It could very well be the case that from a mobility perspective, non-zoning is preferable to the exclusionary zoning ordinances of most American suburbs. Houston's experiences certainly seem to lend credence to this proposition.

Pedestrian circulation within activity centers

While many of Houston's activity centers have very high densities by suburban standards, paradoxically, they tend to be ill-suited to walking. A study by the Rice Center (1987) found that only around 20 per cent of non-work trips made by workers of these centers were by foot; CBD employees, by comparison, walked for two-thirds of all non-work journeys. Two factors seem to account for the difference. One, there is an undersupply of sidewalks in most suburban centers. While 100 per cent of streets in downtown Houston have sidewalks, only 77 per cent of those in Post Oak do. Along the Energy Corridor, less than one out of every four miles of roadway is bordered by sidewalks. Of the sidewalks that do exist, many fail to connect, offering pedestrians a discontinuous pathway of pavement intermixed with dirt and grass.

The second deterrent to walking in Houston's suburban centers has been the vast spaces separating most buildings. Even in mixed-use centers, activities tend to be so far apart that most people find it easier to hop in their car when traveling beyond one-quarter of a mile. The lack of amenities, such as benches and canopied building fronts, has also discouraged foot travel in many outlying centers. In general, most employees of these centers are only willing to walk within buildings or to the adjoining parking lot.

The infrequency of pedestrian travel in Post Oak is particularly noteworthy given that it resembles a large downtown in so many ways. Post Oak has several distinct nodes of high-rise towers, interspersed with a variety of retail shops and other mixed-uses. Most buildings, however, have been designed on the premise of vehicular access, offering few direct pedestrian connections to adjoining properties. Post Oak's long block faces, moreover, result in a high incidence of pedestrian–auto conflicts at mid-block points. In addition, heavy traffic volumes result in long waits at most signalized intersections. With 45,000 parking spaces in the Post Oak area (double that in downtown Houston) and only 3.7 per cent of workers having to pay for parking, the automobile has become the mode of choice when traveling beyond 500 feet. Not only is parking plentiful and cheap in Post Oak, it is also convenient. The Rice Center (1987) study found, for instance, that 86 per cent of Post Oak workers park "zero blocks" (i.e., virtually right next to their offices), compared to only 25 per cent of downtown workers.

Perhaps what epitomizes Post Oak's pedestrian-free environment is the lack of foot traffic to the Galleria, the combined mall–office–hotel complex that is Uptown's centerpiece. While everyone travels by foot once inside the Galleria complex itself, virtually no one walks to get there, except from the parking lot. The sea of parking surrounding the Galleria, and the relative isolation of surrounding office towers, has made walking simply too burdensome for many. The nearest major high-rise tower to the north, Post Oak Central, is 2,000 feet away from the main structure of the Galleria, farther than many Americans are prepared to walk even under the most favorable conditions (Rice Center 1987, Untermann 1984).

The Uptown Association, the "chamber of commerce" for the Post Oak area, has recognized the problems facing pedestrians who try to circulate in the area and has sought to correct the situation. The current plan calls for the addition of new sidewalks, the building of mid-block skybridges, and the embellishing of the streetscape with benches, artwork, and other amenities. Perhaps the key policy lesson offered by Post Oak and other Houston area activity centers is that density and mixed-use developments, by themselves, are not enough to get people out of their cars, even for short distances. Unless efforts are made to contain parking and interlink buildings with suitable pathways, most suburban office workers will remain wedded to their automobiles for both long and short distance travel.

Case summary

Houston's suburban office market has been one of the fastest growing in the country during the course of the 1980s. New office developments have generally been quite varied, ranging from low-profile parks to towering office centers. On the whole, however, suburban office development has been denser and more integrated with complementary uses than in other parts of the country. One consequence appears to be relatively high levels of vehicle-pooling and comparatively short commuting distances. One explanation for Houston's high-density, nodal style of suburban office growth is the absence of zoning. With deeds, there appear to be fewer constraints on density, building heights, and land use mixing. Despite the high-rise profile of Houston's suburbs, there tends to be relatively little pedestrian traffic between buildings, even in mixed-use environments like Post Oak. The prevalence of free parking and the shortage of interesting pathways has discouraged foot travel in many of Houston's higher density suburban centers. Here, a useful policy lesson seems to be that parking containment and pedestrian amenities are important ingredients in reducing auto-dependency, even in a higher density, mixed-use environment.

7.5 Summary

These three cases provided a cross-section of land use and transportation issues currently affecting suburban office centers in the United States. The Bellevue case suggests what can be achieved when suburban centers are transformed to places where people take priority over automobiles. Parking containment has been a pivotal part of Bellevue's concerted program to create a pedestrian-friendly downtown. Bellevue's system of density bonuses has also been instrumental in encouraging private sponsorship of pedestrian amenities, such as public squares and street level retail functions. While many of Houston's suburban centers have densities that match Bellevue's, foot travel tends to be less frequent in these places mainly because the long spacing between buildings and abundance of free parking invite car traffic. Nonetheless, Houston's high suburban employment densities and multi-use environs have enticed many workers to commute via vanpools and bus transit. Finally, the Chicago case emphasizes the importance of careful site planning and jobs–housing coordination in areas experiencing strip-like development of office parks and freestanding buildings. Shortages of affordable housing near some of Chicago's suburban office corridors have displaced some workers, setting the stage for long-distance freeway commuting. Initiatives that might be taken to remedy problems such as these are discussed next in Chapter 8.

Note

1. The statistics in this section are estimates provided by the Transportation Task Force of the Houston Chamber of Commerce in the *Regional Mobility Plan for the Houston Area*, 1982.

8
Linking land use and transportation in SECs

8.1 Overview of research findings

For the most part, the hypotheses posited at the beginning of this study appear to be borne out by both the empirical and case study findings of this research. SECs with the smallest shares of work trips made by private automobile are generally relatively dense and varied in their land use make-up. Large-scale MXDs and sub-cities, such as Bellevue, Washington and Post Oak west of Houston, were found to have particularly high shares of their workers commuting via carpools, vanpools, and buses. On-site and near-site retail services, like restaurants, shops, and banks, are especially important if suburban workers are to be lured out of their cars. Where such facilities are absent, many workers find it necessary to drive in order to have a car available for running midday errands, meeting a colleague for lunch, or going to the bank. Mixed-use environments also allow parking to be reduced through shared parking arrangements. Reductions in surface parking, in turn, can shrink the dimensions of a project and thus make walking more attractive.

Many suburban office projects were found to be insensitive to the needs of pedestrians, cyclists, and transit users. Site layouts that segregate buildings and land parcels many times create prohibitively long walking distances. Most corridors of unrelated office projects have disconnected series of sidewalks surrounded by unattractive spaces. The combination of wide setbacks and separate access roads, moreover, discourages the entry of transit vehicles into these properties. Where foot travel and transit usage are relegated to a second-class status, not surprisingly, solo-commuting predominates. While spacious site designs enable vehicles to circulate freely once they are inside an office compound, thoroughfares which serve these developments are all too often saturated by vehicles hauling a single occupant. Many office complexes with the best on-site circulation suffer the worst off-site congestion.

Two other sources of worsening suburban congestion have been the abundance of free parking and widening jobs–housing mismatches. The provision of free, convenient parking zoned at more or less one space per employee is an open invitation for most suburban workers to drive to work. Those centers where parking is restricted and prices are charged consistently achieve the highest rates of vehicle-pooling and transit usage. The jobs–housing imbalance problem has been a significant source of the freeway congestion encountered upstream and downstream from major suburban job centers. Growing numbers of non-professional workers are being forced to live distances farther than they might otherwise because of the relatively high cost of housing near many suburban centers. In general, SECs with the most expensive nearby housing average the highest shares of moderate salaried service workers. The farther away these workers live, the greater the likelihood that suburban freeways will become congested since more miles are logged by more people on the same few beltloops and thoroughfares.

All of these influences, it should be emphasized, do not operate independently of one another. Most suburban workplaces with low densities, for instance, also tend to have a single dominant use and an abundance of free parking. Increasing densities while retaining a surfeit of parking will probably only serve to worsen congestion as more workers descend upon the same work area each morning. Higher densities, alone, will normally heighten congestion around suburban workplaces in the near term. In tandem with market-rate parking fees and mixed-use development, however, increased density is apt to make transit and ridesharing attractive enough so as eventually to bring about a net reduction in ambient levels of congestion.

In light of these findings, the sections which follow suggest various institutional, legislative, and land use policy initiatives that offer promise for creating suburban workplaces that enhance mobility. Examples where some of these recommended initiatives are taking shape are also discussed.

8.2   Institutional responses

One of the major obstacles to forging a consensus on land use issues in suburbia is the multitude of government bodies involved. Most of the metropolitan areas studied in this work have a tradition of strong local control in all matters of land use planning. Unfortunately, all of the local choices made by independent bodies do not always add up to what is best for an entire region. While land use decisions are made locally, their transportation impacts are felt regionally. A community's decision to convert residentially zoned land to office use in a setting where jobs far exceed housing might be in the interest of that community's financial balance sheet, however the increase in cross-town commuting is likely to run counter to the interests of the region at large. Each community's land use choices might make sense initially, but over time, cumulatively they can create tremendous mobility problems for neighboring communities and the region as a whole.

The lack of cooperative land use planning among jurisdictions is a root cause of many of the mobility problems faced in America. Over the past several decades, job growth and residential growth have generally occurred independently of each other in most regions of the US, all too often along different growth axes, producing acute jobs–housing imbalances. A regional focus, some argue, is necessary if spillover problems like countywide traffic jams are to be dealt with successfully and jobs–housing imbalances narrowed.

While regional governance makes sense in theory, in reality local governments are unlikely ever to give up their control of land use decisions. Two legislative initiatives, however, could accomplish many of the objectives of regional governance by reducing fiscal disparities and competition among communities and promoting jobs–housing integration:

(a) *Tax–base sharing.* Regional sharing of municipal tax revenues could remove much of the fiscal incentive communities have to zone for commercial growth at the expense of residential development. Under tax-base sharing, certain tax revenues would be pooled at the regional level and redistributed according to a community's ratio of workers to employed residents. In principle, tax-base sharing would result in municipalities made up predominantly of industrial and commercial uses to reimburse those communities that end up housing their workers. The only US metropolitan area practicing tax sharing is Minneapolis–St. Paul, Minnesota, where local jurisdictions share about 28 per cent of the region's property tax base. Under this program, local jurisdictions share tax bases, not tax dollars. Each community in the Twin Cities area must contribute 40 per cent of the increase in its commercial and industrial property tax base into a metropolitan pool, which is then redistributed according to population and tax base. As a result, many more affluent communities have stopped zoning out low tax generators such as small houses (Fulton 1987, Reschovsky & Knaff 1977).

(b) *Fair-share housing requirements.* Statewide requirements imposed on communities to provide a fair share of a state's affordable housing needs could narrow the gap between where suburban employees work and live. The model for affordable housing programs is that instituted by the state of New Jersey. There, a Council of Affordable Housing was formed in response to the Mount Laurel II court decision which found that most municipal zoning ordinances discriminated against low- and moderate-income families, *de facto*, by precluding affordable housing. The Council has subsequently set an affordable housing quota for each municipality based on a formula that fairly distributes the responsibility of meeting the State's need of 145,000 new affordable units by 1993. If other states were to follow New Jersey's lead, major progress could be made in ensuring that at least some suburban housing additions are targeted to the earnings levels of most clerical and service-industry workers.

It is no coincidence that in both of these cases, state government took the initiative to launch these programs. Only states can prod municipalities into coordinating their growth policies. Extraterritorial sharing of tax resources likewise requires state intervention. Any significant step toward subregional land use planning and tax sharing must clearly begin in our state capitols, be it through the passage of enabling legislation or through strong leadership.

Besides government initiatives, the private sector can help coordinate land use decisions which are in keeping with regional mobility objectives. Many SECs have business associations already in place that could serve as a vehicle for coordinating land use programs. Local chambers of commerce and trade associations could also encourage their members who develop and build offices and housing to coordinate their respective projects. Individual company initiatives can also encourage closer jobs–housing balance. In the San Francisco Bay Area, for instance, several large companies that recently moved to the Bishop Ranch office complex have offered employee relocation bonuses to encourage workers to reside close to their job sites. One company grants relocation allowances on a sliding scale, with the largest contribution going to workers who move the closest to their offices.

8.3   Legislative and regulatory responses

Among the instruments available to local government for encouraging more integrated land development, those which produce zoning and tax incentives would likely yield the most lasting mobility dividends. Some of the possible tools available for shaping land use changes around suburban employment centers are outlined below.

(a) *Traditional zoning.* Zoning allows a jurisdiction to control the densities, uses, and platting of land. Zoning for higher employment densities, mixed uses, and multi-family residences near suburban employment centers could reduce solo-commuting. Higher densities are the key to providing affordable, non-subsidized suburban housing since only then can fixed land costs be spread over more units.

(b) *Performance zoning.* Under this arrangement, certain standards governing the density, site characteristics, traffic impacts, and other features of a development can be pre-established. Performance zoning gives the developer considerable flexibility in designing a project as long as he meets agreed-upon standards. To the extent a developer is held accountable for ensuring that his project will not aggravate traffic below level of service D, for instance, the likelihood of on-site housing units being built increases.

In the US, performance zoning as a tool to mitigate traffic congestion has been pursued most aggressively in Fort Collins, Colorado, a predominantly suburban community some 80 miles north of Denver. During the 1970s, Fort Collins was one of the fastest growing communities in the country. Although a 1979 citizen-initiated referendum to limit new housing starts lost 2:1, city leaders realized that bold new measures were needed to ensure quality growth. What they came up with was a performance zoning system which, basically, replaces strict zoning bylaws with bargaining between developers and city officials. Developers bring their proposals to the planning board and are challenged to accommodate Fort Collins's goals: mixed land uses, high shares of pedestrian and bicycle commuting, and 100 per cent private financing of new infrastructure needed to support new growth. Commercial developers are granted higher densities if they locate near residential areas and transit routes, and institute vanpool programs.

While grumblings over rapid growth have not vanished in Fort Collins, nearly everyone prefers performance zoning to across-the-board bans on new construction. The idea is to manage growth carefully through performance criteria that are consonant with the interests of both the development community and the public at large. As long as the business community continues to assume major responsibility for containing traffic and financing additional public improvements, the Fort Collins approach to growth management will work.

(c) *Inclusionary zoning.* Here, developers are required to include certain activities or improvements as a precondition to project approval. In a way, inclusionary zoning is the antithesis of traditional exclusionary zoning practiced by most suburban communities in the US. Rather than excluding land uses, zoning is used instead to require the coalescing of functions. Inclusionary zoning, for instance, could be used to encourage the joint development of offices, housing units, and retail services in all master-planned business parks.

The Edinborough project in Edina, the hottest suburban office/retail market in the greater Minneapolis area, is a good example of inclusionary zoning: 392 moderately priced condominium units, a 203- unit apartment structure, and a 7-story office tower were recently erected on the 26-acre site. A survey of people buying condominiums in the mixed-use project showed that half are from, or employed in, Edina (Bachman 1987).

(d) *Conditional use zoning.* This form of zoning sets standards and conditions to allow land uses normally prohibited in a zone. In a way, then, it is an *ad hoc* approach to achieving land use mixing. Conditions might include allowing a new office project only if it is located within a specified radius of an existing high-density residential area.

(e) *Incentive zoning.* Developers can also receive bonuses, normally in the form of increased FARs, for providing certain amenities and uses. Taller office towers, for example, might be allowed if a certain number of housing units are built within the development. As practiced in Bellevue, Washington, commercial densities might be increased if a developer sponsors a vanpool program for all tenants in lieu of standard levels of parking.

(f) *Transfer development credits.* This system allows densities to be distributed among multiple projects in such a way that high density uses are clustered together. A developer, for instance, could increase densities near employment centers by transferring density credits from areas whose densities will be kept below the permitted ceiling. With the ability to shuffle densities within a prescribed area, it is probable that more urban-like cores, with densities that taper as one moves to the periphery, would evolve in suburban centers.

(g) *Zoning swaps.* Here, the zoning classifications of two different parcels within a community are switched to encourage a richer mixing of land. The city of San Jose, California, for instance, recently instituted a zoning swap policy by rezoning an industrial area into residential at the northern end of the city while rezoning an equivalent-size residential land parcel to industrial usage. The intent of this and other zoning swaps is to scatter employment growth, promote mixed-use development, reduce commuting distances, and relieve the city's over-taxed freeway network.

8.4 Density initiatives

Higher densities were shown to be crucial in creating suburban work environments conducive to transit and other commute alternatives. A problem encountered in a number of suburban employment areas is that office densities fall in the 0.5 to 2.0 FAR range – in general, 2.0 is too low to support intensive transit services, yet 0.5 is high enough to create nodes of development that are congestion points (Regional Transportation Authority 1987). The effects of density, of course, varies in a number of contexts. In a setting where free parking encourages nearly everyone to drive, bunching workers together in a high-rise structure will only lead to traffic jams on roads leading to the building. Over time, however, if market prices for parking were charged and frequent transit services were operated, the high-rise structure could prove successful at enticing workers into buses and carpools.

This dual nature of density accounts for the varying zoning programs adopted by local decision makers in their attempts to stave off congestion. Along the rapidly developing Route 206 corridor in central New Jersey, for instance, officials of local jurisdictions have agreed to allow a tripling of current office–commercial densities in hopes of stimulating higher transit patronage. In Minnesota, on the other hand, the city of Edina brought a court action to enjoin the city of Bloomington from approving a dense office project, alleging that the development would cause congestion in adjoining Edina. In Santa Clara County, California, furthermore, a special task force of elected officials from five office–industrial cities collectively agreed to limit FARs to under 0.35 when approving new developments in hopes of spreading out trip ends.

To the extent that increases in transit usage and vehicle pooling are desired, SECs should generally aim for FARs above 2.0, at least over the long term. This could be done through a combination of zoning strategies cited above. Transfer development credits, for instance, could be used to create a wedding-cake pattern of densities, with high rises concentrated in the core of an SEC and building heights tapering off toward the perimeter. Other measures that might be considered for increasing densities include the introduction of: (a) lower right-of-way and pavement width requirements in areas where traffic volumes are modest; (b) zero-lot line developments; (c) reduced parking space dimensions; and (d) shared-use parking arrangements in mixed-use developments (Bookout & Wentling 1988, Cervero 1986b).

In some instances, market forces themselves are bringing about higher density suburban workplaces. At the Denver Tech Center, Perimeter Center, Tysons Corner, and several other suburban downtowns, rising land values have resulted in most one- and two-story offices that were built in the 1970s being replaced by new high-rise structures. In the case of the Tech Center, the original suburban like densities of 0.25 FAR have risen to nearly 2.0 over the past two decades (Galehouse 1984). All future buildings in the Tech Center will range from 4–24 stories, configured into clustered villages. In general, where suburban land remains cheap enough, developers will continue to slash construction costs by spreading buildings laterally, since costly elevators and extra foundation supports can be eliminated. When the marketplace commands land to be used more productively though, retrofits of original park-like designs to denser clusters, such as at the Denver Tech Center, will become more commonplace.

8.5   Site design initiatives

While the affects of factors such as density and land use composition on commute choices are reasonably well understood, less is known about the relationship between site design and travel behavior. Based on this research, several guiding principles can be offered for creating SEC environments which could encourage workers to travel in some manner other than by private automobile:

(a)   Suburban office developments should have a well-defined, centralized core which serves as a focus for surrounding development;
(b)   people-oriented facilities should be placed in this core, such as restaurants, shops, and banks;
(c)   buildings should be sited so as to invite access between them; self-contained, inwardly focused worksites should be discouraged;
(d)   setbacks between building entrances and sidewalks should be narrowed to shorten walking distances;
(e)   on-site roads and trailpaths should link directly into off-site facilities surrounding the development.

In general, we need to design workplaces more like commercial centers of yesteryear, when walking was the primary mode of travel – ones with higher densities, identifiable cores, and a lively mixture of activities. Only by placing offices, shops, banks, restaurants, health clubs, and hotels side-by-side will we create the kinds of pedestrian-friendly environments that might make appreciable numbers of suburban workers want to leave their cars at home.

Anderson (1986) and Potter (1984) have suggested a number of design treatments that could encourage different modes of travel to and within employment centers. Borrowing from their work, the following site practices seem appropriate for SECs.

Transit-sensitive designs

Mass transit operates best where the circulation network allows vehicles to be routed directly through a development without requiring extensive backtracking. This implies that roadways within SECs should be highly interconnected, avoiding branching access roads and cul-de-sacs which require buses to retrace their path on the way out (see Fig. 8.1). Similarly, access to a site should be provided at two or more points to separate entrance and exit locations and improve through routing (Anderson 1986).

To make transit usage convenient, several other design practices might be considered:

(a) transit stops should be positioned to minimize the walking distance for the greatest number of passengers;
(b) bus connection points should be provided near the front entrances of major buildings;
(c) waiting areas should provide full amenities, including benches, all-weather protection, and passenger information.

Overall, transit users should be as close to their offices when they are let off a bus as motorists are when they park their cars. This means

Cul-de-sac routes .... Poor transit access   a   Loop road .... Improved transit access   1 acre

Figure 8.1 Alternative road layouts within an office development.
Source: Anderson [1986].

providing sheltered bus stops that are situated approximately 100 feet
or so from the main entrances of major office buildings.

Vehicle-pooling design considerations

Carpools and vanpools essentially have the same access and parking
requirements as solo-occupant automobiles. Ridesharing can be made
more attractive in several ways, nevertheless. Preferential parking for
vehicle-pools is important in large complexes where average walking
distances from parking lots to building entrances tend to be long. Where
decked parking exists, sufficient vanpool parking should be reserved at
the main level and adequate overhead clearance should be provided to
accommodate vans' added height. As with bus transit, canopied drop-off
zones and staging areas near building entrances should be set aside for
carpools and vanpools as well.

Pedestrian and cycling design considerations

A separate internal circulation system for pedestrians and cyclists should
be provided where possible. At mid-block junctions with major arteries,
grade-separated crossings should be provided (see Fig. 8.2). Paths
should also be efficiently routed through adjacent parcels and between
major trip origins and destinations rather than along the perimeter of a
site. Attractive landscaping, adequate lighting, and assorted pedestrian
amenities such as benches, shade trees, and public art can invite
suburban workers to walk when they might otherwise drive.

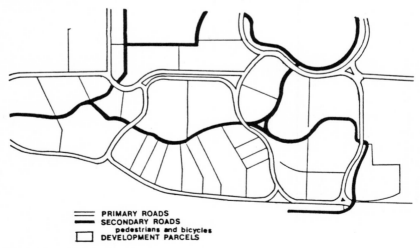

PRIMARY ROADS
SECONDARY ROADS
pedestrians and bicycles
DEVELOPMENT PARCELS

Figure 8.2 Separate pedestrian and cyclist path system.

Bikepaths are generally most appealing to cyclists when they follow curvilinear alignments and are bordered by berms, trees, and other plantings. There should also be a clear connection of any internal bikeway to the network beyond the boundaries of a site. Other on-site amenities that can encourage workers to cycle to work include secure bicycle lockers and storage areas and facilities for showering and changing into work clothes. In many mixed-use developments health clubs offer such services.

The Opus 2 office complex south of Minneapolis has introduced a pedestrian and cyclist trail system that stands as an exemplar. Opus 2 has a one-way loop road system that snakes through the 554-acre compound, funneling cars in a "figure eight" type of movement pattern. Developers realized, however, that if sidewalks were built which hugged the serpentine roadway system, pedestrians would add extra distances to their walk between any two points. Accordingly, project designers superimposed a more lineal footpath on to the loop network, providing grade-separated skybridges at major junctions. This secondary pedestrian and bicycle system follows several nicely landscaped linear parks throughout the Opus 2 complex. Not only have more direct trails been provided, the dissociation of foot and vehicular traffic has enhanced pedestrian safety and made walking more visually enjoyable.

Another bicycle-friendly work environment is the Bishop Ranch office development east of San Francisco. Besides providing wide sidewalks and designated curb lanes for cyclists, developers of the project have also written covenants into land sales specifically requiring all buildings with large concentrations of employees to contain showers and lockers. At one site, a locker is available for every 50 workers and a shower for every 200.

8.6 Parking considerations

Parking supplies have been shown to be a critical factor influencing the travel choices of workers in suburban and urban settings alike. A number of studies show that the likelihood of workers commuting *via* transit or some other alternative is far more sensitive to parking supply and costs than to such incentives as lower fares or improved transit connections (Meyer & Gomez-Ibanez 1981).

The practice of zoning for roughly one parking space per employee at most suburban workplaces is a significant obstacle toward making ridesharing, transit, and other commute alternatives work. Zoning for one space per worker encourages most workers to fill their allotted parking spot by driving to work. Today's parking standards generally need to be relaxed to give developers and builders greater flexibility in gauging how much parking they provide. While there is tremendous resistance to reducing parking supplies in most suburban settings, a number of communities have taken bold steps to do exactly that. Besides the case of downtown Bellevue, programs to contain parking are currently under way at the Denver Tech Center, the North Dallas Parkway, Warner Center, and a number of communities in central New Jersey along the Route 1 corridor, among other places. Some areas have switched from a minimum requirement of parking to a maximum ceiling under the premise that developers will not cut their own throats by supplying too few spaces. The Denver Tech Center, moreover, has encouraged the retrofit of parking lots where feasible. The Center's Design Criteria manual notes that "consideration should be given to designing parking structures for future alternative uses in the event parking demand diminishes."

Since parking facilities tend to be land-hungry, efforts to reduce their size and dimensions should be pursued where possible. Shared-parking programs are one way to shrink parking lots. In Portland, Oregon, for instance, a progressive parking ordinance offers density bonuses to uses in MXDs that are able to share parking. Another way to reduce parking's affects on site density is to put it underground. In most instances, land prices have to be fairly high to justify this. Density bonuses, however, can make underground parking more attractive. As noted in chapter 7, the city of Bellevue grants an additional 1 square foot of office space for every 2 square feet of parking placed underground. Some firms appear willing to incur the higher expense of below-surface parking on aesthetic grounds, moreover. For example, at the headquarters of a computer firm in Redmond northeast of downtown Bellevue, 1,680 parking spaces have been built beneath seven main buildings, even though all buildings are only two stories in height. As a result, a considerable volume of foot traffic flows between buildings.

In sum, initiatives that could contain parking include: the switch from minimum parking floors to maximum parking ceilings; the design of parking structures to allow future alternative uses in the event parking demand diminishes; in lieu of provisions which enable employees to substitute vanpools and other commuting alternatives for parking stalls; and ordinances which allow mixed-uses to share their respective parking facilities, thus modulating total parking supplies.

8.7   Mixed-use and jobs–housing initiatives

A central finding of this research is that suburban work settings with mixtures of uses are essential if workers are to be lured out of their private automobiles. Synchronization of job and housing growth near suburban centers, moreover, could relieve suburban congestion by internalizing more travel within well-defined subregions.

Mixed-use development

Many of the zoning instruments already discussed could encourage multi-use development. Tax concessions could likewise induce such projects. Performance standards might also be introduced to create heterogeneous work environments. In Cupertino, California, for instance, a program has been instituted that encourages developers to diversify their projects. Prior to formal permit application, a developer is informed how many trip ends his project is allotted at a given time in the future. The developer can then propose whatever mixture of land uses will contain trip-making within the allotted ceiling. Since the trip generation rates applied in making the projections are considerably lower for multi-use than single-use projects of comparable size, developers have a built-in incentive to add retail, restaurants, and housing into their proposals.

Fortunately, a growing number of developers no longer need to be prodded into building mixed-use suburban projects. The market itself is encouraging this. At the Denver Tech Center, for instance, developers have decided to sell land below market price for on-site housing, childcare services, and selected retail functions in order to create a more integrated mixture of complementary uses. While losses are being sustained in the near term, developers are convinced that a more lively mixed-use work setting will prove more profitable in the long run.

Jobs–housing balances

This study has argued that the prohibitive cost of much of suburbia's housing and restrictive zoning, among other factors, have contributed to a widening jobs-housing imbalance in America's suburban labor markets as well as worsening traffic congestion. In addition, extreme jobs–housing imbalances have been shown to be associated with high levels of motorized trip-making and congested freeway conditions at the nation's largest suburban employment centers.

While in the industrial era there was a logic to separating homes from smokestacks, slaughterhouses, rendering plants, and other nuisances, in today's work environment of pollution-free offices, the rationale for separating homes and workplaces by ribbons of superhighways is less clear. In fact, one could argue that since congestion produced by jobs–housing imbalances is one of the most serious public nuisances today, zoning should be "turned on its head" to encourage the integration rather than the segregation of land uses. Given the option of living far from one's workplace and commuting in bumper-to-bumper traffic or living close enough to stroll to work along a nicely groomed pathway, most breadwinners would surely go for the latter option.

Closer coordination of suburban job and housing growth can be encouraged in a number of ways. State legislation, such as New Jersey's, can require all communities to zone for some multi-family housing. State funds can also be tied to local housing policies. In the Commonwealth of Massachusetts, for instance, Executive Order 215 denies state development assistance to any community found to be unduly restrictive of housing growth. Some state initiatives, however, have been less peremptory. Connecticut distributes handbooks explaining the benefits of affordable housing to local officials. California, moreover, has passed enabling legislation which allows local governments to create zones where accessory units can be developed in existing single-family sites.

Localities can take a number of initiatives themselves to promote multi-family and moderate-income housing. Inclusionary zoning and density bonuses, for instance, could encourage new apartment construction. Tax-exempt municipal bonds could also be issued to finance housing additions. In Orange County, California, developers are required to provide 25 per cent of all new units in unincorporated areas of the county at prices which low- and moderate-income families can afford. Density bonuses and below-market financing raised through revenue bonds have been introduced to encourage low-cost housing production. In the communities of Costa Mesa and Santa Ana within Orange County, moreover, building permits are regulated to ensure that jobs and housing growth occur at the same pace. In both communities, the amount of commercial and industrial floorspace for which building permits are issued in any one year is set according to how much housing was built in the previous year. In addition, both places require large office developers to build or contribute to the production of residential units within city limits that will house at least 20 per cent of their tenants' employees. Similar office–housing linkage programs have been created in San Francisco and Boston (Porter 1985).

Finally, as part of the development review process, localities are in a position to bargain for jobs–housing linkages. Credits against impact fee obligations, for instance, could be granted in exchange for developers agreeing to build affordable housing units within office complexes (since in theory jobs–housing integration reduces the need to widen streets). Where no impact fee ordinances exist, jurisdictions could negotiate for such linkages as part of the permit approval process. Several California communities have taken noteworthy steps in this direction. The cities of Novato and San Rafael in Marin County, for instance, not only require that all developers of large–scale office projects build on-site housing, developers must also give employees who work in these projects the "right of first refusal" – i.e., the chance to purchase market-rate units before they are opened to the general public. In Burlingame and Menlo Park in San Mateo County, moreover, city officials routinely negotiate with developers and employers during the project review process to give hiring preference to local residents as a means both of shortening commutes and increasing local employment. Several other California communities, in addition, sponsor skill training and referral programs to match residents to jobs.

Jobs–housing balance, it should be emphasized, does not mean the ushering in of a new era whereby merchants live atop stores, suburban homes abut offices, or cottage industries flourish. It relates more to providing workers with the opportunity to reside close to their job sites if they so choose. Clearly, jobs and housing growth are out of kilter when workers commute well over an hour each day because housing is neither affordable nor in sufficient supply within reasonable proximity to their workplaces. The spirit of jobs–housing balancing is to break down the exclusionary barriers that are forcing more and more Americans to reside farther from their workplaces than they would prefer, and in so doing to reduce regional congestion, conserve energy, and enhance environmental quality.

8.8   Closing remarks

Historically, land use and transportation have shown how closely related they are to one another. The reason why most European cities are so compact, with many residents living near their workplaces, is that they evolved in an era when walking was the primary means of travel. Cities like Los Angeles and Houston, on the other hand, grew most rapidly during a period when the auto-highway system was gaining ascendancy, producing a sprawling settlement pattern. There is no reason to believe that the same kind of relationships between land use and transportation will not hold for suburban work settings as well. To the extent suburban workplaces are built primarily to accommodate the automobile, the prevalence of solo-commuting will simply reinforce the low-density, single-use character of these places. An environment where appreciable numbers of workers spend considerable time in traffic jams each morning and evening will be firmly set into place. While it is unlikely that the private automobile ever will, and perhaps ever should, fall from its reign as the dominant mode of commuting, at the same time steps need to be taken to make ridesharing, mass transit, walking, and cycling respectable alternatives. As suburbia continues to become the destination of more and more travel, it is essential that the joint influences of land use and transportation be carefully weighed when designing workplaces of the future. Future levels of mobility and overall quality of suburban living could very well depend on it.

The reason why the planning and design of suburban workplaces is of such paramount importance is that many employment centers in both the US and abroad are just beginning to take form. It is imperative that developers and planning professionals seize the opportunity to coordinate transportation and land use while many projects are at a fairly embryonic stage and there is still time to take steps which will enhance future mobility. For once the vast majority of projects in an area are on the ground, the stage is already set for how workers will commute for years to come and the opportunities to build environments which induce workers to choose certain commuting options will become quite limited. The physical design characteristics of workplaces, it must be remembered, is one of the few areas where the public sector maintains direct control of the development review process. Unlike other traffic mitigation strategies, such as staggered work hour initiatives and vanpool programs, which fall almost totally under the purview of local developers and employers, public officials can directly influence the size, scale, densities, and tenant mixes of future workplaces when plans are being designed and negotiated. Unless these matters are taken seriously, draconian growth controls are apt to become the primary land use tool for dealing with traffic congestion in America. To the extent that public policy-makers exercise their prerogatives and work toward creating suburban environments that feature a lively mix of activities and are sensitive to the needs of pedestrians, cyclists, bus riders, and vehicle-poolers, lasting mobility dividends will accrue to those who live, work, and do business in the suburbs.

APPENDIX 1
National Survey on land use and travel characteristics of Major suburban employment centers.

Please answer all questions as fully as possible. If you are unsure about your response, please make your best estimate and indicate that it is an estimate by placing an (E) after the response.

Name of Project or Development:_____

1. Land Use, Employment, and Site Characteristics of Development

1.A. Please provide information on the following **scale** and **locational** characteristics of the development:

Total land acreage _____

Approximate number of miles to the primary and largest downtown (central business district) in the metropolitan area _____

Current total square footage of floorspace for entire development _____

Future total square footage of floorspace at build-out (final completion) of development _____

Expected year of project build-out (completion) _____

1.B. Please provide information on the following **employment** characteristics of the development:

Current number of employees in the entire development _____

Expected number of employees at build-out (final completion) of development _____

Approximate percent of workforce in the development currently employed in the following occupations:

Management	_____
Administration and Accounting	_____
Professional and Technical (e.g., R&D, engineering, etc.)	_____
Clerical and Secretarial	_____
Sales	_____
Assembly and Manufacturing	_____
Other (_____)	_____

Total: 100 %

APPENDIX I (Cont.)

1.C. Please provide information on the following **density** and **design** characteristics of the development:

Average floor area ratio (i.e., ratio of floorspace to land area -- for instance, 2:1 means twice as much floor area as land area) _____

Maximum allowable floor area ratio under current zoning _____

Percent of land covered by buildings, on average (i.e., footprint of buildings to total land area of sites -- for example, a 33% coverage rate means one-third of land is taken up by buildings) _____

Average front lot setback of buildings from property or site lines _____

Average side lot set-back of buildings from property or site lines _____

For the entire development, what are the number of stories of:
Typical or "average" building _____
Lowest building _____
Tallest building _____

Please describe the "typical" building in the development (in terms of size, scale, length, depth, and general design features): _____
_____
_____
_____
_____

For the entire development, what are the approximate dimensions (in feet) of:
Typical or "average" lot _____
Smallest lot _____
Largest lot _____

Please describe the general lot pattern and propinquity of buildings in the development (e.g., large, rectangular lots with buildings perpendicular and far apart; lots of varying shapes and sizes with buildings relatively nearby; etc.) : _____
_____
_____
_____
_____

Has the evolution of the development: (please check most appropriate response)
Been according to the original master plan _____
Been according to annual or periodic revisions to the master plan _____
Occurred incrementally or in a step-by-step fashion _____
Other (_____) _____

Number of different conditions, covenants, and restrictions (CC&Rs) that are affixed to the land in the entire development _____

APPENDIX I (Cont.)

1.C. (cont.)

Describe the development by checking as many of the following categories that apply:

Master-planned project _____
Campus-style _____
Urban village _____
Suburban downtown _____
Business park _____
Office park _____
Executive park _____
Industrial park _____
Technology park _____
Mixed-Use complex _____
Speculative buildings _____

Describe the overall design philosophy, if any, behind the project:

_____
_____
_____
_____
_____
_____

1.D. Please provide information on the following **land use** characteristics of the development:

Percent of total floorspace in project devoted to:

Offices _____
Retail and Commercial _____
Industrial/Manufacturing _____
Warehousing _____
Residential housing _____
Other (_____) _____
Total: 100%

Number of housing dwelling units currently in the development _____
-- Number of detached single-family units _____
-- Number of attached multi-family units _____

Expected number of dwelling units at project build-out (completion) _____

Number of restaurants currently in the development _____

Number of banks currently in the development _____

Number of shopping clusters, retail centers,
or shopping malls in the development _____

APPENDIX I (Cont.)

1.D. (cont.)

Within a three mile radius of the development:
Approximate square footage of retail development _____
Number of shopping centers or shopping malls
    with over 100,000 square feet of floorspace _____
Number of residential dwelling units _____
    -- Number of single-family units _____
    -- Number of multi-family units _____
Approximate purchase price of "average"
    or typical single-family home _____
Approximate monthly rental of "average"
    or typical apartment unit _____

1.E. Please provide information on the following **land ownership** characteristics of the development:

Of the development's total land area, what share is:
    Owned by the developer or developers _____
    Owned by private firms and companies _____

Number of different property owners in the development _____

2. Transportation Characteristics of Development

2.A. Please provide information on the following **travel characteristics of workers** in the development.

Average home-to-work travel time of employees (in minutes) _____

Average home-to-work one-way travel distance of employees (in miles) _____

Percent of total workforce that commutes to work by:
    Driving alone _____
    Carpool _____
    Vanpool _____
    Mass transit _____
    Walk _____
    Other (_____) _____
                Total: 100%

Percent of workforce that participates in:
    Flexitime program _____
    Staggered work hours program _____
    Work-at-home program _____

Average time of arrival of workforce in morning _____ (a.m.)

Average time of departure of workforce in evening _____ (p.m.)

APPENDIX I (Cont.)

2.B. Please provide information on the following **transportation facilities and service** characteristics at or near the development:

Number of freeway miles (in one direction) within
a five mile radius of the development _____

Number of roadway miles (in one direction) within
the development itself _____

Number of freeway interchanges within
a three mile radius of the development _____

Daily traffic volume (in one direction) of the principal freeway or
arterial that serves or leads into the development _____

Average level-of-service on principal freeway or arterial that serves
or leads into the development on typical weekday _____
(where traffic volumes as a percent of capacity are:
A = < 60%; B = 60-69%; C = 70-79%;
D = 80-89%; E = 90-99%; F = 100% or >)

Average level-of-service on major surface streets
within a three mile radius of the development _____

Designated or generally accepted peak hour (e.g., 7:30-8:30 a.m.):
-- For morning peak _____
-- For afternoon peak _____

Percent of daily trips by workforce in the development that occur during:
-- Morning peak hour _____
-- Afternoon peak hour _____

Typical or "average" number of parking spaces in the development:
-- Per 1,000 gross square feet of floorspace _____
-- Per employee _____

The current parking ratios in the development are: (check whichever apply)
-- Below the ratios found at comparable developments in the area _____
-- At or above the ratios found at comparable developments _____
-- Below maximum zoning requirements _____
-- Above minimum zoning requirements _____

Number of mass transit bus runs that operate during the main peak hour:
-- Within the development _____
-- Within a three mile radius of the development _____

Average daily ridership of bus service(s) that
operate(s) within the development _____

APPENDIX I (Cont.)

2.B. (cont.)

Do the owners of the development operate or support: Yes   No
     -- A shuttle or circulator within the complex   ___   ___
     -- Commuter bus runs outside the complex   ___   ___
     (If yes to either, please describe: _____
_____
_____
_____)

Number of privately owned and operated subscription or
     commuter buses that serve the development daily _____

Number of companies in the development that provide vans for
     their employees as part of a formal vanpool program _____

Current number of company-sponsored vans
     that serve employees in the development _____

Within the development, is there: Yes   No
     A designated rideshare coordinator   ___   ___
     A special office for rideshare coordination   ___   ___
     A separate, internal bikepath system   ___   ___

3. Survey Respondent Information

Title or position of respondent _____

Name and phone of possible contact person _____

THANK YOU FOR YOUR TIME AND ASSISTANCE

** Please return the questionnaire in the stamped, return envelope **

APPENDIX 2
Cluster analysis summary

This Appendix briefly discusses the empirical results for the cluster analysis of SECs summarized in Chapter 4, section 4.3. Changes in the coefficients (i.e., squared Euclidean distances) from one step of grouping to another formed the basis for deciding at what stage to stop merging clusters. For instance, the two SECs that were paired at the first stage to form the initial cluster were Bishop Ranch and Corporate Woods since they had the lowest distance coefficient – 0.0875. The second stage involved the grouping of BWI and East Garden City, whose distance coefficient was 0.123. This process continued, with coefficients getting larger at each step. Between the 42nd and 43rd stages, the coefficients rose from 6.69 to 6.88, a modest 2.8 per cent increase. Between the 43rd and 44th stages, there was a marked increase in the coefficients from 6.88 to 8.38, a 21.8 per cent jump. The sharpest rise, however, was between the 44th and 45th stages, whereby the coefficients rose 32.3 per cent, from 8.37 to 11.08. At this stage, the coefficients were getting comparatively high, nearly two-thirds more than what they had been just two stages earlier – an indication that the merging process should cease. This was confirmed by the fact that the coefficients increased by less than one-tenth of 1 per cent between the 45th and 46th stages.

Table A.2 presents the dendrogram produced from this analysis. The dendrogram, which is read from left to right, portrays the formation of clusters in sequence, scaled so that distance coefficients fall between 0 and 25. Vertical lines denote joined clusters. The position of the line on the scale indicates the distance at which clusters were joined. Since many of the distances at the beginning stages are similar in magnitude, it is difficult to tell the sequence in which some of the early clusters are formed. (For instance, it is clear that Bishop Ranch, Corporate Woods, Hacienda, and Inverness combined early to form a cluster; however, at exactly what stage this occurred is not discernible.) More relevant, however, is the formation of clusters at the later stages, i.e., to the right side of the dendogram, since this is where the cut-off is usually set for merging clusters. All clusters formed after the normalized distance score of 15 were ignored. This meant that some of the more idiosyncratic cases (e.g., The Woodlands) that entered in the far late stages had to be judgementally assigned to a cluster. This was generally done so that

Table A. 2 Dendrogram of Cluster Analysis of 57 SECs

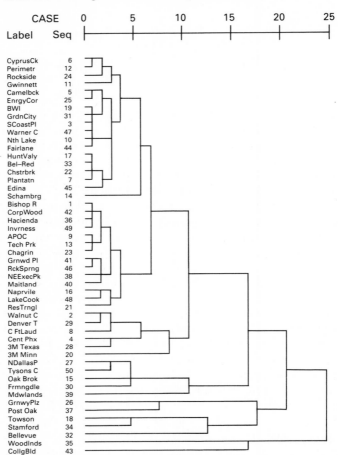

Label	Seq
CyprusCk	6
Perimetr	12
Rockside	24
Gwinnett	11
Camelbck	5
EnrgyCor	25
BWI	19
GrdnCity	31
SCoastPl	3
Warner C	47
Nth Lake	10
Fairlane	44
HuntValy	17
Bel–Red	33
Chstrbrk	22
Plantatn	7
Edina	45
Schambrg	14
Bishop R	1
CorpWood	42
Hacienda	36
Invrness	49
APOC	9
Tech Prk	13
Chagrin	23
Grnwd Pl	41
RckSprng	46
NEExecPk	38
Maitland	40
Naprvile	16
LakeCook	48
ResTrngl	21
Walnut C	2
Denver T	29
C FtLaud	8
Cent Phx	4
3M Texas	28
3M Minn	20
NDallasP	27
Tysons C	50
Oak Brok	15
Frmngdle	30
Mdwlands	39
GrnwyPlz	26
Post Oak	37
Towson	18
Stamford	34
Bellevue	32
Woodlnds	35
CollgBld	43

these cases fell within the ranges of some of the key density and size variables for a group. Additionally, in order to ensure that the final groups had roughly comparable numbers of cases, in several instances large clusters that had merged in fairly early stages were separated, in one case below the normalized coefficient of 8. Thus, as used in this study, cluster analysis, in and of itself, is not an end result. Rather, it is helpful for providing an overall framework for grouping cases. When combined with one's best judgements, it provides a useful foundation for generating interpretable clusters.

BIBLIOGRAPHY

Adams, John S. 1970. Residential structure of midwestern cities. *Annals of the Association of American Geographers* 60, 37–62.

Alonso, William 1964. *Location and land use*. Cambridge, Mass.: Harvard University Press.

Anderson, Charles 1986. *Site design and traffic generation in suburban office park developments*. Berkeley, Ca: Department of City and Regional Planning, University of California, Master's thesis.

Association of Bay Area Governments 1985. *Jobs/Housing balance for traffic mitigation*. Oakland: Association of Bay Area Governments.

Atlanta Regional Commission 1985. *Transportation problems and strategies for major activity centers in the Atlanta region*. Atlanta: Atlanta Regional Commission.

Atlanta Regional Commission 1986. *Population and housing estimates for the Atlanta region, 1986*. Atlanta: Atlanta Regional Commission.

Ayadalot, P. 1984. *The reversal of spatial trends in French industry since 1974*. In *New spatial dynamics and economic crisis*, J.G. Lambooy (ed.). Helsinki: Finnpublishers.

Bachman, G. !987. Edinborough MXD: providing affordable housing on a prime tract in the Minneapolis region's hottest office market. *Urban Land* 46, 16–20.

Baerwald, Thomas J. 1982. Land-use change in suburban clusters and corridors. *Transportation Research Record* 861, 7–12.

Baker, Carol 1983. Tracking Washington's metro. *American Demographics* 5, 30–5, 40.

Barton-Aschman, Inc. 1983. Shared parking demand for selected land uses. *Urban Land* 42, 12–17.

Ben-Akiva, Moshe & Steven R. Lerman 1985. *Discrete choice analysis: theory and application to travel demand*. Cambridge, Mass.: MIT Press.

Berry, B. J. L. 1959. Ribbon developments in the urban business pattern. *Annals of the Association of American Geographers* 49, 120–43.

Berry, B. J. L. and Q. Gillard 1977. *The changing shape of metropolitan America*. Cambridge, Mass.: Ballinger.

Blalock, Hubert M. 1979. *Social statistics*. Revised 2nd edn. New York: McGraw-Hill.

Blumenfeld, Hans 1964. The urban pattern. *Annals of the American Academy of Political and Social Science* 352, 8–24.

Bookout, L. W. & J. W. Wentling 1988. Density by design. *Urban Land* 47, 10–15.

Briggs, Dwight, A. Pisarski & J. McDonnell 1986. *Journey-to-work trends*. Washington, D.C.: COMSIS Corporation. Report prepared for Federal Highway Administration, US Department of Transportation.

Brown, Malcom, John Morrall & Alison Wong 1984. *The Impact of transit on suburban office travel characteristics*. Compendium of Technical Papers. San

Francisco: 54th Annual Meeting of the Institute of Transportation Engineers.

Burby, Raymond J. & Shirley F. Weiss 1976. *New communities U.S.A.* Lexington, Mass.: Lexington Books.

Burgess, Ernest W. 1925. The growth of the city. In *The city*, R.E. Park, E.W. Burgess, & R.D. McKenzie (eds.). Chicago: University of Chicago Press.

California Department of Finance 1986. *Summary Report: Alameda County controlled population estimates, 1980–1986.* Sacramento: California Department of Finance.

Carroll, J. Douglass, Jr. 1952. The relation of home to work places and the spatial patterns of cities. *Social Forces* 30, 271–82.

Castles, S. & G. Kosack 1985. *Immigrant workers and class structure in western Europe.* London: Oxford University Press.

Catanese, A. J. 1971. Home and workplace separation in four urban regions. *Journal of the American Institute of Planners* 37, 331–7.

Cervero, Robert 1984. Managing the traffic impacts of suburban office development. *Transportation Quarterly* 56, 533–50.

Cervero, Robert 1986a. *Jobs–housing imbalances as a transportation problem.* Research Report 86–9. Berkeley.: Institute of Transportation Studies, University of California.

Cervero, Robert 1986b. *Suburban gridlock.* New Brunswick: Rutgers University. Center for Urban Policy Research.

Cervero, Robert 1988. Congestion, growth and public choices. *Berkeley Planning Journal* 3, 55–75.

Cervero, Robert & Bruce Griesenbeck 1988. Commuting choices in suburban labor markets: a case analysis of Pleasanton, California. *Transportation Research* 22A, 151–61.

Chapin, F. Stuart & Edward J. Kaiser 1979. *Urban land use planning.* Urbana: University of Illinois Press.

Church, George J. 1987. The boom towns. *Time*, June 15, 1987, 14–17.

Clark, F.P. 1954. Office buildings in the suburbs. *Urban Land* 13, 8–14.

Clark, W. A. V. & James E. Burt 1980. The impact of workplace on residential location. *Annals of the Association of American Geographers* 70, 59–67.

Communications Technologies 1987. *The commuting behavior of employees of Santa Clara County's Golden Triangle.* San Francisco: Report prepared for the Golden Triangle Task Force, Santa Clara County, California.

Commuter Transportation Services 1987. *Warner Center transportation survey results.* Los Angeles: Commuter Transportation Services, Inc.

Daniels, P.W. 1974. New offices in the suburbs. In *Suburban growth*, J. Johnson (ed.). Westmead: Gower.

Delaware Valley Regional Planning Commission 1986. *Route 130 corridor study.* Philadelphia: Report prepared for the New Jersey Department of Transportation.

Diamond, Susan 1985. A transportation system management ordinance: Developer-requested regulation. *Land Use Law* 37, 3–6.

Dingle Associates, Inc. 1982. *Ridesharing programs of business and industry.* Washington, D.C.: Report prepared for the Federal Highway Administration, US Department of Transportation.

DKS Associates 1987. *Bellevue CBD implementation study: transportation/circulation element.* Oakland, California: Report prepared for the City of Bellevue Planning Department.

Dowall, David E. 1984. *The suburban squeeze.* Berkeley: University of California Press.

Dowall, David E. 1987. Back offices and San Francisco's office development growth cap. *Cities*. 1, 119–27.

Dunteman, George H. 1984. *Introduction to multivariate analysis*. Beverly Hills: Sage Publications.

Dunphy, Robert 1985. Urban traffic congestion: a national crisis? *Urban Land* 44, 2–7.

Dunphy, Robert 1987. Suburban mobility: reducing reliance on the auto in DuPage County, Illinois. *Urban Land* 46, 6–9.

DuPage County Development Department 1986. *DuPage County growth trend report*. Wheaton, Illinois: DuPage County Development Department.

Erickson, Rodney A. 1983. The evolution of the suburban space economy. *Urban Geography* 4, 95–121.

Everitt, Brian 1980. *Cluster analysis*, 2nd edn. New York: Halsted Press.

Federal Highway Administration 1986. *Highway statistics*. Washington, D.C.: US Department of Transportation, Federal Highway Administration.

Fothergill, S. & G. Gudgin 1982. *Unequal growth: urban and regional employment change in the U.K.* London: Heinemann.

Freeman, Kemper, William R. Eager & Christina J. Deffebach 1987. A market-based approach to transportation management. *Urban Land* 46, 22–6.

Fulton, Philip 1986. Changing journey-to-work patterns: the increasing prevalence of commuting within suburbs in metropolitan areas. Paper presented at the 65th Annual Meeting of the Transportation Research Board, Washington, D.C.

Fulton, William 1986. Silicon strips. *Planning* 52, 7–12.

Fulton, William, 1987. Boundary fights lead to tax-sharing debate. *California Planning & Development Report* 2, 1,5.

Galehouse, Richard F. 1984. Mixed-use centers in suburban office parks. *Urban Land* 43, 12–16.

Garreau, Joel 1987. From suburbs, cities are springing up in our back yards. *Washington Post*, March 8, 1987, A1, A26–30.

Gauldin, R. 1979. Developing a suburban office park. *Mortgage Banker* 49, 40–6.

Giuliano, Genevieve & Roger F. Teal 1985. Privately provided commuter bus services: experiences, problems, and prospects. In *Urban transit: private challenge to public transportation*, C.A. Lave (ed.). San Francisco: Pacific Institute for Public Policy Research.

Greenwood, M.J. 1982. *Migration and economic growth in the United States: national, regional and metropolitan perspectives*. New York: Academic Press.

Gruen Gruen & Associates 1985. *Employment densities by type of workplace*. San Francisco: Gruen Gruen & Associates.

Gruen Gruen & Associates 1986. *Employment and parking in suburban business parks: a pilot study*. Washington, D.C.: Urban Land Institute.

Harris, Chauncy D. & Edward L. Ullman 1945. The nature of cities. *Annals of the American Academy of Political and Social Science* 242, 7–17.

Hartshorn, Truman A. & Peter O. Muller 1986. *Suburban business centers: employment implications*. Washington, D.C.: US Department of Commerce, Economic Development Administration.

Houston Chamber of Commerce 1982. *Regional mobility plan for the Houston area*. Houston: Chamber of Commerce, Transportation Committee.

Hoyt, Homer 1939. *The structure and growth of residential neighborhoods in American cities*. Washington, D.C.: US Government Printing Office.

Hughes, J. W. & F. James 1975. Changing spatial distributions of jobs and residences: transportation implications. *Growth and Change* 6, 20–5.

Hughes, J. W. & G. Sternlieb 1986. The suburban growth corridors. *American Demographics* 8, 17–22.

Institute of Real Estate Management 1984. *Office buildings: income/expense analysis, downtown and suburban*. Chicago: Institute of Real Estate Management.

Institute of Transportation Engineers 1976. *Transportation and traffic engineering handbook*, J.E. Baerwald (ed.). Englewood Cliffs, New Jersey: Prentice Hall.

Institute of Transportation Engineers 1985. *Planning urban arterial and freeway systems*. Washington, D.C.: Institute of Transportation Engineers, Publication RP–015.

Institute of Transportation Engineers 1987. *Trip generation*, 4th edn. Washington, D.C.: Institute of Transportation Engineers, Seminar Workbook

Jones, D. W. & F. Harrison 1983. *Off work early: the final report of the San Francisco flex-time demonstration project*. University of California, Berkeley: Institute of Transportation Studies.

Kasarda, J. D. & J. Friedrichs 1985. Comparative demographic–employment mismatches in US and West German cities. *Research in the Sociology of Work* 3, 1–30.

Kenyon, K. L. 1984. Increasing mode split through parking management: a suburban success story. *Transportation Research Record* 980, 5–11.

Klinger, Dieter & J. R. Kusmyak 1986. *1983–1984 national personal transportation study*. Washington, D.C.: US Department of Transportation, Federal Highway Administration.

Knack, Ruth E. 1986. The once and future suburb. *Planning* 52, 6–12.

Kroll, Cynthia A. 1986. *Suburban squeeze II: responses to suburban employment growth*. Berkeley: Center for Real Estate and Urban Economics, University of California, Working Paper 86–110.

Lea, Elliott, McLean & Co. 1985. *Dallas Parkway Center: land use and transportation study*. Dallas: Report prepared for North Dallas Chamber of Commerce and the City of Dallas, Texas.

Leinberger, Christopher B. & Charles Lockwood 1986. How business is reshaping America. *Atlantic Monthly*, 1986, 43–51.

Lenny, Ann 1984. Canyon Corporate Center – From RVs to R&D: transition to a higher use. *Urban Land* 43, 23–6.

Levinson, H.S. 1976. Urban travel characteristics. In *Transportation and traffic engineering handbook*, J.E. Baerwald (ed.). Englewood Cliffs, New Jersey: Prentice Hall.

Ley, David 1985. Work–residence relations for head office employees in an inflating housing market. *Urban Studies* 22, 21–38.

Liepman, K. 1944. *The journey to work: its significance for industrial and community life*. London: Kegan, Paul, Trench, & Trubner.

Lindley, J.A. 1987. Urban freeway congestion: quantification of the problem and effectiveness of potential solutions. *Institute of Transportation Engineers Journal* 57, 27–32.

Louis Berger & Associates 1986. *Route 73–38–79 Corridor Study*, Part 2. Trenton. Report prepared for the New Jersey Department of Transportation.

Lynch, Kevin & Gary Hack 1984. *Site planning*. Cambridge, Mass.: MIT Press.

McKeever, J. Ross 1970. *Business parks*. Washington, D.C.: Urban Land Institute, Technical Bulletin 65.

Margolis, Julius 1973. Municipal fiscal structure in a metropolitan region. In *Urban economics: readings and analysis*. R.E. Grieson (ed.). Boston: Little Brown, 379–95.

Masotti, Louis H. & John K. Hadden (eds.). 1973. *The urbanization of the suburbs*. Beverly Hills: Sage Publications.

Meyer, John R., John F. Kain & Martin Wohl 1965. *The urban transportation problem*. Cambridge, Mass.: Harvard University Press.

Meyer, John R. & Jose Gomez-Ibanez 1981. *Autos, transit and cities*. Cambridge, Mass.: Harvard University Press.

Mills, Edwin S. 1972. *Studies in the structure of the urban economy*. Baltimore, MD.: Johns Hopkins University Press.

Northeastern Illinois Planning Commission 1984. Transportation availability and employment opportunities. Chicago: Northeastern Illinois Planning Commission.

Norusis, Marija J. 1986. *Advanced statistics: SPSS/PC+*. Chicago: SPSS Inc.

Office Network 1987. *National office market report*. Houston.

O'Mara, W. Paul & John A. Casazza 1982. *Office development handbook*. Washington, D.C.: Urban Land Institute, Community Builders Handbook Series.

Orski, C. Kenneth 1985. Suburban mobility: the coming transportation crisis? *Transportation Quarterly* 39, 283–96.

Orski, C. Kenneth 1986a. Toward a policy for suburban mobility. In *Urban traffic congestion: what does the future hold*? Washington, D.C.: Institute of Transportation Engineers.

Orski, C. Kenneth 1986b. Transportation management associations: battling suburban traffic congestion. *Urban Land* 45, 2–5.

Orski, C. Kenneth 1987. "Managing" suburban traffic congestion: a strategy for suburban mobility. *Transportation Quarterly* 91, 457–76.

Pisarski, Alan E. 1987. *Commuting in America*. Westport, Conn.: Eno Foundation for Transportation, Inc.

Porter, Douglas R. 1985. The office/housing linkage issue. *Urban Land* 44, 16–21.

Potter, Steven 1984. The transport versus land use dilemma. *Transportation Research Board* 964, 12–18.

Puget Sound Council of Governments 1984. *Regional travel characteristics*. Seattle: Puget Sound Council of Governments.

Pushkarev, Boris & Jeffrey Zupan 1977. *Public transportation and land use policy*. Bloomington: Indiana University Press.

Quigley, John & D. Weinberg 1977. Intraurban residential mobility: a review and synthesis. *International Regional Science Review* 1, 41–66.

Regional Transportation Authority 1987. *Transportation options for suburban Cook County*. Chicago: Regional Transportation Authority.

Reichert, James P. 1979. Wanted: national policy on suburban transit. *Transit Journal* 5, 37–42.

Reimer, Paul 1983. Future high-tech parks. *Urban Land* 42, 19–22.

Reschovsky, Andrew & Eugene Knaff 1977. Tax base sharing: an assessment of the Minnesota experience. *Journal of the American Institute of Planners* 43, 361–70.

Rice Center 1983. Houston metropolitan area. In *Development review and outlook: 1983–1984*. Washington, D.C.: Urban Land Institute.

Rice Center 1987. *Houston's major activity centers and worker travel behavior.* Houston: Rice Center, Joint Center for Urban Mobility Research.

Robert Charles Lesser & Co. 1987. *The new map of metropolitan America.* Sante Fe: Robert Charles Lesser & Company.

Rodriquez, Carlos G., James J. McDonnell, Robert W. Draper & Edward McGarry 1985. *Transportation planning data for urbanized areas: based on the 1980 Census.* Washington, D.C.: US Department of Transportation, Federal Highway Administration.

Rolleston, Barbara 1987. Determinants of restrictive suburban zoning: an empirical analysis. *Journal of Urban Economics* 21, 1–21.

Ruth & Going, Inc. 1983. *South Coast metro area pilot transportation management program.* San Jose, California: Report prepared for the Orange County Transportation Commission.

Sachs, Margaret 1986. *Transportation in suburban job growth areas.* Chicago: Northeastern Illinois Planning Commission.

Schnore, L. F. 1959. The timing of metropolitan decentralization: a contribution to the debate. *Journal of the American Institute of Planners* 25, 200–6.

Schwanke, Dean, Eric Smart & Helen J. Kessler 1986. Looking at MXDs. *Urban Land* 45, 20–5.

Shoup, Donald 1982. Cashing out free parking. *Transportation Quarterly* 36, 351–64.

Solow, Robert M. 1973. On equilibrium models of urban location. In *Essays in modern economics,* J. M. Parkin (ed.). London: Longmans.

Taaffee, E. J., B. J. Gardner & M. H. Yates 1963. *The peripheral journey to work.* Evanston, Illinois: Northwestern University Press.

Thurstone, L.L. 1947. *Multiple factor analysis.* Chicago: University of Chicago Press.

US Bureau of Census 1982. *The journey to work in the United States.* Washington, D.C.: US Government Printing Office, Current Population Reports.

US Bureau of Census 1984. *Statistical abstract of the United States.* Washington, D.C.: US Government Printing Office.

US Department of Transportation 1985. *The status of the nation's highways: conditions and performance.* Washington, D.C.: Report of the Secretary of Transportation to the United States Congress.

Untermann, Richard K. 1984. *Accommodating the pedestrian: adapting towns and neighborhoods for walking and bicycling.* New York: Van Nostrand Reinhold.

Urban Land Institute 1984. *Development review and outlook.* Washington, D.C.: Urban Land Institute.

Urban Land Institute 1986. *Development trends 1986.* Washington, D.C.: Urban Land Institute.

Urban Land Institute 1987. *Market profiles 1987.* Washington, D.C.: Urban Land Institute.

Urban Land Institute 1988. *Market profiles 1988.* Washington, D.C.: Urban Land Institute.

Vernon, R. 1963. *Metropolis 1985.* Garden City, New York: Anchor Books.

Warner, Sam Bass 1962. *Street car suburbs.* Cambridge, Mass.: Harvard University Press.

Warner, A.M. 1972. Estimates of journey to work distances from census statistics. *Regional Studies* 6, 211–19.

Wasylenko, Michael 1980. Evidence of fiscal differentials and intrametropolitan firm relocation. *Land Economics* 56, 339–49.

Webster, F. V., P. H. Bly, R. H. Johnston, N. Paulley & M. Dasgupta 1985. *Changing patterns of urban travel*. Paris: OECD, European Conference of Ministers of Transport.

Wegmann, F. J. & S. R. Stokey 1983. Impact of flexitime work schedules on an employer-based ridesharing program. *Transportation Research Record* 914, 9–13.

Willemain, Thomas 1981. *Statistical methods for planners*. Cambridge, Mass.: MIT Press.

Windsor, D. 1979. *Fiscal zoning in suburban communities*. Lexington, Mass.: Heath.

Wingo, Lowdon, Jr. 1961. *Transportation and urban land*. Washington, D.C.: Resources for the Future.

Work, Clemens, G. Witkin, L. J. Moore & S. Golden 1987. Jam sessions. *U.S. News and World Report*, September 7, 1987, 20–7.

INDEX

activity centers 17, 184–5, 187–90
administrative workers 32, 62, 107, 146, 152, 183
affordable housing 50, 69
agglomerations 16, 82
aggregation biases 135, 154
analysis of variance 104–5
Atlanta, Georgia 6–7, 15, 17, 25, 47, 53, 96–7
Aurora, Illinois 180
automobile
  circulation 3, 33
  design biases 3, 33, 58–9, 62
  disincentives 58
  dominance of 40, 62, 122, 125, 195
  mode shares 61–5, 125–8
  usage in suburbs 3, 8, 62–4

back-office functions 5, 32, 36, 157, 164
balanced communities 46–7, 53
ballot box zoning 184
banks 41–2, 44–5, 92, 94, 116, 118, 127, 139
Bay Area Rapid Transit (BART) 59, 64, 87, 89–91
bedroom communities 4, 49, 74, 155
Bellevue, Washington 27, 33, 39, 57–8, 63–6, 85, 169–76, 193, 195, 200
Bel–Red corridor, Washington 27, 65, 169, 171
bicycling, see cycling
Bishop Ranch Business Park, California 6, 24, 49, 59–60, 63–4, 87, 198, 205
Boston, Massachusetts 5, 7, 10, 25, 100–1
Boulder, Colorado 10
boundary issues 19, 81, 83, 99
building
  coverage 33, 36, 79, 172
  heights 6, 34, 38, 67, 74, 80, 83–4, 94, 108–10, 171, 190, 193

layouts 23, 36, 39, 56, 60, 68, 112, 192, 202
lines 34, 39, 172
moratoria 9–10, 101
placement 43, 54, 68, 80, 84, 179, 192, 203
tenancy 66–7, 80, 82, 156, 158–61, 164
build-out 30, 32, 105
bus transit, see transit.
business associations 19, 28, 83, 198
business parks 31, 36, 40, 56–7, 63, 99

Camelback corridor, Arizona 83
campus-style designs 6, 33–6, 77, 80, 91, 101
carpools, see ridesharing
case study sites
  listing of 21–3
  location of 22–3
  selection of 18–20
  summaries of 86–101, 168–94
Central Avenue Corridor, Arizona 82, 89
central business districts (CBDs) 16–17, 21, 43, 57, 106, 149, 151–2, 170–1
Chesterbrook, Pennsylvania 26, 51–3, 93–4
Chicago, Illinois 7–8, 25, 50, 53, 66, 176–84, 193
child care facilities 89, 172, 207
citizen opposition 9–10, 49, 84
City Post Oak, Texas 6, 17, 26, 37–9, 58, 60–1, 63–5, 78, 84–5, 185, 187–8, 192, 195
class A office space 38, 69, 87, 92–3
class segregation 50
classification 72–4
clerical workers 5, 31–2, 36, 50, 53, 92, 107, 152–3, 157, 161, 164, 166, 183
Cleveland, Ohio 26
cluster analysis 78–9, 102–3, 217–18
College Boulevard, Kansas 94–5

communities
  balanced 46–8, 53
  bedroom 4, 49, 74
  corporate 49
commutersheds 51, 183
commuting
  cross-town 1, 7–8, 12, 14, 73, 183
  distances 46, 50–1, 53, 61–2, 69, 98,
    125–6, 139, 157–8, 162–3, 191
  factors related to 32–3, 58, 125, 130–1,
    135–42
  patterns 1, 7–9, 12, 14, 73, 183
  modes 59, 62–5, 127–8, 157, 165, 191
  speeds 61–2, 125–6, 142–3, 186
  travel times 61–2, 125–6, 143–4
company size 159–64
concentric zones 72–3
conditional use zoning 200
conditions, *see* covenants
condominium 51–3, 85, 119
congestion
  citizen revolts against 8–10
  index 8–9
  suburban 1–4, 6–9, 67–8, 90–1, 98, 100,
    129–31, 165, 183, 196
Contra Costa County, California 50
corporate communities 49
Copenhagen, Denmark 10
correlations
  land use factors 76–7, 109, 113–14, 117,
    119
  land use-transportation factors 3,
    148–50, 209–10
corridor associations 28, 99
counterurbanization 73
covenants 36, 60, 87, 91, 112, 191, 205
coverage ratio 34–6, 57, 69, 77, 80, 89,
    108, 110
cross-hauling 8, 14, 73
cumulative impacts 7
Cupertino, California 207
Cypress Creek, Florida 25, 63, 68, 83, 92
cycling
  design considerations 41, 60–1, 64–5,
    204–5
  levels 64, 127, 151, 165
  paths 60, 64, 202, 204–5
  provisions 60, 202, 205

Dallas, Texas 6, 8, 26, 47
data sources 18–21, 168–9, 211–16
decentralization 1, 4–6, 9, 11, 73
dendogram 79, 217–18
density
  bonuses 172–3, 193, 199–200, 206, 208
  effects on congestion 2–3, 130–1, 145–7,
    165, 195, 201
  factors 20, 75–7

population and residential 52
relationship to mode choice 2, 33, 66,
    127, 132, 134, 147, 165, 190–1
strategies to create 131, 201–2
tapering 172, 201
Denver, Colorado 1, 24, 48
Denver Technology Center, Colorado 24,
    39, 57, 63–5, 85, 202, 206–7
derived demand 2, 18
design
  aesthetics and amenities 33, 60, 69, 77,
    172, 192, 205
  approaches 2, 36, 195
  considerations 20, 179
  controls on 40, 79, 112, 153–4
  coordination 79–80, 83, 112, 153–4
  factors 76–7
  guidelines 179–80
  impacts on travel mode 2–3, 18, 33, 39,
    62, 210
Detroit, Michigan 7, 9, 26–7
developers
  attitudes of 56
  land controls by 40, 108, 112, 153–4
development fees, *see* impact fees
downtown, *see* central business districts
downzoning 9, 49
drive-alone commuting 2–3, 42, 62–4,
    125–8, 134–8, 156–7, 165, 196
dual wage-earners 46, 50
DuPage County, Illinois 7, 180–4

East Farmingdale, New York 24, 31, 63,
    83
East Garden City, New York 24, 92–3
eateries 42, 44–5, 70, 116, 118
Edinborough project, Minnesota 200
Edina, Minnesota 26, 83, 200–1
employment
  composition 20, 31–2, 106–7, 143–4
  densities 34, 36, 110–11, 142–3, 151–4
  growth 4–6, 9, 186
  sizes 31, 105–6, 119, 140–1, 148–9,
    158–60, 162–4
employment centers
  criteria for 16–17, 28
  locations 24–7
energy consumption 51, 209
Energy Corridor, *see* West Houston
    Energy Corridor
entropy index 77–8, 81–6, 115–16, 143–4
exclusionary policies 49, 183, 200
extended commuting 8

factor analysis 75–8, 102
factor scores 75, 78, 102
Fairfax County, Virginia 97–8
Fairlane Town Center, Michigan 26–7

fair-share housing programs 198
female labor 5, 46, 157
FIRE (financial-insurance-real estate) 5, 48, 96
fiscal zoning 49, 197
flex-time 146, 157–8, 160–4
floor area ratio (FAR) 20, 28, 33–5, 38, 69, 75–7, 81–6, 101, 108–9, 146, 148–9, 154, 165, 171–2, 201
footloose 11, 73
footpaths 60, 87 *see also* pedestrian movements, trailpaths, walking
Forrestal Center, New Jersey 99–100
Fort Collins, Colorado 199
France 11
freeway
  congestion 1, 67–8, 129–30, 145–7, 186
  facilities 54–5, 68, 121–2, 142–4
  interchanges 54–5, 122, 136, 139
  networks 68, 89, 121–2
frontage roads 54

Galleria, Georgia 56
Galleria, Texas 60, 84, 187, 192
Golden Triangle, California 24, 31, 47, 61, 68
Gwinnett County, Georgia 7
Great Britain 10–12, 46, 73–4
Greenway Plaza, Texas 17, 26, 38, 51, 57, 63, 65, 82, 110, 185, 188, 190–1
Greenwood Plaza, Colorado 24, 48, 82
growth classifications 74
growth controls 9–10, 49, 84, 90–1, 101, 199

Hacienda Business Park, California 24, 49, 52, 59, 64–5, 155–6
Helsinki, Finland 10
hierarchical clustering 78–9, 217–18
high technology
  growth 4, 10, 49, 99
  parks 7, 39, 77, 101, 177
horizontal skyscrapers 2, 35–6
Houston, Texas 1, 6, 9, 26, 32, 42, 57–8, 61, 64, 184–93
housing
  affordable 4, 50, 53, 69, 98, 153, 194, 198, 209
  linkage programs 208
  multi-family 49–50, 52, 115, 118–19, 127
  prices 50, 52–3, 115, 120, 131, 151–2, 166
  provisions 43, 51–3, 115, 118–20, 145, 172
  single-family 50, 119
  supply 50, 115, 119–20
Howard Hughes Center, California 56–7
Hunt Valley, Maryland 25, 63, 95

hypotheses 3–4, 134, 142, 164–6, 195–6

impact fees 101, 176–7, 207–8
incentive zoning 172–3, 200
inclusionary zoning 206–8
industrial development 11, 74
industrial parks 7, 74
infilling 74
Institute of Transportation Engineers (ITE) 17, 41, 66, 69, 71
institutional responses 180, 196–201
interchanges 54, 122, 136, 139
international comparisons 10–12, 46
Interstate-5, Oregon 31, 98–9
Interstate-88, Illinois 83, 177, 179, 182
intra-suburban commuting 7–8, 46, 181–3

job turnover rates 50–1
jobs-housing balance
  benefits of 46, 51, 141–2, 207
  definition of 46–7, 70
  factors related to 51–3, 165–6
  inside SECs 52–3, 99, 139, 152–3, 207, 209
  near SECs 53, 99, 139, 152–3, 207, 209
  programs to promote 151, 172–3, 197–8
jobs-housing imbalances
  reasons for 48–51
  scope 3, 46–8, 61, 86, 119, 166, 180–4, 196
journey to work, *see* commuting

Katy freeway, Texas 1, 189

labor force *see* employment
Lake-Cook corridor, Illinois 25, 66, 178
land
  conversion 117, 207
  lotting 34, 38–9
  ownership 20, 40, 112
  size 34, 111–12
land use
  composition 20, 43
  coordination 2, 49, 208
  definition of 17–18
  entropy index 77–8, 81–6, 115–16
  factors 77–8
  industrial 74, 114
  mixes 2, 40–3, 45, 49, 68, 113–18, 138, 165, 190–1
  office 43–5, 66, 68, 77–8, 81–6, 113–14, 136–7, 139–41, 153–4
  planning 49, 180, 197–8
  residential 43–5, 49, 77–8, 97
  retail 44–5, 113–14, 137, 141, 148–50, 152–3, 165
  segregation 48, 191, 200, 207–8
landscaping 33, 39, 79, 85, 99, 204

large office growth corridors 19, 79–80, 98–101, 129
Las Colinas, Texas 6, 95
level of service 67–8, 71, 91, 133, 144–6, 199
light-industrial uses 44, 107, 110, 114
location theory 73
logit analysis 158–64
London, England 10–12
Long Island Expressway, New York 8
Los Angeles, California 8, 24, 59
lot
  dimensions 34, 38–9, 112
  shapes 38–9, 111
lotting patterns 34, 38–9, 108, 111–12, 172
Luxembourg 10

Maitland Center, Florida 87–8
management staffs 32, 152–3
Manchester, England 11–12
Manhattan, New York 31, 92–3
manufacturing decline 6, 11–12, 73–4
marketing strategies 58, 107, 173
master-planned projects 6, 19, 51, 54, 77, 79–80, 93–4, 200
Meadowlands, New Jersey 24, 31, 51, 59, 63–4, 83, 93
megacomplexes 6, 74, 84, 114
megacounties 7
metropolitan
  form 72–4
  planning organizations 19, 100
Minneapolis, Minnesota 26, 59, 74, 197, 201
mixed-use
  advantages of 41–3, 64, 69
  developments, *see* MXD
  effects on ridesharing 42, 69, 118, 131, 137–8, 142, 165, 195, 206–7
  examples 92–5, 169–75, 190–1, 200
mobility crisis 1–2, 67
mode of travel
  distributions 62–4, 69, 125–8
  factors influencing 2, 8, 54, 56, 58, 122, 125, 127–8, 130–2, 134–42, 147, 158–62, 165, 196
  levels among SECs 62–5
Mount Laurel II court decision 100, 198
multicollinearity 76, 79, 102, 135
multi-tenancy 156, 158–61
multiple nuclei growth 73–4
MXD
  extent of 43, 69
  large-scale 79–80, 82–3, 92–3, 101, 105, 107, 112, 114–20, 122, 125–8, 131, 148, 165
  moderate-scale 79–80, 83–4, 93–5, 101, 122, 129–31

Naperville, Illinois 25, 50, 66, 176–7, 179–80
negotiations 199, 209
New England Executive Park, Massachusetts 25, 88–9
New York metropolitan area 24, 49, 92–3
new towns 10, 12, 19, 93–4
North Belt, Texas 190
North Dallas Parkway, Texas 26, 47, 51, 68, 84, 95–6, 119, 206

Oak Brook, Illinois 25, 48, 66, 83, 177, 179, 181–4
Oakland County, Michigan 7
occupational breakdowns 31–2, 107, 129, 157
off-site
  housing 52–3
  road facilities 54
  traffic impacts 6–7
  transit services 59
office boom 4–7, 12
office concentrations 6–7, 16, 79–80, 89–91, 101, 109, 113, 150
office decentralization
  reasons for 4, 73
  scope of 5–6, 72–4
office growth
  corridors 79–80, 98–101, 129
  rate of 1, 4, 10, 73
  reasons for 4–6, 73
  share in suburbs 4–5, 9, 43
office parks
  campus-style 6, 31, 68, 77, 79–82, 87–9, 101
  design standards 33, 36, 56, 60
O'Hare Airport, Illinois 178–9
on-site
  amenities 42–5, 92, 94
  child-care 89, 172, 207
  hotels 84, 93–7, 116
  housing 51–3, 83–4, 95–7, 99, 115, 118–20
  parking 54–8, 69–70
  restaurant 42, 44–5, 92, 97, 141, 165
  retail 42, 44–5, 92, 97, 141, 165
  road facilities 54, 120–2
  transit services 59, 121, 204
open space 36, 87
Opus II project, Minnesota 205
Orange County, California 6, 44, 50, 208
Palo Alto, California 47–8, 57, 70
Paris, France 10, 12
park-and-ride lots 90–1
parking
  cost of providing 56–7, 70
  design considerations 43, 201, 205–6
  factors related to 54–9, 147–54

free 3, 58, 60, 64, 69, 91, 122, 192–3, 195
    on-site 54–8
    ordinance 171, 173, 175
    phasing in 56–7
    preferential 58, 180, 204
    price 54–5, 58, 122–3, 132, 147, 173, 192
    provisions 43, 55–8, 70, 81–6, 121–3
    restrictions 57–8, 173, 175–6
    shared–use 42–3, 150, 201, 206
    space consumption 43, 56–7
    standards 33, 56, 148, 150, 173, 175, 205
    structures 37, 57, 70, 148, 175
    suburban 3, 122, 173
    supply 33, 43, 54–60, 69–70, 79, 81–6, 122, 146, 150, 165, 171, 173, 175, 192, 205
    underground 171, 206
    walking distances for 57–8, 70
peak travel 65–6, 126, 129, 131, 160, 162–5
pedestrian movement
    encouragement of 60, 172–3, 175, 193, 202
    pathways for 60, 87, 191–2, 204–5
    skywalks for 60, 188, 192, 204
    see also trailpaths, walking
performance zoning 199, 207
Perimeter Center 15, 25, 47, 51, 57, 84, 96–7, 103, 202
Petaluma, California 10
Philadelphia, Pennsylvania 5, 26, 33, 56, 93
Phoenix, Arizona 89
Pittsburgh, Pennsylvania 7, 21
planned unit development (PUD) 19, 49, 60
Pleasanton, California 27, 35, 61, 154–65
political context 10, 180, 196–8
Portland, Oregon 7, 98–9, 206
post-industrialization 5–6, 21, 50, 73
Post Oak, see City Post Oak
Princeton, New Jersey 7, 99–100
private commuter buses 59, 123, 188
private sector initiatives 198
project
    coordination 40, 180
    evolution 40, 82
    expansion 30, 105
    size 30–1, 91, 105–6, 145–7, 165
property ownership 34, 40, 108, 112, 153–4
public opinion polls 8, 186

questionnaire 20–1, 211–16

Ramapo, New York 10
rail transit 64
Reading, England 10

Redmond, Washington 169–70, 206
regional growth patterns 48–9, 197
regression analysis 134–5, 144–5, 167
regulations 198–201, 208
reindustrialization 11
research and development 36, 80, 91, 100–1
research methods 13, 18, 27, 74–9, 104, 168, 217–18
Research Triangle, North Carolina 15, 18, 33, 77, 82, 91
restaurants 41–2, 44–5, 115, 127, 139
restrictive zoning 10, 49, 101, 197
retail
    land use 43–5, 56, 116–18, 141, 195
    intensities 44, 115, 118, 137–8, 153–4
    plazas 44, 60, 116–17, 171–2, 175
residential
    buy-outs 96–7
    land use 43–4, 173
ridesharing
    company sponsorship of 59, 123–4
    coordinators 59–60, 124, 136, 138, 157, 175, 188
    design considerations 58, 204
    effects of flex-time on 158, 160, 164
    factors influencing 42, 58, 63, 118, 127, 138–40, 158–62, 164–5
    levels among SECs 59–60, 63–4, 127
    mode share 58, 63–4, 125–8, 188, 195
    parking preferences for 58, 180, 204
roadway
    configurations 8, 12, 68, 203
    facilities in SECs 54, 120–1, 125, 203
    facilities near SECs 54, 121–2
    functions 51, 54
Route 1, New Jersey 7, 26, 31, 47, 99–100, 206
Route 101, California 1, 7, 68
Route 128, Massachusetts 7, 25, 31, 89
Route 495, Massachusetts 10, 25, 31, 49, 100–1

Saint Louis, Missouri 5, 7
sample frame 18–21
San Francisco, California 1, 6, 8, 24, 27, 33, 47, 56, 155, 158, 198
San Jose, California 7, 24, 200–1
San Ramon, California 35, 57, 87
Santa Clara County, California 47–9, 61, 68, 201
satellite centers 10, 15, 74, 84
scatterplots 109, 114, 117, 119, 149–50
Schaumburg, Illinois 25, 44, 48, 83, 176–8, 181–4
Seattle, Washington 27, 65, 169–76
SEC
    build-out 30, 32

definition of 17–18, 30
density 32–6, 68, 108–11
designs 32–6, 60, 68–9, 105–12
evolution 82, 86
groups 79–87, 104–5
location 18, 21, 24, 30, 105–6
occupational breakdowns 31–2, 106–7
size 18, 30–1, 69, 82, 105–6, 109, 147, 165
sector growth 72
sensitivity analysis 160–3
service-based economy 5–6, 11, 21, 73
setbacks 39, 68, 89, 111–12, 172, 192, 202
shared parking 42–3, 150, 201, 206
shopping malls 4, 74, 83, 85–6, 89, 96, 99, 114–15, 117, 177, 180, 190
sidewalks 87, 172, 180, 191–2, 202
signature building 39, 112
Silicon Valley, California 7, 47, 49–50
single tenant buildings 39, 112
site design
  guidelines 179–80, 184
  organization of buildings 35, 39, 179
  strategies 179–80, 202–5
size factors 76–7, 145–6
smart buildings 5, 33, 99
solo-commuting, *see* drive-alone
South Coast Metro, California 6, 24, 42, 44, 51, 57–8, 64, 68, 78
sprawl 73
staggered work hours 126, 129
Stamford, Connecticut 24, 58, 63, 84
state initiatives 198, 208
stepwise analysis 134–5
streets, *see* roadways
Stockholm, Sweden 10, 12
study outline 3, 12–14
sub-cities 79–80, 95–8, 101, 105–10, 112, 114–15, 119, 122–3, 125–6, 128–9, 131, 133, 150, 169
subregional
  balance 46
  planning 48–9, 197–8
suburban
  activity centers 16, 184–5
  boundaries 15, 81, 83, 99
  centers 6, 16–17, 74, 79–80, 89–91, 101, 150, 202
  clusters 6, 16–17, 74, 202
  commute patterns 1, 7–8
  corridors 7, 10, 79, 98–101
  definitions 15–16
  downtowns 6, 74, 84, 95, 202
  employment centers, *see* SEC
  employment growth 1, 4–7, 11–12, 73, 176, 186
  parking standards 3, 54–8, 148
  traffic 1, 4, 8

suburbanization
  commercial 4, 73, 186
  residential 4, 73
  waves 4, 74
suburb-to-suburb commuting 7–8, 12, 46
sunbelt growth 5, 9, 11
Sunset Corridor, Oregon 7, 99
superblocks 39, 172, 192
supply-side factors 136, 138, 140
survey instrument 19–21, 211–16

tax-base sharing 197
tax incentives 198–9, 207–8
technical staffs 32, 92, 107, 146, 151–2
Technology Park, Georgia 6, 25, 77
telecommunications 5, 99
tenant compositions 63, 66–7, 158–61, 164
Tennessee Valley Authority 59, 160
terminology 15–18
toll roads 96–7, 187, 190
townhouses, *see* condominiums
Towson, Maryland 25, 84
Transco Tower, Texas 37–8, 187
trailpaths 60, 202
traffic boom 7–10
traffic
  congestion 1, 7–9, 67–8, 90, 98, 100, 129–31, 165, 183, 196
  conditions 9, 21, 68, 129–30, 142–6, 165
  volumes 68, 126, 129–30
transfer development credits 200–1
transit
  access 58, 203
  center 64, 174–5, 204
  design considerations 57–8, 203–4
  inducements 173
  private operation of 59, 64, 123, 188
  ridership levels 59, 63–4, 123, 128, 175
  service on-site 55, 59, 121, 204
  service off-site 55, 59, 123
  shuttles 59, 70, 87
  stops 58, 87, 203–4
transit-hostile environments 3, 179
transit-sensitive designs 179–80, 203–4
transportation management association 83
transportation systems management
  ordinance 156–7, 166, 175
travel
  clashes 51, 166
  distances 46, 61–2, 69, 125–6, 139, 158–60, 162–3, 191
  factors related to 32–3, 135–42
  modes 2, 59–60, 62–5, 69, 125–8, 165
  patterns 1, 7–9, 12, 14, 73, 181–3
  times 61–2, 125–6, 142–3
  speeds 61–2, 69, 125–6, 142–3, 186
  subsidies 58, 122
  surveys 19, 157

trip generation rates 41–2, 66–7, 69, 207
trip-making
  circuity 7–8
  cross-town and lateral 1, 7–8, 14, 73, 183
  distances 46, 50, 61–2
  intra-suburban 7–8, 46, 181–3
  metropolitan 7–8, 137–8
  peaking 41, 65–6, 126, 129, 131, 133
  see also travel
Tysons Corner, Virginia 6, 16, 25, 57, 60, 65, 84–5, 97–8, 119, 202

unemployment 183–4
underground parking 171, 206
Uptown, *see* City Post Oak
Urban Land Institute 18–19, 31, 43, 69
urban transit, *see* transit
urban village 6, 74, 84

vanpools 58–9, 121, 123, 127, 136–41, 167, 188, 191, 204
  see also ridesharing
vehicle occupancy levels 65
vehicle-pooling *see* ridesharing
volume-to-capacity ratios, *see* level of service

wage-earners
  primary 50
  secondary 5, 46, 50
wage-housing price match-ups 48, 53–4, 61, 69, 120, 153, 166, 183, 196

walking
  designing for 60–1, 202–5
  distances 38–9, 57–8, 60–1, 192, 203–5
  effects of building placement on 2, 38–9, 191–3
  factors influencing 41, 51, 120, 131, 140–1, 165–6, 191–2
  levels among SECs 64–5, 126–8, 151
Walnut Creek, California 24, 48, 70, 87, 89–91
warehousing 114
Warner Center, California 24, 28, 42–3, 53, 58, 68, 85, 206
Washington, D.C. 8, 15–16, 25, 64, 97–8
West Germany 11–12
West Houston Energy Corridor 17, 26, 28, 61, 65, 185–6, 188–91
white-collar workers 31–2, 92
Woodlands, Texas 26, 51–3, 59, 188, 190
work environment 137, 163, 165, 209
workplace
  design 4, 162–4
  quality 6, 79–82

zero lot lines 201
Zip Strip, New Jersey 7, 99–100
zoning
  conditional use 200
  incentive 172–3, 200
  inclusionary 200, 208
  ordinances 172–3
  performance 199, 207
  swaps 200–1